Also by Joanna Denny

Anne Boleyn

JOANNA DENNY

Katherine Howard

A TUDOR CONSPIRACY

PORTRAIT

Visit the Portrait website!

PORTRAIT Portrait publishes a wide range of non-fiction, including biography, history, science, music, popular culture and sport.

If you want to:
- read descriptions of our popular titles
- buy our books over the internet
- take advantage of our special offers
- enter our monthly competition
- learn more about your favourite Portrait authors

VISIT OUR WEBSITE AT: www.portraitbooks.com

First published in 2005 by **Portrait**
an imprint of
Piatkus Books Ltd
5 Windmill Street
London W1T 2JA
e-mail: info@piatkus.co.uk

This edition published in 2007

The moral right of the author has been asserted

A catalogue record for this book is available from the British Library

ISBN 0 7499 5120 6

This book has been printed on paper manufactured
with respect for the environment using wood from
managed sustainable resources

Edited by Richard Dawes
Text design by Paul Saunders

Data manipulation by
Action Publishing Technology Ltd, Gloucester
Printed & bound in Great Britain by
Mackays Ltd, Chatham

Contents

House of Tudor

м. *married*   b. born   d. died   ex. *executed*

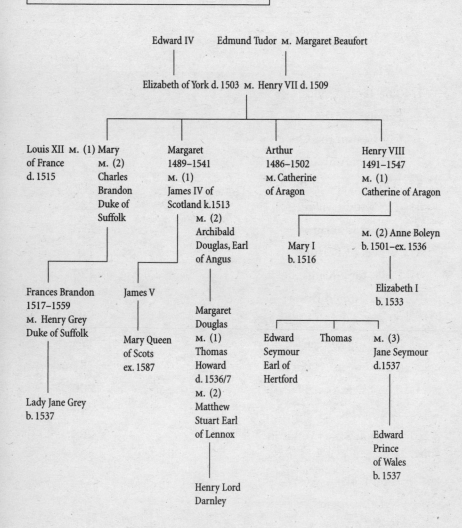

Edward IV   Edmund Tudor м. Margaret Beaufort

Elizabeth of York d. 1503 м. Henry VII d. 1509

Louis XII м. (1) Mary	Margaret	Arthur	Henry VIII
of France м. (2)	1489–1541	1486–1502	1491–1547
d. 1515 Charles	м. (1)	м. Catherine	м. (1)
Brandon	James IV of	of Aragon	Catherine of Aragon
Duke of	Scotland k.1513		
Suffolk	м. (2)		
	Archibald		м. (2) Anne Boleyn
	Douglas, Earl	Mary I	b. 1501–ex. 1536
	of Angus	b. 1516	

Frances Brandon
1517–1559
м. Henry Grey
Duke of Suffolk

James V

Elizabeth I
b. 1533

Margaret
Douglas

Mary Queen
of Scots
ex. 1587

м. (1)
Thomas
Howard
d. 1536/7

Edward
Seymour
Earl of
Hertford

Thomas

м. (3)
Jane Seymour
d.1537

Lady Jane Grey
b. 1537

м. (2)
Matthew
Stuart Earl
of Lennox

Edward
Prince
of Wales
b. 1537

Henry Lord
Darnley

The Howards

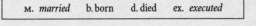

M. *married*   b. born   d. died   ex. *executed*

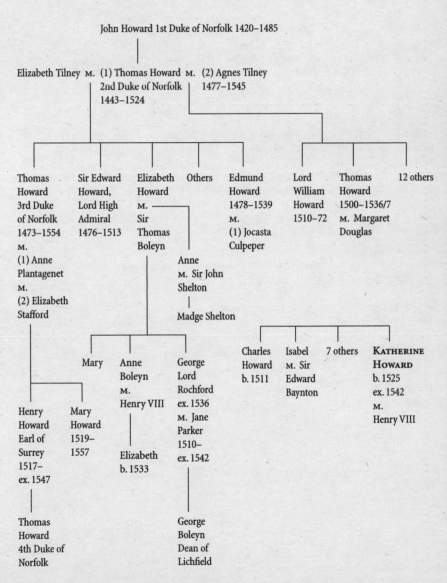

John Howard 1st Duke of Norfolk 1420–1485

Elizabeth Tilney M. (1) Thomas Howard M. (2) Agnes Tilney
2nd Duke of Norfolk 1477–1545
1443–1524

Thomas Howard 3rd Duke of Norfolk 1473–1554 M. (1) Anne Plantagenet M. (2) Elizabeth Stafford

Sir Edward Howard, Lord High Admiral 1476–1513

Elizabeth Howard M. Sir Thomas Boleyn

Others

Edmund Howard 1478–1539 M. (1) Jocasta Culpeper

Lord William Howard 1510–72

Thomas Howard 1500–1536/7 M. Margaret Douglas

12 others

Anne M. Sir John Shelton

Madge Shelton

Mary

Anne Boleyn M. Henry VIII

George Lord Rochford ex. 1536 M. Jane Parker 1510– ex. 1542

Charles Howard b. 1511

Isabel M. Sir Edward Baynton

7 others

KATHERINE HOWARD b. 1525 ex. 1542 M. Henry VIII

Henry Howard Earl of Surrey 1517– ex. 1547

Mary Howard 1519– 1557

Elizabeth b. 1533

Thomas Howard 4th Duke of Norfolk

George Boleyn Dean of Lichfield

(The signature of Katherine Howard)

CALENDAR

All dates given are according to the Julian calendar which was kept until February 1582, with New Year starting on 25 March. In 1582 Pope Gregory XIII introduced the Gregorian calendar with New Year starting on 1 January but Protestant England ignored these changes, remaining ten days behind Europe until 1751-2.

Prologue

ON A COLD AND BRIGHT Sunday morning in early November, the sweet sound of singing echoed from the Chapel Royal, Hampton Court. All along the corridors courtiers bowed low as Henry, King of England, passed by on his way to hear mass.

A dazzling presence, he took his place in the royal pew, his cloth of gold doublet and jewelled collar rivalling the ornate gilt ceiling above. The corset he wore underneath creaked as he knelt with difficulty because of a leg ulcer.

He was alone, his face set and sullen, his mind drifting away from the singing of the choir to the woman who was only yards away, a prisoner in her own chamber.

The fact that she was the Queen and his wife of little more than a year made it even harder to forget her.

Was that a noise from the corridor outside, a disturbance at the door? The King's attention never wavered. His face was set in stone, unmoving as the sounds of screaming broke through the formal music, unsettling the choir. Heads were turning now, alarmed glances exchanged, but the King continued to fix his eyes on the figure on the crucifix, as determined as his guards to shut her out.

She saw him for one brief moment before they slammed the doors in her face.

She had run the whole length of the gallery just to reach him, to try to talk to him, calling out her name, *Katherine, the Queen.*

Surely he had heard her and if he heard her then he must come and tell her what was wrong, why they had kept her away, refusing to let her see him, or talk to him.

For he was her husband and somehow he would save her.

As the doors shut, crossed halberds barred her way and suddenly she was seized brutally by the guards and pulled back. She struggled, indignantly protesting how dared they touch her, lay hands on her.

Once more she cried out a name, her husband's name, knowing that he must have heard her.

Gone suddenly was the hope she had cherished in these last days, snuffed out like a candle. Gone was the illusion that it was all a mistake or a plot by her enemies. Now she understood at last just who the enemy was.

Her husband the King.

She shook off her guards, freeing herself to walk with dignity the length of the gallery back to her apartments, her prison.

That night Henry left Hampton Court in secret by river and returned to London.

They would never see one another again.

Chapter One

The Tenth Child

THERE WAS A GROWING expectation at the great house. The entire family, staff and friends gathered to cheer their lady on her way to her lying-in as once again she faced the hazards of childbirth. Everyone present was conscious that this could be their final farewell, for so many women did not come out from confinement alive. Childbirth was the most dangerous time in a woman's life and there was no guarantee that either mother or child would survive the experience.

Lady Jocasta was now 45 and this would be her tenth child, but no easier for that. Five by her first husband, five by her second, and – should she survive the ordeal once more – there might be more to follow, God willing. Many mothers bore 15 or even 20 children.

The lying-in room was the traditional sanctuary of married women. The chamber was freshly swept and laid with clean rushes and sweet-smelling herbs chosen for their medicinal qualities and the appropriate time of the year: basil, lavender, tansy or penny royal. The family cradle awaited its new occupant. It was a handsome heirloom of polished wood, set with rockers and a hooded canopy to protect the baby from draughts. The great bed had been hung with the very best curtains and covers, in preparation for the time when the mother would show off her newborn child.

According to the rituals of childbirth, the midwives now shut the door in the face of the expectant father as he stood by the stairs with the rest of the family, the household servants, friends and neighbours who had gathered to await the birth of yet another Howard into the world.

In the inner sanctum, the shutters were firmly closed and a good fire built up and kept burning to create a high temperature. Childbirth was a curious ritual mingling practical obstetrics with a good deal of myth and superstition. The Catholic Church taught that women must suffer in childbirth to pay for the original sin committed by Eve. The pain was God's gift to bring women to redemption, but it was the work of a skilled midwife to save lives.

The chief midwife massaged the mother's belly with warm potions such as oil of lilies or almonds. She had learnt her craft from her own mother and grandmother, skilled in the secret mysteries that were passed down through the generations. The women then helped Jocasta onto the birthing stool the midwives had brought with them, standing around to lend her support and encouragement on all sides. As the child's head was just beginning to crown, the midwife crouched and held out a cloth as the baby slithered into the world. It was a girl.

The midwife quickly cleared the baby's mouth to aid her first breath and rubbed her little red body to encourage her cry. Next, she cut the umbilical cord and bathed her in a mixture of warm milk and wine. A coin was placed on the baby's buttocks to drive the devil away then she was swaddled, long linen strips being bound tightly around her body to keep her still and ensure the limbs grew straight during the first year. She was then handed over to her mother, the lady of the house.

As Jocasta was helped into the great canopied bed and took the tiny child in her arms, prayers were offered up for the blessing of a safe delivery, but the women gathered there looked upon her with pity. Everyone knew that another girl was surely a sore disappointment.

Jocasta prepared to put on a brave face before her husband and the world. The little girl in her arms was insignificant in the

Howard family order, just another mouth to feed, another daughter who one day would require a dowry and a husband.

Who could ever imagine that she would find such a husband and such a destiny as Queen of England?

Katherine Howard was born at a great turning point in history – as Henry VIII first met and fell obsessively in love with her cousin Anne Boleyn. This stormy and tragic relationship was to provide the catalyst for the English Reformation and the creation of English nationalism.

By 1525, the Tudor dynasty had been in power just 40 years, since Henry Tudor wrested the crown of England from Richard III, the last of the Plantagenet kings, in 1485. Henry VII's new regime ruled with an iron hand, but when Henry VIII inherited the kingdom from his father in 1509 there were many at home and abroad who still regarded the Tudors as upstarts and usurpers. England was an island state that had lost its French territories piecemeal during the Hundred Years War. Predominantly rural, with extensive wild woods and forests, verdant with lush fields and orchards, England's very isolation ensured its prosperity. The continual waves of plague, famine and warfare that swept across the European continent were kept at bay by 22 miles of rough water in the Channel.

With a population of less than three million, of whom 90 per cent lived in the countryside, and most in the southern counties, England was prosperous: '… in all the shops of Milan, Rome, Venice and Florence together, I do not think there would be found so many of the magnificence that is to be seen in London'. The people had enough food to eat, they lived in relative peace and had the prospect of improving their lives. Half a century before, the introduction of the printing press had encouraged a revolution in literacy and education, aiding the spread of new reformist beliefs. The opinionated and independent English took advantage of the new spirit of the age, grasping the opportunity to grow as a nation and a people, to carve out a role on the international stage.

In this 'garden of England', Kent was a rich landscape of soft hills and gentle river valleys blossoming with orchards, far more than in any other region, as Lambarde records. Where Katherine was born is unknown, but her mother Jocasta's house at Oxon Hoath in Kent seems most likely. Near Tonbridge, a town with just a few hundred houses – but then even most cities had populations of less than five thousand – it was originally built during the reign of King Henry V by Sir John Culpeper as a royal park for oxen and deer.

Born in 1480, Jocasta or Joyce Culpeper married twice. She was the daughter of Sir Richard Culpeper, Sheriff of Kent, a descendant of Princess Joan of Acre, daughter of Edward I. Her entire life was ordered according to the desires of her family, to build and reinforce their influence throughout the county. When her father died on 4 October 1484, she was only four. Her widowed mother, Isabel Worsley, was left with three daughters, Margaret, Jocasta and Elizabeth, as heiresses to the manors of Oxon Hoath, Siflton Manor and Borough Court at Ditton also called Brooke Court.

Isabel soon took a second husband, Sir John Legh of Stockwell, Lambeth, Sheriff of Surrey in 15 and 1515–1516. The Sheriff collected rents and royal revenues, summoned juries, served writs, enforced the law and ran the local assizes. A Sheriff was elected on the morrow of All Soul's Day (2 November) by the King's Council to serve his county for one year at his own expense. They were therefore wealthy and well-connected esquires and members of the gentry, of which there were about 5,000 families in 1540.

When Jocasta was barely 12 years of age her mother arranged her marriage to her stepson Ralph Legh, the Under-Sheriff of London. Twelve was the legal age for marriage for girls, the 'flower of a female's age'. Jocasta fulfilled her family's expectations, dutifully producing two sons, John and Ralph, and four daughters, Isabel, Joyce, Margaret and Mary, in quick succession. After Ralph's death, Jocasta's mother arranged for her to make a second and even more prestigious alliance with the Howard family and she married Lord Edmund Howard in about 1513.

Lord Edmund was the son of the second Duke of Norfolk, one of 22 brothers and sisters. The Howards were the greatest aristocrats in England and could boast family alliances with the Duke of Buckingham and the Earls of Sussex, Bridgewater, Oxford and Derby. There was hardly a noble family in England to whom they were not related and, given Henry VIII's lack of a male heir, the Howards remained contenders for the throne, a possibility not missed either by them or by the King.

The Howards took inordinate pride in their heritage through Joan of Cornwall, a descendant of King John and their enemies said that they were 'puffed with insatiable pride'. Many of those who could have helped Edmund Howard to advance were alienated by his conceit and overbearing arrogance of character. One such was Sir Thomas Palmer, a 'citizen and mercer of London', who came from an old Sussex family whose purchase of Preston Manor in February 1525 for £500 established them as gentry. He had little but contempt for Edmund Howard, acidly remarking, 'Though he be a lord, yet he is not God.'

A common proverb of the time noted, 'There is more to marriage than four bare legs in bed.' Marriage was the lifeblood of society, ensuring continuity and advancement as property and land deals were made as part of the marriage contract. It was normal for the extended family and friends to play a major role in arranging matches and taking part in the negotiations to draw up what was really a business merger. A profitable marriage could bring the whole family greater standing and considerable economic benefits.

A Howard catch was an excellent match for a widow of Jocasta's status, with five or six small children, although Edmund was a younger son, without any titles or lands to inherit. In 1514 or 1515 the newly married couple were already in their mid-thirties but without visible means of support.

The old order of Norman aristocracy typified by the Howards was beginning to give way before a dynamic and ambitious generation of gentry who sought status by intermarrying with the lower branches of noble houses. The ranks of the old aristocracy had been thinned by prolonged civil war and by 1509, when Henry VIII succeeded to the throne, England had only one duke

(Norfolk), one marquis, ten earls and thirty barons. In contrast to the old order, the gentry were inclined towards the new reform faith, whereas the Howards remained staunchly Catholic. The Leghs were part of such a new wave of rising men who were eager to obtain recognition.

Edmund had no objection to marrying a widow with children, anticipating that his marriage to Jocasta would eventually bring him part of the inheritance left by Sir Richard Culpeper. He knew that her son John, by her first marriage to Ralph Legh, was heir to the Legh family fortune, but the lands were held in trust and Jocasta's stepfather, Sir John, appears to have distrusted the Howards. In his will, he left strict instructions regarding his daughter-in-law's inheritance, on 'condition that her husband redeem all lands (that are) the inheritance of my daughter in the county of Kent from her father, Richard Culpeper, and her brother, Thomas Culpeper, so that the lands descend to her heirs'.

Sir John further stipulated that 'if the Howards trouble the Executors they are to have nothing'. It appears that the Howards did trouble the executors and Edmund got nothing, since after his mother-in-law Isabel's death in 1527 the manors were sold to Francis Shakerly.

Without a family home of their own, Edmund and Jocasta were forced to move frequently, descending on family members with their ever-expanding brood of young children. By 1525, it seems that Jocasta was pregnant with her tenth child.

The confusion over the number and parentage of Jocasta's many children makes it almost impossible to ascertain either their order or their correct birth dates, but the Legh family papers show that Sir John made his last will and testament in 1524, listing Jocasta's sons Charles, Henry and George.

Although the date of Katherine's birth is unknown, when Sir John Legh died on 18 April 1527 his widow Isabel, Katherine's grandmother, made a new will. This records Katherine by name, suggesting that she was born after 1524 but before 1527.

This is much more credible than the traditional view that she was born in 1520 or 1521, which was based on unreliable guesswork by the French Ambassador Marillac in 1541. Other writers noted the fact that she was exceptionally young. The anonymous *Chronicle of Henry VIII* reports Katherine as 15 when she first met the King in late 1539, making her year of birth 1524 or 1525. This five-year discrepancy between the traditional date given for her birth and that suggested by her grandmother makes a vital difference to our view of Katherine. It has always been accepted that she was very young when she first came to public attention, a fact pointed out by contemporary chroniclers who would not have made an issue of it had she been a woman of 20 rather than a girl of 15.

Surrounded by such a large family, another daughter must have seemed like an added burden to her father. The great troop of children proved tough survivors in an age when half the babies born died in their first year and a quarter of the survivors died before their 15th birthday.

Life in the early 16th century was brief, often tragic, regularly punctuated by the death of siblings, parents, wives and children. The number of babies who did not survive delivery meant that home midwives were often called upon to perform hasty rites of baptism in order to save a soul. In such cases, lay persons were officially permitted by the Church to fulfil duties normally reserved for the all-male priesthood.

England remained a Catholic country even though the winds of reform were spreading rapidly from Northern Europe. The Church maintained its grip over the vast majority of people, who were still illiterate, particularly in country areas where the reach of Lollardy and new evangelical tracts and English translations of the scriptures had not yet created a Protestant movement. The mass, penance and the confessional were entrenched as part of everyday life.

It was believed that a child who died unbaptised would be lost in limbo, *limbus puerorum*, caught between heaven and hell. Sir Thomas More was typical of those who believed 'those infantes be dampned onely to the payne of losse of heauen'. Death was always waiting to threaten the newborn and infants. Priests taught that the newborn child was contaminated by original sin, vulnerable to the Devil's wiles until brought within the safe fold of Holy Mother Church through baptism. This ceremony usually took place within hours of the birth at the family's parish church. The mother was therefore not present, remaining at home to recuperate for a set period of 40 days, until she was 'churched' in a special ceremony of purification, following the ancient rites recorded in the Bible in Leviticus 12.6. Only then was she considered fit to rejoin society.

The father led the baptismal party in procession to the door of the parish church. Here the priest stopped them, demanding to know whether the child was baptised or not. According to the ritual, he must first exorcise Satan by cleansing the baby's mouth with salt and making a blessing over its head. The family had already selected godparents for the new baby, to act as sponsors for the future and guides for the child's spiritual upbringing. Being a godparent was considered the closest link outside that of blood ties, and marriages between godparents and godchildren were forbidden. For a boy there would be one godmother and two godfathers, for a daughter one godfather and two godmothers. These were questioned by the priest on their own Christian faith and credentials and only then was the baptismal party permitted to enter the church.

The tiny child was taken down to the stone font and immersed three times in cold water in the name of the Father, the Son and the Holy Spirit. Then the priest pronounced her name. The child was now rescued by the godmother who wrapped the new little Christian in a special white robe, or *crysom*, often an heirloom that had been passed down through the family from child to child. After a blessing at the high altar, candles were lit and the party eagerly returned home to celebrate.

Jocasta may never have survived to be churched. As was frequently the case, given the poor medical and sanitary conditions of the time, she failed to recover from the ordeal of childbirth, apparently worn out by her endless round of pregnancies. Almost half the female population died before they reached the age of 50 and once into the menopause a woman was considered old.

Jocasta's death was announced by the tolling of church bells, denoting her age. She was laid out in her black-shrouded coffin in one of the main rooms, so that family, friends and neighbours might process by to pay their respects. The whole house, including its entrance and courtyard, was draped in black cloth. All mirrors were turned to face the wall. Mourners were given money to buy black clothes. The mourning period was three to four years for a deceased father or mother, but a surviving husband or wife dressed in black until they remarried or until they died.

A 'widow's weeds' often included a pleated headdress or *barbe*, similar to a nun's habit. Mourning jewellery included rings and lockets, which could hold a lock of hair from the dear departed.

A Catholic funeral required a mass said at home over the coffin, which was then taken out to a black-draped cart to be pulled in procession to the local church. Often professional mourners led the way, holding lighted candles. The family would follow the coffin, to hear requiem mass and witness the burial, either in the church if there was a family vault, or in the churchyard outside. After the funeral, a feast or 'wake' was traditional.

Edmund was left with their surviving children, including the newborn Katherine.

It was not a sentimental age. There was little time to mourn. In the weeks following her birth and her mother's death, the upbringing of his latest daughter was immediately passed to the care of servants and wet-nurses while he began the search for a suitable stepmother.

About a third of marriages were second marriages, with discussions about possible candidates often beginning at the funeral feast. The Howard men had each married several times following the death of wives in childbirth and for a younger son like Edmund, with a great name but little or no prospects, it was vital that he married again and married well in order to finance his ever-expanding family.

Edmund's second wife was Dorothy, the daughter of Thomas Troyes, a widow with eight children of her own. Far from clearing his increasing debts, their situation became so desperate that in 1527 he was obliged to send Dorothy to the King's chief minister,

Cardinal Wolsey, begging for assistance, possibly a lucrative post. In a letter, he told the Cardinal that he had ten children to provide for and the family was starving. He argued, 'If I were a poor man's son, I might dig and delve for my living', but because he was a Howard he 'could not labour without bringing great reproach and shame to himself and all his blood'. He was 'utterly undone', he claimed, and dared not come to London for fear that his creditors would put him in jail. Imprisonment for debt was common, and in some cases by choice as it kept a man's possessions safe for his heirs, since death cancelled all debts.

Little Katherine was far from his thoughts. At a time when half of all newborn infants died in their first year, her survival was a gamble. She was placed in the care of her wet-nurse, a local woman who had recently given birth herself and was hired to feed her employer's child along with her own. Many wet-nurses chose to take up lucrative employment bringing up middle class and noble children, depriving their own baby in favour of the noble child or paying relatives in the countryside to bring up their own.

In large households, children might be brought up entirely by servants and tutors, scarcely ever seeing their parents except on formal occasions. Nurses took the mother's place, looking after their charges and providing the affection that may have been missing in their lives. Elizabeth I was later to acknowledge her debt to Blanche Parry, the girl who had rocked her cradle, who was to stay in her service for the next 57 years: 'We are more bound to them that bringeth us up well than to our parents, for our parents do that which is natural for them, that is bringeth us into this world; but our bringers up are a cause to make us live well.'

As a result, parents rarely saw their children, with the wealthy passing their sons and daughters over to trusted servants to bring up according to strict guidelines, rarely troubling even to see their children except in the case of severe sickness or death.

By the time they could stand, children would be more formally dressed. Boys and girls alike wore long dresses, appearing identical until fully weaned and toilet-trained. Often boys would remain 'unbreeched' until the age of five or six, when they were given their first pair of hose and their long hair was cut. Once weaned, children were dressed in the same kind of clothes as their parents, appearing as mini-adults.

In their early years, parents provided small children with toys and gave them time to play games. John Trevisa wrote in 1398 of babies playing with 'a child's brooch', or rattle. Spinning tops are known to have existed from ancient times, one being found in an archaeological dig at Winchester. Two toy soldiers were discovered in London, little knights in armour on horseback, holding swords. Thomas More records simpler games such as Knucklebones, played with marrowbones or cherry stones. Little girls like Katherine played with dolls, called *poppets* or *mammets*, which were carved from wood or made of cloth and dressed in homemade costumes. By the 14th century such dolls were being sold commercially at fairs all over England.

The kind of games that Katherine would have played with her brothers and sisters can be seen in Pieter Brueghel's 1560 painting, *Children's Games*. It depicts a whole variety of pastimes, from Blind Man's Bluff and Tug of War to Leap Frog. Both boys and girls are playing with hoops, bowls and nine pins. There is a game of tag going on and Follow the Leader. Other children walk on stilts or stand on their heads. Boys climb trees or go skinny-dipping. Girls play at weddings and christenings.

After All Saints' Day, 1 November, it was the practice to slaughter animals for winter food, making pigs' bladders available for footballs. The game was looked down upon, described as 'nothing but fury and external violence' by Sir Thomas Elyot in his book, *The Governor* (1553). It was banned in 1349 but continued to be played and enjoyed new popularity at one time as it distracted boys from archery practice, which was compulsory for all males from the age of seven. Archery, although enjoyed equally by girls and women (including Anne Boleyn), was a military requirement, with butts set up on village greens and open spaces such as Finsbury Fields in London to practice every Sunday or feast day after church. Legal statutes and fines enforced this very English skill, which was needed on the battlefield.

Come winter, children would dress up as boy-bishops on Childermas or the Feast of Holy Innocents parading around, singing and collecting money for the church, but these customs associated with Catholic saints' days were to be banned in England in 1541 by government edict.

Edmund was left with John, Ralph, Isabel, Joyce, Margaret, Mary, Charles, Henry, George and little Katherine. Whether these ten children were all his, or those who survived from his wife's earlier marriage to Ralph Legh, or even included some of Dorothy's own children, they were all regarded as family now, taking the Howard name.[31] Ten was a burden but a family the size of Edmund Howard's was not unusual. His own father had married twice and produced at least ten children with each of his wives, the vast majority healthy and living well into adulthood to make profitable marriages.

Given Edmund's own pride in his ancestry, it is probable that all the children in his care were brought up to have a strong sense of solidarity. The children of the gentry were taught at an early age to appreciate their own genealogy and to understand their place in society. Many families across the social classes had children from various marriages ranging widely in ages, all living together in the same house, often in cramped conditions. The fact that the Howards were of the nobility – albeit somewhat impoverished in their finances – did not mean that sisters did not have to share beds. It was virtually unheard of for anyone, including the royal family, to sleep in a room alone. The Lisle family letters show that children and stepchildren were regarded as part of the same family, recognising one another as brother and sister and referring even to a stepfather as 'my lord my father'.

The English family was a large, loose network based on kinship. A household might include 20 or 30 people, often cousins and nephews or nieces who had come to be educated and even to work for relatives. Foreigners found it strange that families chose to send their own children away while taking in those of other family members.

As Edmund had complained to Cardinal Wolsey, children were a drain on a family's finances until they became old enough to become sources of income. At some time around their seventh birthday, both sons and daughters were generally considered of an age to make a break with childish things and to take their first step into the adult world. Edmund must have been grateful when his children grew old enough to be 'placed out'.

In families of high rank this meant starting education or training for a position in their future lives. Since feudal times boys of the nobility had been sent away to be educated and trained in the use of arms, acting as pages and waiting at table, learning the etiquette of court and the requirements of warfare. Girls were sent to become 'maids of honour' and serve noble ladies. For the lower classes – and that was the vast majority – it meant the beginning of apprenticeship for service as indentured servants. [33] This 'placing out' was seen by some foreign visitors as a sign of the English 'want of affeccion' towards their children, but in large families such an interchange was a necessity. The system not only provided a constant supply of labour but offered patronage, the prospect of advancement and even future marriages.

In noble households the day started with mass or formal prayers at dawn. Afterwards the fast was broken with a meal of cold meat cuts and bread, washed down with ale or small beer. While their parents were often out hunting or at business, the older children would go to their studies with their tutor, to learn Latin passages of the Bible by rote, or ancient Greek if they were more progressive. Dinner was usually the main meal and taken at any time between eleven and one. More lessons followed, usually archery or dancing practice, needlepoint or playing musical instruments. Supper was taken about five or six, separately from the adults, and all children were well abed, after more prayers, by nine at night.

The correct manners and modes of good behaviour were set out in the best instruction manuals. There were a crop of these popular works designed to teach parents how to bring up their children, such as *How the Good Wife Taught Her Daughter* and *The Book of Nurture*:

Reverence thy father and mother as Nature requires.
If you have been out of their presence for a long while, ask their blessing.
At dinner, press not thyself too high; sit in the place appointed thee.
Sup not loud of thy pottage.
Dip not thy meat in the saltcellar, but take it with a knife.
Belch near no man's face with a corrupt fumosity.
Scratch not thy head with thy fingers, nor spit you over the table.
If your teeth be putrefied, it is not right to touch meat that others eat.
Wipe thy mouth when thou shalt drink ale or wine on thy napkin only,
not on the table cloth.
Blow not your nose in the napkin where ye wipe your hand. [35]

Discipline was also important. It was believed that children were born sinful and required strict measures to erase their intrinsic wickedness. It was held that 'Foolishness is bound in the heart of a child but the rod of correction shall drive it far from him.'

Parents and masters needed to impose strict rules and transgressors were firmly punished: 'Spare the rod and spoil the child.' Children were 'broken in', as some might train a horse or dog. For errant boys and girls beating and flogging were common. Sometimes such retribution was particularly severe, as in the case of the defiant Elizabeth Paston who wanted to choose her own husband. The girl was imprisoned at the family home where 'she hath since Easter the most part been beaten once in the week or twice, and sometimes twice on a day, and her head broken in two or three places'.

Lady Jane Grey also defied her parents' choice of husband and was beaten violently until she agreed to marry. She once described her parents' harsh treatment:

For when I am in presence of either Father or Mother, whether I speak, keep silence, sit, stand or go, eat, drink, be merry or sad, be sewing, playing, dancing, or doing anything else, I must do it as it were in such weight, measure and number, even so perfectly as God made the world; or else I am so sharply taunted, so cruelly threatened, yea presently sometimes with pinches, nips and bobs and other ways (which I will not name for the honour I bear them), so without measure misordered, that I think myself in hell.

Young wards and heiresses were soon married off, often before they were old enough to consummate the marriage. By contrast, daughters with little or no dowry were seen as encumbrances for whom husbands were hard to find. As for boys, it was so difficult for some young men without good prospects to find wives that they remained living at home under their parents' authority well into their thirties, still treated like children.

But the eldest boy from Jocasta's first marriage, John, was the heir to the Legh fortune through his father Ralph Legh, while his brothers and sisters were now approaching marriageable age with the hope of making beneficial and profitable matches with the nobility or, failing that, with the rich and up-and-coming merchant class.

Their stepfather lost no time in seeking to arrange husbands for the girls, with Margaret married to Sir Thomas Arundel in November 1531, Joyce to John Stanney, Isabel to Henry Boynton of Bromham, and Mary in 1532 to the widower Sir Edward Baynton, possessor of a 200-acre estate in Wiltshire. With no dowry to offer, these were the best matches that could be expected. The prestige of the Howard name was sufficient to attract the interest of many from the new mercantile class, which sought social and political status through the ownership of land and prestigious marriages.

Edmund himself was not averse to marrying into these rising families. When his second wife Dorothy died in May 1530, he found a wealthy widow, Margaret Jennings, the daughter of Sir John Mundy who had bought extensive lands in Derbyshire to create a family seat, Markeaton Hall, and was Lord Mayor of London in 1522. It does not appear that any further children were born of these marriages.

Through such alliances, Edmund struggled to provide for his family, forever in debt and obliged to call for favours and loans from those about him. Most notably of all, he turned to his eldest brother Thomas, head of the Howard dynasty.

Chapter Two

Family

THE HOWARDS may have been renowned for their pride and arrogance, but for years they were regarded as enemies of the Tudor regime. Their support for the House of York was still remembered by Henry VIII, who continued to view the family with suspicion, aware of their great ambition. It was only through war and their willingness to serve their country that they recovered sufficiently to restore the status of a family in close proximity to the throne. Yet scarcely more than a century before, the Howards, like the Tudors, had been insignificant minor country gentry.

The name Huard, Heward or Haward has ancient roots, meaning 'guardian' or 'hardy' and 'brave'. The Huardus were first mentioned in Cumberland in the Domesday Book of 1086 and a certain *Willelmus filius Huward* is recorded in Northumberland in the Pipe Rolls for 1170. The family moved south to become farmers in the flatlands of East Anglia. Howard fortunes steadily increased and by the early 14th century William Howard was a lawyer and made Justice of the Court of Common Pleas. His eldest son, Sir John Howard, married the heiress Joan of Cornwall and became Sheriff of Norfolk and Suffolk and governor of Norwich Castle.

The transformation of the family's fortunes came with the

marriage of Sir Robert Howard of Stoke Neyland to Lady Margaret, daughter of the feuding Thomas Mowbray, Duke of Norfolk, who had been disgraced and banished by King Richard II. Their son John Howard was born about 1421 and was a soldier all his life, supporting the Yorkist dynasty during the so-called 'Wars of the Roses'.

His influence grew and he became a friend of Richard, Duke of Gloucester, with whom he served during campaigns in the borders against Scottish marauders.

When John Mowbray, Duke of Norfolk, died without a son, John Howard had every right to expect to inherit both land and title through his mother, Lady Margaret Mowbray. But although he had served the King so well, Edward IV cheated him by forcing Parliament to allow his own son Richard, Duke of York, to keep the inheritance of his dead child wife, Anne Mowbray. When Edward died, John Howard gave his whole-hearted support to his ally Richard of Gloucester in the 1483 crisis of state during which Parliament acclaimed him as King Richard III.

Subsequently, Howard was raised to the vacant dukedom of Norfolk and his heir was made Earl of Surrey. The Howards adopted the motto, *Sola virtus invicta*, 'Virtue alone invincible'. Their coat of arms was 'red with a silver stripe between six silver crosses', with the crest of a lion 'on a chapeau'. Like the paternalistic barons of old, John Howard took pride in the management of his estates and the welfare of his tenants. His account books show his generosity to the poor, the sick, children and clever students whom he supported to go to the University of Cambridge. Among his followers was his deputy, Sir William Boleyn, grandfather of the future Queen Anne Boleyn.

When in August 1485 Henry Tudor, backed by a French mercenary force, invaded Wales, Norfolk led support for King Richard. The armies clashed at the battle of Bosworth where the Duke, then aged over 60, led the royal forces with his son and heir Surrey. Through treachery, Richard and Norfolk were both killed and Surrey taken prisoner. Henry Tudor seized the crown as King Henry VII.

The Howard family now faced a difficult future. With the dramatic regime change, the suspicious new monarch viewed them as potentially dangerous enemies. Along with all the men who fought for their King at Bosworth against the rebel forces, the Howards were accused of treason under attainder and Surrey was not permitted to inherit the Norfolk title.

Surrey had eight surviving children by his first wife, Elizabeth Tilney, notably Thomas, the heir, born in 1473; Edward, born in L476; Elizabeth, who married Sir Thomas Boleyn and gave birth to Anne; and Edmund, the future father of Katherine Howard. When his first wife died in 1497, Surrey then married Agnes Tilney, a much younger cousin of his first wife, who was later to bring up Katherine. Together Surrey and Agnes produced another eight children. It was through this vast family that the Howards effectively interconnected with most of the great houses such as Sussex, Oxford, Devon, Derby and Wiltshire.

While their father remained in prison, the three brothers were obliged to serve the new King at court where they received the traditional medieval education of martial training in arms together with some Latin, French and law. Under the previous regime, Thomas the eldest, had been betrothed when he was 11 to Anne, a daughter of Edward IV and sister of Elizabeth of York, who married Henry VII after Bosworth. But this connection to the royal Plantagenet line was too close for comfort for the Tudors and the betrothed couple were not permitted to marry until 1495. Married to the parsimonious Henry VII, Queen Elizabeth had to provide for her sister and her new husband out of her own purse, paying them 20 shillings a week.

Before long, the Tudors needed Surrey's services. As a loyal subject, he was expected to produce armed troops to defend the country at his own expense. He was released to deploy to the Scottish border and later proved his loyalty to the House of Tudor as Treasurer. As a result of the peace he had secured with Scotland, in 1503 he escorted Henry VII's daughter Margaret to her marriage with the Scots King James IV. The Howard family went with him. Young Thomas also accompanied his father on an embassy to Flanders in 1507.

In 1509 the crown passed to the young and vigorous Henry VIII. The 17-year old King was relatively unknown, having been kept out of the public eye during his adolescence. As a second son, Henry had never been expected to inherit and was not trained to become King, possibly being destined for the Church. But when his elder brother Arthur, Prince of Wales, died in 1502, Henry became the focus of his father's attention. Their relationship was strained, with the King keeping his heir in tight seclusion, as the Spanish Ambassador Fuensalida reported in 1508, and controlling his public appearances. The Ambassador claimed that their relationship was violent, with the King 'beset by the fear that his son might during his lifetime obtain too much power...and sought to kill him'.

At six foot two, Henry was vain about his figure and the red-gold hair inherited from his maternal grandfather, the Yorkist King Edward IV. Clean-shaven until 1518, as he gained weight he grew a beard to disguise his full face. He had a small, petulant mouth and piercing blue eyes, but they were weak and later he required spectacles to read. The Venetian Ambassador Sebastian Giustinian recorded: 'Nature could not have done more for him ... His Majesty is the handsomest potentate I ever set eyes upon: above the usual height, with an extremely fine calf to his leg, his complexion very fair and bright, with auburn hair combed straight and short in the French fashion, and a round face so very beautiful that it would become a pretty woman, his throat being rather long and thick ...' His clothes were of cloth of gold or rich silks, ablaze with jewels; 'his fingers were one mass of jewelled rings, and around his neck he wore a gold collar from which hung a diamond as big as a walnut'.

The new King agreed to marry his brother Arthur's widow, Catherine of Aragon. He had serious doubts about the validity of this arrangement but was reassured that her first marriage had not been consummated. Although Catherine was six years older than her new husband, at first the couple seemed happy enough.

Pleasure was now the order of the day. Henry surrounded himself with a clique of hard-drinking, whoring and sporting followers, including Edward Howard and Charles Brandon, whose resemblance to Henry had led to him being called the King's 'bastard brother'. Brandon was Henry's partner in tournaments and accompanied him drinking and whoring. The nobility loathed him as a upstart but Henry overlooked his scandalous married life and in February 1514 made him Duke of Suffolk, one of the three greatest nobles in England, alongside the Dukes of Norfolk and Buckingham. 'From a stable-boy into a nobleman', commented Erasmus scathingly.

The King was proud of his athletic skill, being highly competitive in everything he did, and always had to win. Foreigners regarded the English as 'licentious in their disposition' and drunkenness was common. Henry's vices were 'lechery, covetousness and cruelty, but the two latter issued and sprang out of the former'. As he grew older, he surrounded himself with younger men as if to cling to his fast-disappearing youth. In May 1519 Cardinal Wolsey objected to these 'minions' and their 'French vices', reporting they 'were so familiar and homely with him, and played such light touches with him that they forgot themselves'.

All three Howard brothers were often at court but Henry favoured Edward over his brothers and he made a reputation competing in great jousting tournaments with the King, notably at Greenwich Palace in October 1510, when he felled a gentleman of Almain (Germany) called Gyot. Henry appointed him to his own household as a standard-bearer with a salary of £40 a year. No such honours were given to Thomas.

All his life Edward was aware of being second to Thomas, the heir, knowing he would inherit nothing. Edward was the risk-taker and adventurer of the family, with a charming capacity for making friends and marrying money. His first wife Elizabeth was the daughter of Sir Miles Stapleton of Ingham Manor in Norfolk. She died on 18 February 1504 and was buried in White Friars, Norwich. By 1506 he was married again, to Alice Lovel, *suo jure* (in her own right) Baroness Morley, widow of William Parker, who was old enough to be his mother.

Edward was eager to prove himself in battle and stirred up

renewed conflict with Scotland. In 1511 Bishop Richard Fox reported that Edward had 'marvelously incenseth the king against the Scots, by whose wanton means his grace spendeth much money and is more disposed to war than peace'.

He got his chance in June when a Scottish fleet under Andrew Barton appeared off the English coast. Barton was a privateer, but regarded as little more than a pirate by his enemies, who complained to the King of harassment. Thomas Howard and his brother Edward were commanded to equip three ships of war to remove the threat.

After paying to equip the little expedition, Surrey sent his sons in search of the Scots admiral. The encounter took place off the coast of Kent on 2 August 1511. Barton's flagship *The Lion*, with 36 guns, was a prize worth taking. The English assaulted the Scots and made a lucky strike against the enemy captain. Although wounded, Barton continued to lead his men to the bitter end, when he was felled by a cannonball and his ships were captured. The engagement was celebrated in a ballad:

> 'Ffight on my men', sayes Sir Andrew Bartton
> 'These English doggs they bite soe lowe;
> Ffight on ffor Scottland and Saint Andrew
> Till you heare my whistle blowe!' ...
> My Lord Haward tooke a sword in his hand,
> And smote off Sir Andrew's head.

The Lion was borne as a trophy into the Thames and became, after the *Great Harry*, the largest man-of-war in the English navy. Edward Howard was later appointed 'admiral of England, Ireland and Acquitane'.

As Sir Andrew had been a special favourite of James IV of Scotland, the naval battle caused increased tension with Scotland, perhaps as Edward Howard had hoped all along. James, who was married to Henry's fiery and controversial sister, now sent a demand for redress to his brother-in-law, but Henry haughtily replied that princes should not concern themselves with the fate of pirates.

The following year the English allied with Spain to attack the French, hoping to recover their lost territories in Guienne. Now that Surrey was in his late sixties, the command was given to the Marquess of Dorset, with Thomas Howard as his deputy and Edmund Howard among his officers. Edmund was now 32 and still looking for a role in life. Unlike Thomas, who would one day inherit everything, and Edward, who had carved an active and lucrative life for himself, Edmund had no inheritance or demonstrable talents to provide security. He was always short of money and throughout his life singularly failed to match his finances to his Howard aspirations.

In 1510 he had attempted to make a career in the law, joining the Middle Temple in London, but gave it up after less than a year.[18] Left without any means of earning a living, he grew embittered at the poor hand that Fate had dealt him.

He joined his elder brothers Thomas and Edward at the royal court, but his personality proved to be a barrier to intimacy with the King's inner circle.

The chronicler Edward Hall records the optimism with which the English set out against the French:

> To see the lords and gentlemen so well armed and so richly apparelled in cloths of gold and of silver and velvets of sundry colours, pounced and embroidered, and all petty captains in satin and damask of white and green and yeomen in cloth of the same colour, the banners, penons, standards ... fresh and newly painted with sundry beasts and device, it was a pleasure to behold.

A two-fold attack was planned: the fleet would harry the north coast of France and then convey an expeditionary force to northern Spain, to join up with the troops of Ferdinand, Henry's father-in-law. The dashing Edward Howard was now at the peak of his fame and fortune. He was made 'Admiral of the Sea during this voyage and enterprise to be made against the French King in Guyen', taking charge of the King's new flagship, the *Mary Rose*, which had been built in Portsmouth in 1510.

The 600-ton technologically advanced carrack was named for the King's younger sister, the Duchess of Suffolk, wife of Henry's close friend Charles Brandon. The *Mary Rose* was an innovative and purpose-built warship, armed with the latest guns manufactured by the Belgian Hans Poppenreuter, including bronze culverins and sakers. On taking command, Edward reported to the King: 'Sir, she is the noblest shipp of sayle and grett shipp at this hour that I trow be in Christendom. A shipp of 100 tonne wyl not be soner ... abowt then she.'

Edward Howard's accounts list expenses incurred to outfit a Tudor warship:

> The Mary Roose: – Fyrst to Syr Edward Haward, knyght, chief captain and admyral of the Flete for his wages and vitayle at 10s. a day by the seid iij mounthes amountyng to £42 ... Also for the wages and vitayle of 2 lodesmen alias pylottes ych of thiem at 20s. a mounth by the seid iij mounthes £6. Also for the vitayle of 411 souldiours, 206 maryners, 120, gonners 20, and servitours 20, in the same ship, every man at 5s. a mounth by the seid tyme £308 5s. Also for wages of the same 411 persons every man at 5s. a mounth by the seid tyme £308 5s. Also for 34 deddeshares demi at 5s. a share by the seid tyme £25 17s. 6d. Also for toundage aftyr 3d a ton a weke by the seid tyme 500ton, nil quia navis Regis.

In April he was in Plymouth complaining of the paucity of rations:

> I pray Godde that we lynger no longer, for I assure you was never army so falselie vitailled. They that received their proportion for 2 monthes flesche can not bring about for 5 weeks, for the barrels are full of salt ... many came oute of Themys with a monthe's bere, trustyng that the vittelers shulde bringe the rest, a here commyth none ... Sir for Godd's sake, sende by post all along the coste that they brew bere and make biskets that we may have some refresshyng to kepe us together uppon this cost.

But the hastily planned expedition failed to fulfil Henry's

expectations. When Dorset fell ill with fever, Thomas Howard suddenly found himself at the head of the English army in a hostile land, short of supplies and with the whole winter ahead. His men were soon threatening mutiny. A letter from Sir William Knight to Cardinal Wolsey warned that 'The army is idle; a large band has refused to serve under 8d a day.'

The mutiny was pacified, but one man suffered death and 'many bands now declare that they will go home at Michaelmas, if they should die for it'.

The expedition had turned to disaster. Edmund's hopes of glory on the battlefield soon disappeared when his brother Thomas made the fateful decision to bring the troops home.

The King was furious. His Spanish allies were accusing the English of cowardice by deserting the field. Ever vengeful, Henry unreasonably blamed Thomas Howard for this humiliation and was to remember it and hold it against him for years.

Thomas retreated to the countryside where his wife Anne Plantagenet was dying of consumption. Although she had borne him several children, none had survived to provide him with an heir. Thomas viewed her death as an opportunity and within just weeks had made a highly profitable marriage with the heiress of Edward Stafford, Duke of Buckingham.

The military disaster was somewhat alleviated by naval success. On the way home from the convoy, Edward and the English fleet took enemy ships and burned Conquet in Brittany. After refitting at Portsmouth, they sailed to attack the French fleet at Brest and on 10 August 1512 a fierce sea battle took place. Edward Howard destroyed or took captive more than 30 enemy ships and 800 prisoners, but others fared less well. Sir Thomas Knyvet, who had married the Howards' sister Muriel, was in command of *The Regent*. As she moved in to grapple the French ship *Marie La Cordelière*, ready to board her, the French suddenly sabotaged their own powder store. In the explosion, both ships and crews were engulfed in flames. The French lost 1,500 men and the English were left with just a handful of survivors. These did not include the captain, the Howards' brother-in-law. Edward vowed revenge for his death, declaring that 'he will never see the King in the face till he hath revenged the death of the noble and valiant knight, Sir Thomas Knyvet'.

The French were now reinforcing their fleet, introducing galleys from the Mediterranean under Chevalier Prégent de Bidoux or 'Prior John' of the Order of St John. These galleys were heavily armed, shallow-draught vessels rowed by banks of slaves and therefore not subject to the vagaries of wind and weather. By the following spring this new fleet had assembled in the port of Brest, where Edward discovered them. Instead of blockading the harbour where they lay, the Lord Admiral elected to assault the enemy.

On 25 April 1513 the English attacked. Edward Echyngham wrote later to Cardinal Wolsey to describe the scene:

> On St Mark's day, 25 April, the Admiral appointed four captains and himself to board the [galleys]. The Admiral himself, with 160 men … These enterprised to win the French galleys with the help of boats, the water being too shallow for ships. The galleys were protected on both sides by bulwarks planted so thick with guns and crossbows that the quarrels and gonstons came together as thick as hailstones.

For all this the Admiral boarded the galley that Prior John was in.

Edward Howard had just boarded one of the enemy ships when he and his men found themselves stranded, 'but the French hewed asunder the cable, or some of our mariners let it slip. And so they left this [noble Admiral in the] hands of his enemies.'

They struck rocks in the bay, facing the full force of French artillery batteries along the coast. Cut off from the rest of the fleet, Edward was severely wounded in hand-to-hand fighting:

> There was a mariner, wounded in eighteen places, who by adventure recovered unto the buoy of the galley, so that the galley's boat took him up. He said he saw my lord Admiral thrast against the rails of the galley with morris pikes…crying to the galleys, 'Come aboard again! Come aboard again!' which when my lord saw they

could not, he took his whistle from about his neck, wrapped it together and threw it into the sea.

Outnumbered, he chose to leap into the sea to avoid being taken captive but, being wounded and wearing a heavy breastplate, he drowned.

His body was later recovered and Prégent de Bidoux had it cut open and preserved with salt before sending it back to the English. Only then was it discovered that the heart was missing. This outrage shocked the English, who were fired up to take vengeance. Henry summoned Thomas Howard from his honeymoon to assuage his earlier disgrace by immediately replacing his valiant brother. Thomas went down to Devon but within a week the King was impatiently demanding to know why he had not sailed with the English fleet. Bishop Fox tried to explain matters to His Majesty: 'the Lord Admiral … with their whole army and their victuallers lie so far within the haven of Plymouth, that they cannot come out of it without a north-west wind and the wind hath been south-west continually three days past'.

When Henry's anger refused to abate, Thomas returned to London and attempted to see the King to explain, but was blocked by Cardinal Wolsey. There was little love lost between the proud Howards and the Cardinal, whom they regarded as an upstart who had risen from the slums to such prominence. Thomas complained that it was Wolsey's fault that the fleet was under-supplied and that he had been obliged to provide his own deliveries from London, but Henry was beyond his reach. Their relationship continued to be one of distrust and suspicion and it was June when Henry himself set out for war with a fleet 'such as Neptune never saw before', led by the *Mary Rose*. Before the expedition set sail from Dover, the head of the Howard clan was summoned before the King, only to be told that he was not going.

Surrey was told, 'My Lord, I trust not the Scots, therefore I pray you be not negligent.' It was reported that Surrey 'could scantly speak when he took his leave'. Stunned though he must have been, he could only acquiesce. The King was relying upon the

70-year-old veteran to keep England safe, under the regency of Queen Catherine, while he and 'the flower of all the nobility' were away on their French adventure. It was left to Surrey's son and heir Thomas to avenge his brother.

In 1512 the 'auld alliance' between Scotland and France had been renewed, designed to attack England on two fronts. Now, in July 1513, James IV sent an ultimatum to Henry: he must withdraw from France or expect an invasion from the north.

During the summer, while the English laid siege to Thérouanne and won a brief skirmish against French cavalry at 'the Battle of the Spurs', Surrey was anxiously recruiting a force to withstand an imminent Scots invasion. It seemed that the real danger lay not in France but on England's northern border. Here Surrey's son, Edmund, hoped to make a name for himself and show that he was the equal of his brothers.

On 22 August James IV and a Scottish army of between 60,000 to 100,000 men launched a full-scale invasion into Northumberland. It was well equipped with artillery brought from Stirling and Edinburgh, including the huge cannon known as Mons Meg. It was also supported by 5,000 regular French troops. They seized the border castles of Etal, Norham and Ford, leaving a wake of destruction throughout the border villages on the English side.

King James was lodged in comfort at Ford, where he is said to have dallied with Lady Elizabeth Heron while his army had a bounty of supplies and livestock looted from the captured English outposts.

The aged Earl of Surrey had been gathering an opposition force from his base at Alnwick. With some 20,000 troops he set out to confront the vastly superior Scottish army already entrenched south of Coldstream on Flodden edge. At his side were his sons Edmund and Thomas, who had been warned of the invasion and set sail from France, landing in Newcastle at the beginning of September with men and artillery salvaged from the French campaign. On 8 September, in foul weather, the tired and weary English made camp in the mud on the banks of the River Till near the village of Branxton.

The conditions were appalling and they were poorly equipped and hungry, about to attack a fresh army of superior strength. A contemporary report notes: 'There was little or no wine, ale, nor beer for the people to be refreshed with but all the army for the most part were enforced and constrained of necessity to drink water ... without comfort or trust of any relief.'

Surrey took control of the left front of his troops, Admiral Lord Thomas Howard the centre, and the inexperienced Edmund Howard the right flank. A reserve of 3,000 men under the command of Lord Dacre was kept to the rear. Then Surrey took his army in a wide sweep crossing the Till by Twizel Bridge. For a time the English army was dangerously exposed, struggling through the mud and marsh on either side of the river. Another section of the army, under Lord Stanley, had forded the river further south near Crookham, taking up a position away to the left of Surrey. This move was later to be decisive.

As Friday 9 September 1513 dawned, the Scots watched as the English advanced across the river. King James then ordered fires to be lit from all the camp refuse so that the dense smoke in the persistent rain might obscure their troop movements. In the confusion, Surrey's *prickers* or scouts reported that the enemy had shifted positions to Branxton Hill, lining up artillery to fire on the English below.

The battle commenced with a duel in which the English were forced to fire uphill. Yet, in the hands of experienced gunners, the English artillery proved much more accurate and by midafternoon the Scots had sustained severe casualties.

A counterattack was launched by the Scots Border Pikes, under Lord Home, at what was perceived to be the weak point of the English force, the right wing under the inexperienced Edmund Howard. His forces outnumbered three to one, the fighting was hand to hand, brutal and vicious. Edmund put up a desperate but losing fight. Many of his men broke the line and scattered, leaving him with a handful of loyal men to stand their ground. His standard-bearer fell dead at his side and he was downed three times but he managed to regain his feet and continue the struggle.

Aware that he could not hold on without reinforcements, Thomas tore the *Agnus Dei* (a holy relic) from his neck and sent it to his father in an appeal for help.

Seeing his advantage, King James now couched his lance and led a cavalry charge downhill against Surrey. But he had not calculated upon the courage and skill of the English bowmen, who stood firm in the valley, launching a storm of yard-long arrows which darkened the skies, finding targets among the flower of Scottish nobility. James himself was felled barely feet from Surrey's position.

Home's Pikes were about to charge Edmund again, when 1,500 of Lord Dacre's Border Lances charged the Scottish flank. A hand-picked group of reivers led by John Heron then hacked their way through to Edmund, 'making even work before them' and killing young Sir David Home.

Meanwhile, on the English left wing, Sir Edward Stanley assaulted Branxton Hill and overcame the highlanders on the right wing under the Campbells and Macleans. Suddenly the battle was over as the English billmen moved in for the kill.

Edmund Howard had survived, holding out against great odds. His father proudly knighted him on the field. The heroic feat is recorded in verse:

> And Edmund Howard's lion bright
> Shall bear them bravely in the fight.

James's corpse was finally identified by his surcoat emblazoned with the royal arms stained by blood. Surrey sent it to London as proof of the victory. Besides their King, the Scots dead numbered an archbishop, three bishops, two abbots, twelve earls, fourteen lords, sixty-eight knights and gentlemen and perhaps 10,000 ordinary foot soldiers. The English lost just 1,500 men.

It seemed like a miracle.

The ballad associated with Flodden, *Flowers of the Forest*, was first recorded in the Skene manuscript of 1620:

We'll here nae mair lilting at our ewe milking,
Women and bairns are heartless and wae,
Sighing and moaning on a ilka green loaning,
The flowers of the forest are a wede away.

Above the Howard family tombs at Framlingham, Suffolk, one can still see the Flodden Helmet, which was borne at the funeral of the victor in 1524.

Flodden was an ignominious defeat for the Scots, leaving the country virtually leaderless, but Surrey's astonishing victory put his own sovereign's French campaign in the shade. Henry was clearly reluctant to acknowledge the debt that he and the nation owed to the Howards and chose not to reward them until February 1514, when the veteran warrior Earl of Surrey finally inherited the title Duke of Norfolk, 29 years after the death of his father in the service of Richard III.

Since Bosworth the Tudors had treated the Howard family with suspicion, resentment festering and often flaring into perilous confrontation. Yet, lacking the necessary skill and experience of warfare himself, the King was obliged to turn to the Howards to safeguard the regime. The Tudors had seized the English crown by conspiracy and invasion. Their claim was tenuous, requiring the imposition of brute force to crush opposition. Even 30 years after Bosworth there were still remnants of the Yorkist party actively working to restore Plantagenet rule.

On the eve of his departure for France Henry had executed one of the White Rose faction, Edmund de la Pole, Earl of Suffolk, whose brothers were in exile but under surveillance. The King told the French Ambassador that he would eliminate the whole House of York, leading Marillac to report 'he will not cease to dip his hand in blood as long as he doubt his people'.

Norfolk's eldest son and heir Thomas now became the new Earl of Surrey at 40 years of age and was ordered straight to France to join the English forces. For his part, Edmund Howard received a reward of just three shillings and four pence a day as a pension and even this was cut off abruptly within a few years. His bragging over his success at Flodden, where he had saved the country from invasion, brought him few friends. In 1514 he received £100 from the royal exchequer 'to prepare himself to do feats of arms' in a tournament to celebrate the marriage of Henry's sister to Louis XII of France. He was also placed on various commissions of the peace where for three years he received a salary of twenty shillings a day for 'taking thieves'.

While Provost-Marshal of Surrey, Edmund came under suspicion of having misused his powers. He was arrested for subverting 'the good rule and execution of justice within the county of Surrey' and was taken before the much-feared court of Star Chamber at Westminster. This was so-called because of the star-spangled ceiling of the room where it met and most of its cases dealt with public law and order, riots, assault and property dealing. Edmund was charged with bribing, threatening and suborning juries in Surrey, 'by the great maintenance, embracery and bearing to the great hurt and damage of the king's subjects'. It appeared that he had favoured his cousin Roger Legh against one John Scotte in a disputed land deal, receiving 80 cartloads of wood as a bribe.

Edmund pleaded with Cardinal Wolsey and the judges 'to be mediators to the king's highness' on his behalf. They were clearly unimpressed and in the end his father had to intervene in order to get him a royal pardon.

The Howards were seen as the hard men of the Tudor regime, summoned to dirty their hands with any unsavoury violence that was required. One such incident was the infamous May Day riot of 1517 when more than 20,000 London apprentices ran amok for three weeks. Thousands of Italians, Flemings and Germans, including Protestant refugees who had fled from persecution, lived and traded in the city, forming large communities. Foreign languages were commonplace on London's streets, causing fierce resentment among the English. A priest denounced the wave of immigrants from the pulpit: 'The aliens and strangers eat the bread from the poor fatherless children, and take the living from all the artificers, and the intercourse from all the merchants, whereby poverty is so much increased that every man bewails the misery of others, for craftsmen be brought to beggary and merchants to neediness.'

Riots broke out over an abducted woman and rich merchants' houses were looted, notably in the St Martin-le-Grand district. In the chaos, the Lieutenant of the Tower of London, Sir Richard Cholmeley, rashly fired cannon into the city. Cardinal Wolsey had to call upon the Earl of Surrey to restore law and order.

With typical heavy-handedness, he quashed the riots, making mass arrests and condemning 13 boy apprentices. According to Edward Hall's *Chronicle* he 'showed no mercy but extreme cruelty to the poor younglings in their execution'.

They were all hanged, drawn and quartered. A further 400 men and 11 women who had been arrested pleaded to the King for mercy at their arraignment in Westminster Hall. John Stow romanticises this scene, describing the prisoners wearing halters around their necks, ready for the gallows, and suggesting that the Queen and Henry's two sisters also begged him to pardon them, which he graciously condescended to do. This was the kind of public show that Henry adored, displaying a regal magnanimity even when he had used Surrey to make the arrests. There were wild celebrations at the King's generosity, boosting his popularity as never before.

As Earl Marshal, Thomas Howard became the King's enforcer. Over the next few years he was dispatched on missions to the peripheries of English power. In 1520 the King gave him the unenviable duty of serving as Lord Lieutenant of Ireland, where the rebels immediately attempted to drive him out. For the next year, he wrote grovelling letters from the rain-lashed island, begging to be allowed home. He was therefore out of the country when the King moved against Edward Stafford, Duke of Buckingham, Surrey's father-in-law, on a charge of high treason.

His father Norfolk, still Lord High Steward at the age of 78, presided over the trial, which shocked the nation and created a scandal in Europe. Buckingham was accused of using sorcery to foretell the King's death, charges which scarcely disguised the vindictive motive of the King to be rid of another rival for his crown. The charges had been fabricated, and the underlying reason was Buckingham's Plantagenet blood. There was a horrified reaction in

Europe, where Emperor Charles V and Francis I believed England was on the brink of revolution.

Buckingham himself complained he would not receive justice, referring to the hostility between himself and the Howards because of his unhappy daughter Elizabeth, who had married Surrey when she was only 17, more than 23 years younger than her husband. She had been hoping to marry Ralph Neville, heir to the Earl of Westmoreland, with whom she was deeply in love. Her feelings were ignored and she endured a bitterly unhappy married life, continuing to write to her first love, Ralph Neville, all her life, even after he took her sister to be his wife.

Now Buckingham denounced Surrey, in court: 'of all men living he hated me most, thinking that I was the man that had hurt him most to the king's majesty'.

Thomas evidently blamed his father-in-law for his lack of popularity at court. His marriage was certainly a disaster, despite the birth of at least four children: Henry, Mary, Thomas and Catherine. The age difference between husband and wife, Thomas's frequent absences and his own infidelities did nothing to sweeten the relationship. He responded to his wife's tantrums with verbal and physical abuse. They made a spectacle of themselves at court with their violent insults and rows, hardly adding to the Howards' favour with the King.

The guilty verdict and Buckingham's subsequent execution were a foregone conclusion that must have satisfied Thomas, who now inherited his wife's fortune. But it was only a renewal of hostilities against the French that rescued him from his enforced exile in Ireland. As Lord Admiral he was called back into service in 1522 to deal with French pirates raiding the coasts, where he successfully launched a retaliatory assault on the port of Morlaix in Brittany.

The French afterwards determined to distract attention by supporting another Scottish attack on the English border. Ten years after Flodden Field it looked as though history was repeating itself. Surrey was immediately ordered by the King to deal with the matter.

During Thomas's enforced absence from court, the King

decided to transfer the hereditary role of Earl Marshal from the Howards to his friend Charles Brandon, Duke of Suffolk. Angry and embittered, Thomas claimed to be ill and insisted that he was needed on the Howard family estates as his father was unlikely to live much longer. He was deeply frustrated at being confined to the fringes of political influence, certain that this was the work of Wolsey, to whom he wrote a desperate appeal to support his family should he be killed in Scotland:

> Most humbly beseeching your Grace that [if] I fortune to miscarry in this journey to be good lord to my poor children, assuring your Grace that without the king's gracious favour and your Grace's showed unto them they are undone. For I have spent so much to serve the king's highness, that if God do now his pleasure [upon] me, I shall leave them the poorest nobleman's children that died in this realm these 40 years, having neither goods nor foot of land to put in feofment to do them good after me. And therefore most humbly I beseech your Grace to be good and gracious lord to them for my poor service done in times past.
>
> Scribbled the 23rd day of October at 11.0 at night.

When this appeal was ignored, Thomas proceeded with the business of sacking the Scots border town of Jedburgh, reporting: 'There is left neither house, fortress, village, tree, castle, corn or other succour for man … Such is the punishment of Almighty God for disturbers of the peace.'

He next relieved the garrison at Wark Castle, chasing off a Scottish force under the Duke of Albany. In December, sure that his bloody work was complete, Thomas started south again, but when he reached York he was intercepted by a royal messenger with curt instructions to get back to his post.

Thomas Howard had finally had enough. He now blatantly ignored the King's order, insisting that he had vital matters of state to discuss with Henry in person. The reason behind his newfound rebellious streak was the news he had just received that his 82-year-old father was dying.

For over 50 years Thomas had been outshone by his warrior father and by his flamboyant brother Edward. Now he was about to inherit the premier title and fortune in England and could no longer be ignored, even by Henry VIII. After an absence of several years, he was able to take his place in the King's Council and at court.

At about the very time that his niece Katherine Howard was born, Thomas finally became third Duke of Norfolk, determined to revive family fortunes and make the Howards a real power in the land.

Chapter Three

My Cousin the Queen

B Y 1526 THE KING was actively seeking a way out of his marriage. Henry had always doubted the legality of his marriage to his brother Arthur's widow, although Catherine claimed her first marriage was never consummated. When she later feigned pregnancy and lied to the court and her father, the King of Spain, Henry was humiliated. Catherine suffered stillbirths and miscarriages, producing only one surviving daughter, Mary, born in February 1516. Henry put on a good face in public, telling the Venetian Ambassador, 'We are both young. If it was a daughter this time, by the grace of God the sons will follow.' But from then on, the King took mistresses, having a son by Bessie Blount and a son and daughter by Mary Boleyn.

During all the years when England was without a male heir, there was growing speculation whether the King would legitimise his bastard son by Elizabeth Blount, Henry Fitzroy. He was just a six-year-old boy in 1525 when he was made Duke of Richmond and Somerset, giving him precedence over everyone else at court, including the Princess Mary.

This snub only served to enrage Queen Catherine, who relayed the insult to her powerful nephew Charles V, ruler of the Holy Roman Empire, which dominated Europe from Spain to

Germany, at a time when Islamic armies threatened the very gates of Vienna. The personal difficulties in Henry's marriage now came to influence international politics.

The King was convinced that his marriage was cursed: the Bible said so in Leviticus: 'If a man shall take his brother's wife, it is an unclean thing … they shall remain childless.' They had sinned, committing incestuous adultery. No wonder God had not sent him a legitimate son.

He fell passionately in love with Anne Boleyn, the younger sister of his mistress. Anne was sophisticated, assured and intellectual, having just returned from the French court where her father had sent her to further her education. The Boleyns were lesser gentry but Sir Thomas Boleyn, a skilled linguist and diplomat, had married Lady Elizabeth, the sister of Thomas and Edmund Howard.

The King pursued Anne relentlessly with letters and gifts, but she resisted him. She had been brought up by her father in the reform faith and her years in France had brought her into contact with other evangelicals. She had no intention of submitting to Henry as her wayward sister had done. Her resistance only served to fire his passions. He sent to Rome to demand an annulment so that he might marry Anne Boleyn.

Anne had hoped that by her refusals Henry would soon tire of stalking an unresponsive prey but her uncle Thomas Howard was soon aware of the King's 'secret matter'. Scenting the potential in the relationship, he tried to persuade Anne to surrender and become Henry's mistress, but Norfolk's religion and morals were diametrically opposed to hers and she would not cooperate.

A staunch Catholic in the traditional mould, Norfolk complained the country was merrier before 'this new learning came up'. He confessed that 'he had never read the Scripture nor ever would' and 'he knew not whether priests had wives but that wives will have priests'.

What kind of man was the third Duke of Norfolk? In the portrait by Hans Holbein, now in the Royal Collection at St James's Palace, he is shown holding the Earl Marshal's baton and the Lord Treasurer's stave. He was the last and most powerful of the old aristocracy, with estates worth £4,000 a year. The Venetian Ambassador Ludovico Falieri noted that he was 'prudent, liberal, affable and astute; associates with everybody, no matter what his origins, has very great experience in political government, discusses the affairs of the world admirably, aspires to greater elevation, and bears ill-will to foreigners ... small and spare in person, his hair is black ...'

Norfolk's private life was notorious. His promiscuity was well known; besides Bess Holland, he had other mistresses and at least two recorded illegitimate daughters, Margaret Howard and Jane Goodman. His views on women were shown by the way he treated his own wife. The Duchess of Norfolk complained to Cromwell that she was 'a gentlewoman, born and brought up daintily' and Norfolk 'chose her for not her dowry'. He seduced younger women, notably Bess Holland, 'that harlot ... the washer of my nursery', as the Duchess described her. In fact, that 'drab', the 'churl's daughter' Elizabeth Holland, who managed the laundry, was sister to the Duke's secretary and related to Lord Hussey of Sleaford. None the less, the Duchess bore her husband four children: Catherine, Henry, Mary and Thomas.

His son Thomas, by Anne Plantagenet, had died in 1508 aged only 12, but an heir was finally born in 1518, Henry Howard, Earl of Surrey, who was brought up chiefly at Kenninghall, near Norwich.

After his own harsh childhood, Thomas was indulgent to his son, his pride and joy. He was very bright and Thomas insisted upon hiring the best tutors for his education at home, notably John Cheke from the University of Cambridge and Stephen Gardiner, an arch Catholic conservative who became Bishop of Winchester. Thomas was proud of his son's 'proficiency and advancement in letters'. Mary Howard, born a year after Surrey, was of equal if not greater intelligence, but as she was just a girl her father did not waste much time in encouraging her talents.

Upon coming into his inheritance, Thomas Howard set out to rebuild the family seat at Kenninghall. Stretching over four acres, this had reputedly been the site of ancient kings and Boadicea's fort. Known variously as King's Hall and East Hall, the manor passed to the Mowbrays and thence to the Howards. Norfolk was determined to make it a great house, exchanging the medieval castle of Framlingham for a magnificent, costly Renaissance palace.

At this time, nobles and gentry were turning from the bleak fortresses of earlier times to more comfortable residences filled with lavish furniture and fittings, often imported from Europe. Some traditional English features were retained, such as the Great Hall where families would dine on festive occasions to display their wealth and status. The head of the household sat on a raised dais with his family and honoured guests 'above the salt', a silver container usually of ostentatious design and great value. Below the salt, in the main body of the hall, the household retainers sat at long trestle tables and benches. A recent innovation was a great window at the far end of the hall to bring in light. The oriel window was often set with coloured glass or heraldic designs, displaying the family coat of arms. The great hammerbeam roof was also richly painted with shields, angels and exotic animals.

An even more modern feature was the addition of an upstairs gallery. This long chamber often ran the length of the house, providing an indoor space for leisure and for the display of tapestries and family portraits, usually protected from the light by curtains. On wet winter days the ladies might promenade up and down the gallery or play bowls for exercise while small children ran about and played.

Just as the King now had his own privy chamber, a nobleman or gentleman had his closet, a small private sitting room or wooden panelled study where he might escape the family to read, write letters or pray. Even a soldier such as Norfolk was capable of adapting to the modern age and, although no scholar himself, he encouraged the intellectual development of his son and heir Henry, who became one of the great poets of the period.

Henry Howard, Earl of Surrey, was brought up together with Henry Fitzroy, the King's illegitimate son by Elizabeth Blount, who was just a year older and was referred to as 'the prince'. The boys became extremely close friends, sharing their studies at

Windsor Castle, which Surrey later recorded in poetry in which he invented a new form of quatrain:

> Where I in lust and joye with a kinges soon
> my childishe yere did passé ...
> frendshippe sworne, eche promyse kept so just,
> Wherwith we past the winter nightes awaye.

In 1529 a legatine court opened in London to judge the validity of the King's marriage to Catherine of Aragon. Nineteen witnesses, including the Duke of Norfolk and his stepmother Agnes, the Dowager Duchess of Norfolk, were summoned to give evidence about the wedding night of Catherine and her first husband, Prince Arthur. The Dowager had attended Catherine and confirmed that the marriage had indeed been consummated, which meant that the Queen had lied about her virginity. Furious, Catherine now appealed to the Pope himself to try her case.

Traditionally, historians have presented Catherine of Aragon as a saintly figure, incapable of lying and deceit, but evidence unearthed in the Spanish archives by Bergenroth in the 1860s disproves this picture. From her own correspondence with her father and the Emperor her nephew, via his ambassador Chapuys, it appears that Catherine deceived Henry VII about the consummation of her first marriage in order to stay in England, and also about her first pregnancy. In February 1510 she had announced she was pregnant, but a letter from her confessor Friar Diego to the King of Spain states that she had a miscarriage in January. On 27 May she wrote to her father herself, claiming she had lost the child 'a few days ago'. For months she kept up the pretence, humiliating the King when it was finally conceded that she had never been pregnant at all.

As her position was undermined, she protested against the honours given to Henry's illegitimate son when he was created Duke of Richmond in 1525, making him the rival to her daughter Mary. She became embittered and desperate to retain her status and ensure that Mary would remain as heir, later even plotting with

Spain through Chapuys and Bishop Fisher over many years to try and seize the throne for her daughter.

The annulment dispute dragged on for years, finally bringing down the powerful Cardinal Wolsey, who had failed to find an acceptable solution to Henry's dilemma. In October 1529 he was deprived of his offices, save the archbishopric of York; in November 1530 he was arrested on charges of treason but died before he could be taken to the Tower.

His replacement as the King's right-hand man was Thomas Cromwell, a careerist and self-made man of genius who had travelled widely, serving as a soldier in Italy, a moneylender in Venice and a banker in Antwerp. He taught himself Italian, French, Latin and some Greek. On his return to England he studied law, became an expert in business affairs and eventually caught the attention of Wolsey and subsequently the King. Ruthless in his climb to power, Cromwell inclined towards the reform religion, although never at the risk of his own career. He witnessed the fall of his former master Cardinal Wolsey with equanimity and soon made himself indispensable as the King's adviser.

The King now sought to break from the foreign authority of the Pope and create an independent Church in England. In this he was encouraged by the Boleyns and Cromwell, who saw ways of diverting the enormous resources of the abbeys and monasteries into the royal exchequer. If Henry broke free from the control of Rome, England would be strengthened as a nation and become a power in its own right: 'This realm of England is an Empire ... governed by one Supreme Head and King.' New legislation would split England away from Europe and ensure her independence, with the King now 'Protector and Supreme Head of the Church of England'. The break with Rome was in this sense a revolution, a major schism in international politics.

Anne had agreed to marry Henry when he was free. For seven long years she kept him at bay, refusing to sleep with him although her enemies called her 'concubine' and the King's whore. Her virginity was confirmed by the Imperial Ambassador to Rome when, perhaps regretfully, he observed: 'There is no positive proof of adultery, none having yet been produced here at Rome but, on the contrary, several letters proving the opposite.'

Now she told the Venetian Ambassador that God 'had inspired his Majesty to marry her' in order to bring in the Protestant religion. It seemed as though it was her destiny to be like Esther, God's chosen instrument, becoming Queen 'for such a time as this'. In late 1532 she was created Marquess of Pembroke in her own right and accompanied the King on a state visit to France. While abroad, she finally surrendered to Henry and in the New Year of 1533 they were secretly married after discovering that she was pregnant.

Anne's rise could only bode well for all her relatives. That summer of 1533 London hosted her coronation, with the large and rapacious Howard family focusing their ambitions on the royal court, where Agnes, Dowager Duchess of Norfolk enjoyed a position of influence.

Edmund Howard took full advantage of this tide in Howard fortunes, persuading the Dowager to take in his daughter Katherine. He had recently been appointed as Comptroller of Calais, thanks to the influence of Anne Boleyn. Calais was the last English outpost on the European mainland, a tiny and beleaguered enclave of 120 square miles from Gravelines to Cape Blanc Nez, known as the English Pale. It had a population of 12,000, including its garrison. The Governor, Lord Lisle, provided intelligence from the continent, passing on news to the King through Cromwell, but also to the Duke of Norfolk. Edmund's new post was not glamorous, involving checking the accounts and ordering supplies, but it paid £80 a year.

Agnes Tilney was the widow of the second Duke of Norfolk, born about 1477 and now in her late fifties. An opinionated second wife, she had resisted all pressure to remarry and was mistress in her own right of vast estates with their annual incomes, an enviable position for any woman and one she was not willing to surrender. She kept control of two great estates, at Lambeth in London and at Chesworth near Horsham in Sussex. These households required a continual influx of servants and retainers, many supplied by her own relatives in the hope that she would advance their prospects.

As a result of her status, wealth and continuing influence, Dowager Duchess Agnes was plagued by relatives for financial assistance. She had borne her husband eight surviving children who, although far from inheriting any lands or money associated with the Norfolk title, all carried the Howard name and made lucrative marriages. She considered that they should be more than capable of building their own lives and fortunes. When her eldest son, William of Effingham, came to her to ask for an advance on his inheritance, Agnes refused him although she kept a secret cache of money at home. She was clearly reluctant to give any of it away to her wastrel children or stepchildren.

She did, however, agree to bring up Edmund's young daughter in her household, to give her a traditional and proper basis for her future life.

It was the golden opportunity. Moreover, it was perhaps the only opportunity for the tenth child of the impoverished, discontented Edmund Howard. At seven years of age, Katherine was brought from obscurity by her ambitious family, to be trained for a glorious future. Now that the King had chosen her cousin Anne Boleyn to become his Queen there were new possibilities at court for pleasant young women such as Katherine.

It was her first time away from home. Although Katherine had travelled before, it had always been in the company of her family, while changing houses to stay with their relatives. It was a time when the vast majority of people rarely travelled beyond their home towns or villages. The furthest most of them went was just a few miles walk to market. Roads were pot-holed and muddy, and no one ever travelled alone or by night. Pack trains of mules took freight on long haul covering 15 to 20 miles a day and blocking the roads. When Katherine had moved house with her family, they had taken their belongings in coffers on carts, perhaps stopping at inns along the way.

Katherine would have ridden a horse or mule. As a small child, she may have been strapped in a pillion, a leather or padded cushion on a wooden frame behind the rider. When she was older, she had the confidence to handle her own horse, a necessary skill for participating in the aristocratic pastimes of hawking and hunting. Women did not ride sidesaddle until it was introduced from France and Italy.

It must have been a nervous time for the seven-year-old girl. Katherine may have had to say farewell to her father but it was exciting to know that she was now old enough to start her education and make her own way in the world. She already seemed to fulfil the ideal that women should be demure and dainty, with peaches-and-cream complexion and blonde hair. We have no reliable portrait, but contemporaries were later to describe her as vivacious with dark blonde hair and of 'diminutive stature'.

Although the traditional picture of Katherine's youth has been painted as one of poverty and neglect, her true situation was rather different. While her formative years may not have been spent in luxurious comfort, from the time she left her father's haphazard care she knew few privations.

Chesworth Park comprised 223 acres, part of St Leonard's Forest, which had passed from the de Braose family. There were five great reception rooms and a warren of chambers and endless corridors that must have been a welcome revelation to the Dowager Duchess's young step-granddaughter. The estate was self-sufficient, a working farm which supplied the household with virtually everything they needed, from bread and beer to rushes and wood for the many fires needed to keep such a place warm.

There were cows in the byre, chickens in the yard, horses in the stables, falcons in the mews and fish bred in ponds for the table. A great herd of deer wandered freely through four acres of orchards and gardens. It was here that Katherine Howard was to live for more than four years.

In many great houses noblemen were being forced to make strict economies, defraying expenses and cutting their enormous households, but it does not appear that this was the case with Dowager Agnes. Her great staff must have included many of the 37 offices reserved to men, as listed in Anthony, Viscount Montague's

Book of Orders and Rules; these included Steward of the Household, Comptroller, General Receiver, Solicitor, Secretary, Gentlemen Ushers, Carver, Sewer (server), Gentlemen of the Chamber, Gentlemen of Horse, Marshall of the Hall, Clerk of the Kitchen, Usher of the Hall, Chief Cook, Yeoman of the Cellar, Yeomen of the Ewery, Pantry, Buttery and Wardrobe, 2nd Cook, Porter, Granator, Bailiff, Baker, Brewer, Grooms, Almoner and Scullery Man. Besides these posts there were of course dozens of female servants, from the Dowager's own ladies-in-waiting and the housekeeper to the poorest laundry maid.

More than half the young people in Tudor England spent their adolescent years as a servant in someone else's house, but only a minority were domestic servants who wore livery embroidered with the master's arms. The rest were agricultural workers: men and boys looked after livestock and worked the fields using horses, while women and girls weeded, harvested and gleaned as required, or were dairymaids. They gave their labour in exchange for lodgings, food and clothing as well as a low wage. In service, they could experience a higher standard of living, more plentiful and better food than they would have had at home.

Servants found work for other members of their family, sometimes sharing the same post or passing on their own job if they moved up in service. They also recommended their poor relations, finding a place for cousins, nieces and nephews, to give them a start in life. Many servants, like apprentices, had to post bonds before entering employment, agreeing to work for a guaranteed period without leaving. Some indentured servants were little better than slaves, being sold into service by their parents who received their wages. This practice was widespread in country areas and continued well into the following centuries with such servants, often young girls, following their masters and mistresses to the New World.

Other members of the household came from the burgeoning middle classes or gentry. Their education and refinement of manners meant that they served as ladies' maids, comptrollers or stewards. Young men who had been educated in the monasteries, and were therefore literate, found work in estate management, handling the accounts or acting as secretary or tutor to a noble family. Those of the highest standing might employ a university graduate.

Many of those who had found a place with the Dowager Duchess were members of her own vastly extended family. Katherine was perhaps among girls already known to her, some of them cousins from the minor fringes of the Howard and Tilney dynasties, such as Katherine and Malena Tilney, daughters of Catherine, Countess of Bridgewater and granddaughters of Dowager Agnes. Even Katherine's own elder sisters and half-sisters had been with the Dowager for short periods, either at the Chesworth house or her mansion in Lambeth. The vast staff meant that Katherine was lost among a great household where up to one hundred girls and women lived communal lives and slept together in rooms like dormitories. There was little or no privacy, with the young girls soon absorbing all that they heard and saw around them from their older companions and instructors.

The Dowager herself was constantly on the move between houses, as the demands and attractions at court required. That year of 1533 she had been away in London, leaving Katherine to be brought up by the women around her. But on her return, Katherine must have heard from her grandmother all the details of Queen Anne's coronation on the feast of Pentecost. The Dowager Duchess played a leading part in the lavish ceremonies, doubtless returning home with eyewitness reports of how, dressed in a robe of scarlet with a coronet of gold on her head, she carried the Queen's train as she entered Westminster Abbey, where Anne Boleyn had uniquely been crowned with St Edward's crown, the same used for the King himself. This effectively made her co-ruler and queen regnant, an honour not bestowed upon any other consort.

At the great banquet that followed the ceremony, the Dowager's son, Lord William Howard, rode into the hall as deputy for the Duke of Norfolk as Earl Marshal of England to challenge anyone who disputed the new Queen's title. How exciting and glamorous it must all have sounded to the young Katherine, listening to the Dowager's account.

By contrast with her older and more prestigious cousin Anne Boleyn, Katherine was given a traditional country education as befitted a girl of her conservative background and station. It was a rare father who accorded the same educational opportunities to daughters as to sons. Such a man was Sir Thomas Boleyn, who went to great lengths to use his connections to arrange that Anne should receive the very best education available, sending her away to be raised in foreign courts in Burgundy and France. He hoped that she would make a brilliant match that would elevate the family, never suspecting that her very difference and vitality would soon obsess the King.

Far from joining in the dissolute lifestyle of Francis I's entourage, as her sister Mary had done, Anne spent her days in attendance on the sickly Queen Claude, keeping her company, reading together, playing music and doing silkwork. Anne associated with women of the highest moral standards, devoting herself to the improvement of her skills in language, composition and the arts. She was 'very expert in the French tongue, exercising herself continually in reading the French Bible and other French books of like effect, and conceived great pleasure in the same'. She also knew some Latin.

Unlike her cousin, there was nothing very remarkable about Katherine at her young age. She did not stand out from the many other girls placed in the Dowager's care. The Howards were traditionalists with conservative attitudes towards women and their role in the world. Norfolk viewed his niece Anne's intellect and independence as reaching beyond her natural place in the world and therefore 'foolish' and subversive.

'I perceive that learned women be suspected of many', warned Juan Luis Vives, whose *Instructions of a Christian Woman* was commissioned by Catherine of Aragon for her daughter Mary. He pointed out to his pupil that 'Men must do many things in the world and must be broadly educated, but only a little learning is required of women.'

Vives warned that the 'frayle kynde' of woman would be tempted to vice by reading. He taught that women were the authors of original sin and, from birth, 'the devil's instruments and not Christ's'. He believed women should not leave the house unaccompanied, and only then with their faces hidden by a veil, for they were naturally promiscuous and deceitful.

Only a handful of girls received an enlightened humanist education. The vast majority were still illiterate, scarcely able to sign their names. Honor, Lady Lisle, the wife of Edmund Howard's employer in Calais, could read but had to dictate letters to a secretary. She sought to improve her children by pulling strings to ensure they were placed out to receive a better education. Only one of her daughters lived at Government House in Calais, while Anne Basset, her daughter by a previous marriage, was sent in November 1533 to be taught French in the household of a family near Abbeville. Her younger sister Mary joined her the following year when she was 11 years old. Very soon, the sisters were writing effusive letters home:

My good sister and friend, I greatly desire to hear good news of you and of my other sisters. If I might have my wish I would be every day an hour with you, that I might teach you to speak French ... I send you a purse of green velvet ... a gospel to my sister Katharine, and a parroquet to my lord my father, because he maketh much of a bird. I beg of you, my sister, to have the goodness to present it to him, and to entreat him to send me some pretty thing for this Easter. He hath yet not sent me anything, although I have never forgot him ... Recommending me as well and as humbly as I may to your good favour ... I pray our Lord to give you a good husband, and that very soon ...
From Abbeville, the xiij of March, Your most loving sister, ever your friend,
Marie Basset.

It was held that the 'principal commendation in a woman [is] to be able to govern and direct her household, to look to her house and family' and 'to know the force of her kitchen'. A manual of 1525 lists a woman's duties:

> When thou art up and ready, then first sweep thy house, dress up thy dish-board, and set all things in good order within thy house; milk thy kine, feed thy calves, sile up thy milk, take up thy children and array them, and provide for thy husband's breakfast, dinner, supper, and for thy children and servants ... ordain corn and malt to the mill, to bake and brew withal when need is ... Thou must make butter and cheese when thou may; serve thy swine, both morning and evening, and give thy pullen meat in the morning, and when time of the year cometh, thou must take heed how thy hen, ducks and geese do lay, and to gather up their eggs.

Girls were routinely instructed in cooking, baking and brewing before they were taught how to read or write. They learnt practical skills, including the salting and preservation of meat for the winter, smoked and hanging from the rafters. Fruit, vegetables, even eggs were pickled and stored.

Besides these tasks, girls were taught how to distil and prepare medicines, and how best to care for children and the sick. It was believed that the body was ruled by four humours – blood, phlegm, choler and black bile. Sickness could be cured by bloodletting to balance the body, or with herbal cures. A good wife knew how to cure toothache, stop worms and banish bad humours. She also had the perfect answer for haemorrhoids:

> Take the sole of an old shoe worn by a man much used to travel; cut it into pieces, and burn it, yet neither to grey or white ashes, but to a friable and tender coal. Reduce it into an impalpable powder. Take then unsalted hog lard, and work it to an ointment, and anoint the afflicted part often therewith.

She could save the family money for a costly physician by diagnosing urine samples and concocting purges. There was 'syrup of poppy' for toothache or to soothe a restless child, burnt feathers or dung for quinsy (tonsillitis), the brains of a hare for teething, while the worms that caused tooth decay could be removed with a boiled green frog. Every good household would have its kitchen garden with tansy, harefoot and pennyroyal and a physic border containing mandrake, wormwood, plantain and valerian. The Dowager Duchess herself was famous for her herbal cures, advising Cardinal Wolsey during the 1528 outbreak of sweating sickness ('the Sweat') to take this recommendation for 'treacle and water imperial, which doth drive it from the heart and thus have helped them that have swooned divers times, and that have received the sacraments of the church'.

Other cures for the Sweat were a mixture of endive, marigold, mercury and nightshade or three large spoonfuls of water of dragons and half a nutshell of unicorn's horn.

Katherine was to be trained in such homely skills so that one day, as a good wife, she could manage her own house. She would be prepared for a suitable marriage to the man chosen for her by her family, very likely a landed country gentleman or perhaps, if she was fortunate, even to someone with a minor place at court.

As Katherine listened to her grandmother's reports of Queen Anne's coronation, no one could have imagined that just a few years later she would be a candidate to replace her cousin in the King's bed.

Chapter Four

Dynastic Ambitions

THE DUKE OF NORFOLK was in France when he first heard that the Pope had excommunicated King Henry on 11 July 1533. He was said to have fainted at the news. The Vatican had not been slow to retaliate against England.

Henry had gambled by breaking with Rome and finally marrying Anne, making her Queen. He anticipated that her pregnancy would deliver the longed-for prince and heir, but that September the child for whom he had created an international crisis, breaking with Rome and incurring excommunication as a result, turned out to be another daughter.

This was a body blow, but Henry concealed his feelings from the world and the Princess Elizabeth was christened, with Agnes, Dowager Duchess of Norfolk, as godmother and the Howard family out in force.

On 23 March 1534 the Act of Succession to 'the imperial crown of England' made it a capital crime to refuse to acknowledge Henry as head of the Church or to contest the new line of succession. Catherine's daughter Mary was declared illegitimate, but the Imperial Ambassador, Eustace Chapuys, described Princess Elizabeth as 'the little bastard'. He denigrated Queen Anne at every opportunity, calling her 'the Concubine', 'the Grand Enemy' of the

Catholic faith, 'more Lutheran than Luther himself' and a 'heretic', for 'whatever is contrary to the Catholic faith is heresy'.

The head of the Howard dynasty, Thomas, Duke of Norfolk, could not accept the separation from Rome. The theological arguments left him unmoved but he feigned support for the King as Henry 'had distinctly declared his will more for one thing than for the other' and therefore Norfolk was prepared to play a waiting game, taking a more prudent role and biding his time. He warned Sir Thomas More of the dangers involved in speaking out too boldly: 'By the mass, Master More, it is perilous, striving with princes. And therefore I would wish you somewhat to incline to the King's pleasure. For by God's body, Master More, *Indignatio principis mors est!*' ('The wrath of princes is death').

His home life went from bad to worse. He was still creating scandal, once informing Cromwell that he could 'be sure of a welcome' with the wife of one of his servants and that he knew of another 'young woman with pretty proper tetins'.

When the Duchess protested about his affair with Bess Holland, he 'came riding all night' to imprison her in her own house, 'taking away all her clothes and jewels and leaving her only a small allowance to support herself and twenty others in a hard country'. The Duchess claimed that she had suffered physical abuse at her husband's hands and that he set the servants to pin her to the floor until her fingers bled with scratching at the boards: 'They bound me and pyanaculled me and satt on my brest tyll I spitt blod, which I have ben worse for ever syns; and all for speking gainst the woman in the Courte, Bess Holand. Therefore he put me out at the doors and kepys the bawd and the harlots still in his house.'

A woman was regarded as the 'weaker vessel', subject to her husband in all things. Wife-beating was not only viewed as acceptable but a necessary curb on a woman's natural, foolish and loose behaviour for, as the old saying had it: 'A wife, a spaniel, a walnut tree: the more you beat them, the better they be.'

In London a by-law had to be introduced forbidding wife-beating after nine at night for fear of disturbing neighbours trying to sleep. But the Duchess of Norfolk was determined to achieve the greatest publicity for her case, writing again to protest to Cromwell: 'He sett hys women to bynde me, tyll blod came out att my fingars endes ... and he never ponyshed them, and all thys was done for Besse Holond's sake.'

Since she had been forced to flee her home in self-defence, she had suffered 'much sickness and cost in physic', trying to survive on what Norfolk sent her. The Duchess actively supported that other discarded wife, Catherine of Aragon, and openly criticised Queen Anne, insisting that she would be the ruin of the Howard family. Unsurprisingly, such comments as those led to her dismissal from court, but she continued to keep in secret correspondence with Catherine, even to the extent of smuggling her messages hidden inside oranges.

The Queen was soon pregnant again, only to miscarry. Henry could not help but be reminded of his past history with Catherine. There were forces at work to subvert his reforms and turn back the clock. Ambassador Chapuys gathered intelligence and provided the covert contact between Catherine and her daughter Mary. His mission was to preserve Catherine of Aragon as Queen, and England as a Catholic nation. In Catholic eyes, Henry, as an excommunicate, had no right or title to the crown. Chapuys told his master there was a way to depose Henry and replace him with Mary. Catherine and Mary were clearly playing with fire, for this was high treason.

The former Papal Nuncio, Uberto de Gambara, believed there was a less dangerous path. He knew that Norfolk was ambitious to link the Howards in marriage with the King's family and therefore into the succession. While Henry remained without a legitimate son and heir, after the King's bastard children, including Richmond and Mary, Norfolk himself stood close to the throne but believed that his true rank and status were not recognised. The Vatican diplomat surely encouraged his prejudice against the 'new men' such as Cromwell, a Protestant, and other 'thieves and murderers' who were usurping his rightful place and influence with the King.

He had placed his son Surrey as companion to the King's son

Richmond, who had an income of about £4,000 a year and maintained an entourage of 500 or 600 followers. Both young men spent a year together at the French court, imbibing the lavish Renaissance atmosphere, playing tennis and causing a certain amount of youthful mayhem by riding through the streets drunk in the middle of the night, firing pistols.

In 1530 Norfolk had arranged the secret marriage of his half-sister Catherine with young Edward Stanley, Earl of Derby. The fact that he had first to kidnap the boy in order to force him to go through with the ceremony had unfortunate repercussions. The lack of royal assent meant that a furious Henry accused Norfolk of abduction and put the marriage on hold. Norfolk was equally outraged, claiming indignantly that the match was 'an alliance essential to his family strength'.

For some years Norfolk had wanted his heir, Henry, Earl of Surrey, to marry the King's daughter Mary but he resigned himself in 1532 to a match with the Earl of Oxford's daughter, Frances de Vere. He then prevented them from living together, aware that the match could thus be easily set aside should a more profitable alliance turn up.

Uberto de Gambara now proposed such a scheme. Norfolk should approach the King again to seek the hand of his daughter Mary for his son Surrey now that she had been declared illegitimate.

Only the duke of Norfolk can persuade him to do this by his influence, and relationship to the new queen, pointing out that the peace of the Kingdom and the settlement of the king's son weighs more with him than the good of his own niece, and that if the king were to die before the son became a man, the next heirs might trouble the succession – the king of Scotland and the sons of the other sister and of the duke of Suffolk ... I think I could point out to him that this course would so endear him to the emperor and the pope that they would enable him to have the princess for his son; whose right would not really be put aside, and they would afterwards help to maintain him by force.

The Pope approved this scheme to promote Mary Tudor's cause, certain that it would 'thus gain many adherents and overthrow her father'.

This plot should have appealed to Norfolk, covering all his options: if Henry chose to make Richmond his heir, or if the King was overthrown by a foreign invasion, his successor was married to a Howard. But, if he was approached, he must have panicked. His relationship with the King was perilous enough without taking the risk of openly coming out in support of Catherine and her daughter.

He withdrew his objections to Surrey's marriage to Frances de Vere and the young couple began living together in 1535, producing five children.

Thomas Howard saw his family as a commodity, ripe for exploitation. As each fresh crop of Howard sons and daughters grew towards puberty they became pawns in the marriage game, tools by which Norfolk could build a dynasty. Romantic love was regarded as an absurd and irrational reason for marriage when financial demands and family ambitions required solid contractual alliances.

Norfolk had placed his daughter Mary Howard as one of Queen Anne's ladies, being cousins. He planned to marry her to the King's son Richmond, certain that this would make him father-in-law of a future King and prospective grandfather to a royal child.

At court, Mary Howard became good friends with other younger women in the new Queen's service, including the King's niece, Lady Margaret Douglas and Mary or 'Madge' Shelton, the daughter of Sir John Shelton and his wife Anne, sister of Thomas Boleyn, the Queen's father. These girls were all related to Katherine Howard and had been selected for places at court to promote family interests. They were of an age, from 14 to 17 years old, lively and flirtatious. They were following in the footsteps of their cousin Anne Boleyn, a path that young Katherine herself would take when she grew older. But unlike Katherine, they were all highly literate and, like the Queen they served, educated to a high degree.

Immediately they attracted a flurry of interest at the court. The young women were supervised by Mrs Marshall and the Queen made it clear to all her household that she condemned any 'licentious libertie'. She insisted that her ladies show 'vertuous demeanor', that they 'take especiall regarde, and to omitt nothing that may seeme to apperteigne to honor' but occupy themselves with 'godly conversation'.

William Latimer reports that the King had 'such pleasure' in theology that he and Anne never dined 'without some argument of Scripture thoroughly debated'. Foxe wrote of Anne's influence on the King: 'So long as Queen Anne, Thomas Cromwell, Archbishop Cranmer, Master Denny, Doctor Butts, with such like were about him and could prevail with him, what organ of Christ's glory did more good in the church than he?'

Queen Anne maintained support for the illegal trade in Scripture coming from abroad. Tyndale's English translation of the New Testament was still banned but Anne bravely kept it on display for anyone to read. Members of her household attended religious service once a day and the Queen gave each one a book of Psalms in English. These were not always appreciated, however. Latimer records how Anne caught her cousin Mary Shelton writing romantic verses in hers, for which she 'wonderfully rebuked her'.

The 'idle poesies' that Mary Shelton wrote in her prayer book were perhaps a response to a love poem from the King, for Mary's name was linked with his in 1535, though whether she actually became his mistress is debatable. On the death of Surrey's friend Thomas Clerc, the poet wrote a sonnet in which he indicated an affair between Clerc and Mary Shelton and Surrey continued the link afterwards.

Mary Shelton's friends Lady Margaret Douglas and Mary Howard also wrote poetry and they are now believed to be the authors of the Devonshire Manuscript, a miscellany of 4,300 lines of courtly love poetry once claimed to be the work of Thomas Wyatt and Henry Howard, Earl of Surrey. Accord to Foxwell, the manuscript originally belonged to Wyatt who gave it to the Duke of Norfolk for his son. Surrey in turn presented it to his sister Mary as a gift on her marriage to the King's son Henry Fitzroy, Duke of Richmond.

Surrey has been much praised for his ability to write poetry from a female perspective, and it has been said that as 'a habitual hearer of the voice of female complaint' (no doubt that of his mother, the long-suffering Duchess of Norfolk), some of his most powerful poems 'adopt and absorb the voices of women'. It is interesting to consider whether these verses in a woman's voice, such as 'Farewell all my wellfare', might actually have been the work of a woman. The handwriting of 'O happy dames' bears a remarkable similarity to that of Surrey's sister, Mary Howard.

The young women at court who wrote about their secret friendships and relationships with suitors sought 'to give themselves a voice' but their involvement in such a literary circle was exceptional and could even be 'potentially dangerous'.

Lady Margaret Douglas had been brought up at the English court, being much in favour with the King, her uncle, for her Tudor good looks, but she had also inherited her mother's feisty temper. The King had fallen out with his sister, the widowed Queen of Scotland, over her scandalous association with Archibald Douglas, the Earl of Angus, Lady Margaret's father. For years there was heated debate about whether their marriage was valid or not and she later sued for divorce, claiming that Douglas had been hand-fasted to another woman who had borne him a child.

Lady Margaret was, after the Queen, the highest-ranking lady in England. She was thus a magnet for Howard ambitions and Norfolk's half-brother Thomas, a son of Dowager Duchess Agnes, secretly paid court to her with love letters and poems. He was 33, she 15 years younger. Mary Shelton acted as go-between for the lovers.

The theme of courtly love was central to the collected poems of the Devonshire Manuscript, displaying the 'liveliness of *amour courtois* in Anne Boleyn's circle'. The 'three ideal regulations of courtly love' were love, loyalty and secrecy, and the Queen's young women were deeply involved in all three. The game required decorum and eloquence which, when combined with the subject of love, provided a dramatic opportunity to display one's wit and cleverness through riddles, jokes, themes, questions and debates. Riddles in particular could be developed to maintain the secrecy that was essential in such dangerous pastimes.

It was not only the young women at court who entered into the 'game of love'. The large and unmonitored household of the Dowager Duchess of Norfolk at Horsham was chiefly composed of both married and unmarried adolescent girls whose ages ranged down to just eight. The Duchess herself was almost 60 and uninterested in the upbringing or instruction of so many of her minor relatives. She was content to leave supervision of the youngest girls to the older women, in the not altogether wise assumption that they would teach them correct and moral behaviour.

Servants often had a reputation for unbridled sexuality, slipping about the house between bedchambers by night. A shrewd housekeeper would try to curb these nocturnal activities by locking internal doors. Some families even tried to prevent any mischief by dividing houses such as Petworth, in West Sussex, with separate staircases built for the male and female servants to use. In other houses it was the master himself, his relatives and guests who regarded the female staff as freely available under *droit de seigneur*. Some serving girls reported affairs or rapes, but it was usually accepted as the hazard of such work.

The young women who entered the service of the Dowager Duchess were not all common servants, the prey of their masters or his guests, but those of gentle birth seeking to profit from their Howard connections. Married or unmarried, enforced chastity was not to their taste and they were likely to take the lead in finding a sexual outlet.

At night, as soon as the rush lights were extinguished, excitement would mount as visitors were smuggled into the women's quarters, bringing with them gifts of wine and sweetmeats.

What followed these midnight picnics might have shocked a sheltered child, but Katherine had been brought up in a vast family of brothers and sisters, stepbrothers, half-brothers and cousins of all kinds and all ages, crowded together into the same house. It is unlikely that she remained for long unaware of sex, whether married or prenuptial.

In the extended family there was really very little privacy, even in the bedchamber.

Katherine would have shared a 'dormitory' with other women, some of who were married and sexually experienced. In these cramped conditions the women and girls had to share beds, only separated from others by bed-hangings and flimsy partitions. With the close proximity of night visitors on every side, eavesdropping or the chance viewing of sexual activity provided young Katherine's initiation.

It seems the mysterious goings-on were presented as a game, a secret and thrilling escapade that had to be kept from the master or mistress of the house, thereby heightening the sense of excitement and enjoyment.

Young Katherine Howard would probably not see any harm in the activities that took place around her, even if these young women were risking their future prospects in nocturnal games, unknown to their families. The Church taught that sex outside marriage was prohibited, while sex within marriage was solely for the procreation of children. Sexual initiation did not change an unmarried woman's status and she remained the legal property of her father until marriage.

Domestic service was a marriage market, a way to get out of the family home or village and meet the opposite sex. Many girls faced the prospect of marriages to much older men, since death in childbirth was so common that a man often went through several wives, as in the case of Katherine's father, Edmund Howard.

Duchess Agnes may have been unaware of the nocturnal games that took place after dark in the long rooms or dormitories, but young Katherine was not. She became a first-hand witness to the clandestine encounters between her companions and certain eligible young men on the fringes of the Howard household.

The age at which Katherine Howard was first initiated into the adult world is determined by her date of birth. Given the evidence that this was probably 1525 or 1526, Katherine was only seven or eight years old in 1533 when she was first sent to the household of the Dowager Duchess of Norfolk. It was a tender age to become party to the uninhibited sexual games of the girls' dormitory at Chesworth. Although she may not have participated herself, it was still a loss of innocence.

Chapter Five

The Shadow of the Tower

O N 7 JANUARY 1536 Catherine of Aragon died, probably
of cancer. Henry was greatly relieved at the news: 'like
one transported with joy'. His ambassador Edward Fox,
Bishop of Hereford, told the Elector of Saxony: 'England is tran-
quil now. The death of a woman has forever terminated all wran-
gling.'

Queen Anne was pregnant for the fourth time and expectations
were high that this time she would bear Henry a son, but at a great
jousting tourney on 24 January the King fell heavily and lay
unconscious for two hours. There were immediate rumours that
he was dead and Norfolk rushed to break the news to Anne. Such
lack of concern for her condition would have been typical of
Thomas Howard and, whether calculated or not, the Queen mis-
carried.

The Imperial Ambassador Chapuys records how Norfolk had
begun working secretly against his niece Anne. His long-term ally
was the Bishop of Winchester, Stephen Gardiner, who had been
tutor of Norfolk's son and remained close to the Howards. He had
been passed over as the King's Secretary by Thomas Cromwell and
later as Archbishop of Canterbury by the reformist Thomas Cranmer. 'Busy Gardiner, the wittiest, boldest, and best learned of his

faculty' never forgave either of them. Norfolk and Gardiner formed a long-lasting alliance of interests that covertly opposed the reforms being introduced as a result of Anne Boleyn's influence upon the King.

Anne and the reform party were active in urging Henry to help the German Protestants in Europe, and the Reformist theologian Philip Melanchthon wrote to Henry: 'Sire, this is now the golden age for Britain.' But Bishop Gardiner 'with his crafty fetches' had got 'into the King's ear' and wrote from France to warn the King against going too far with these 'heretics'. 'Wily Winchester' knew 'his master's nature' but was 'too wise to take upon himself to govern the King'. The reformer Alesius later stated unequivocally that Anne's support for the Protestants was the reason she had to be removed.

The King had overturned a whole system of government in order to bring in a new order confirmed by the Acts of Supremacy and Succession. Cromwell had demonstrated that the income of the government was only two-thirds that of the Church, which was England's greatest landowner with enormous wealth in the form of land, houses and money. His report, *Valor Ecclesiasticus*, initiated an inquiry into the abuses of monasteries and convents. Commissioners paid lightning visits around the country, uncovering instances of moral corruption, debauchery and child abuse. Pregnant nuns were reported in various places; at Cartmel one sister had six children. The Abbot of Fountains Abbey kept six women while a prior had seven children. The commissioners were shocked: 'O Lord God! ... the monstrous lives of monks, friars, and nuns have destroyed their monasteries and churches, and not we.'

The Report of the Commission was presented to Parliament on 4 February. All but the prologue, known as the 'Black Book', was later destroyed by the Catholic regime under Mary Tudor: 'It plainlie appered their filthie lusts were not satisfied with maidens wifes and widows but they also practised one with another that detestable sodomitishe and Romishe unnatural Acte whereof St Paul in the first to the Romans [Romans I, 26-7] writeth which was the Cause that horrible vice was made by parliament felonie without helpe or benefit of Clergie.'

The Queen had visited Syon Abbey, giving the nuns copies of the Scriptures in English, so that they might understand what they were praying instead of learning their offices by rote. Anne attacked corrupt Church practices, revealing the trickery at Hailes Abbey, famous for the 'holy blood' of Jesus Christ collected during the crucifixion, which had never congealed since. Pilgrims had to pay to see it, making a fortune for the abbey. The Queen's chaplains discovered it was in reality duck's blood that ran out by a system of hidden levers worked by the monks.

Anne knew she was the enemy of the Catholic party at court and commented, 'They will not let me live. I am too great an obstacle to their religion.' She asked her chaplain Matthew Parker to watch over her daughter Elizabeth if anything should happen to her. Anne believed Elizabeth had a destiny to rule. Her chief concern was that she should be brought up and educated as befitted a Protestant and future Queen of England. Many years later her daughter Elizabeth was told, 'True religion in England had its commencement and its end with your mother.'

The Catholic faction regarded the Princess Elizabeth as illegitimate and would never accept her as Queen. The Emperor and the Pope would make certain that she was removed, if necessary by foreign invasion, and replaced with Mary. Anne's position was increasingly precarious as her own uncle was plotting her downfall by manoeuvring one of her waiting women into the King's company.

The Seymour family was large, highly ambitious and notorious for a sex scandal in which Sir John Seymour had an affair with his own daughter-in-law, producing two children. When his cuckolded son Edward found out, he sent his wife into a convent and rejected the children. However, this experience did not deter him from using his unmarried sister Jane, now in her mid-twenties, to lure the King away from Anne Boleyn. Chapuys recorded his opinion of Jane Seymour's virtue, or rather, her lack of it: 'You may imagine whether being an Englishwoman, and having been so long at court, she would not hold it a sin to be still a maid.'

There were apparently those who could confirm this and Chapuys suggested that the King 'may marry her on condition she is a maid, and when he wants a divorce there will be plenty of witnesses ready to testify that she was not'.

Jane was untroubled by any qualms of conscience. Chapuys recorded her collaboration in the plot: 'This damsel is quite resolved ... I will endeavour by all means to make her continue in this vein.' She was schooled 'not in any wise to give in to the King's fancy unless he makes her his Queen', for Anne had set the precedent of replacing a foreign princess with an English noblewoman. Once the precedent had been set, it became possible for ambitious families to aspire to promote their own daughters to reach for the crown. The Seymours saw this, and later so did the Howards.

Soon Edward Seymour was appointed to the Privy Chamber, an uneasy ally of Chapuys and the Catholic party. The King had recovered, but he was now 45 and in pain from a leg ulcer, and his volatile moods meant that he was 'of one mind in the morning and quite another after dinner'.

Henry's insecurity had always veered towards paranoia. From his youth he had been imbued with the dark suspicions of his father's court, where every friend was a potential enemy and even the Queen was suspect.

He had risked all to have Anne and it was because of her that he had stood alone against the power of the Holy Roman Empire and the Vatican. It was because of Anne that he was excommunicate, denied the possibility of eternal life, according to Catholic teaching. If Anne was removed and their marriage proved invalid, then he was free to take a new wife, and a new Act of Succession would make all Henry's children equally illegitimate.

Henry now gave Cromwell virtually *carte blanche* to find some means to dissolve the second of his marriages which had failed to provide him with a son. While Catherine was still alive, there had been an impediment to the restoration of relations with the Emperor, but as Chapuys recognised, 'now that the cause of our enmity no longer exists', there was scope for negotiations. On the eve of St Matthias, 23 February, Chapuys and Cromwell met in secret at the Church of the Augustine Friars. They claimed that the King and the Emperor both favoured a revived alliance between their countries to sanction the downfall of the Queen.

The King's Secretary realised that his own life was now on the line. Cromwell had to come up with a solution and aimed to play one side off against another. He had few scruples about destroying Anne in order to save himself. On 3 March Cromwell listed all royal grants to the Boleyns, an ominous sign that he intended the downfall of the entire family.

On 1 May Cromwell's palace coup d'etat took place. The Queen's brother George and their leading supporters at court were placed under arrest and taken to the Tower. Norfolk was sent to arrest Anne. He bluntly informed her that she must come with him to the Tower and she was given no time to even change or collect clothes before catching the tide. Anne was later to say that she had been 'cruelly handled' by her uncle.

Anne had no idea what was happening. She asked her jailer Kingston how she could be expected to defend herself without knowing the charges against her: '"Master Kingston, shall I die without justice?" He told her, "The poorest subject of the King hath justice." And therewith she laughed.'

Overnight, many of those closest to the King were denounced as traitors. News of the great purge was relayed to Calais by John Hussey, Lord Lisle's agent:

This day Mr Norrys, Weston, Bryerton, and Markes hath been arraigned, and are judged to be drawn, hanged and quartered. I pray God have mercy on them. They shall die tomorrow, or Monday at the furthest. Anne the Queen and her brother shall be arraigned in the Tower; some think tomorrow, but on Monday at the furthest. And some doth verily think they shall there even so suffer within the Tower, undelayedly, for divers considerations which are not yet known ....

Rumours abounded but little was known of the charges. On 13 May Hussey wrote:

> Here are so many tales I cannot well tell which to write; for now this day some saith young Weston shall 'scape; and some saith there shall none die but the Queen and her brother; and some say that Wyat and Mr Page are as like to suffer as the others; and the saying now is that those which shall suffer shall die when the Queen and her brother goeth to execution. But I think verily they shall all suffer ...

As Starkey states, 'Their fate was sealed and it remained only to fabricate the detailed charges against them.'

It was not sufficient merely to divorce the Queen; she was to be presented as a traitor and an adulteress whose rapacious appetite meant that she took numerous lovers at the same time. But even this was not sure enough. In order to destroy her reputation, she was also accused of incest with her own brother.

One of those to betray Anne was her sister-in-law Jane, Lady Rochford. The daughter of Henry Parker, eighth Lord Morley, she had married George Boleyn in 1525 and became one of Anne's ladies, although they were never close. She chose to work with Norfolk and Anne's enemies, giving false testimony in court against her own husband, which sent him and the Queen to their deaths. In court George protested, 'On the evidence of only one woman you are willing to believe this great evil of me!'

Cromwell, acting as chief prosecutor, handed him a document and asked if Queen Anne had discussed such a matter with his wife Jane, Lady Rochford. Ambassador Chapuys records: 'I must not omit that among other things charged against him as a crime was, that his sister had told his wife that the King was impotent. This he was not openly charged with, but it was shown him in writing, with a warning not to repeat it. But he immediately declared the matter, in great contempt of Cromwell and some others.'

Knowing that Cromwell was his enemy, George read the note aloud, revealing to the entire court the King's sexual inadequacies:

'*Le Roy n'estoit habile en cas de soy copuler avec femme et qu'il n'avoit ne vertu ne puissance.*' Henry lacked both skill (*vertu*) and power (*puissance*).

The charges preferred against the Queen 'overstepped all ordinary bounds of credulity'. The times and places where Anne was said to have committed adultery – including with her own brother – listed in her indictment were wildly inaccurate but the verdict of the hand-picked jury under her enemy Norfolk was a foregone conclusion.

Chapuys reported that *before* the trial the King was already planning his wedding to Jane Seymour. Immediately after Anne was taken to the Tower, Henry had arranged for Jane to be brought to the house of Sir Nicholas Carew at Beddington, where he could visit her. Although Henry knew very well that Anne was not guilty, he told Jane Seymour on the morning of the trial, 15 May, that Anne would be condemned and all concluded by three that afternoon.

De Carles describes how Norfolk passed sentence on his niece, allegedly with 'tears in his eyes':

> Because thou hast offended our sovereign the King's grace in committing treason against his person and here attainted of the same, the law of the realm is this, that thou hast deserved death, and thy judgement is this: that thou shalt be burned here within the Tower of London, on the Green, else to have thy head smitten off, as the King's pleasure shall be further known of the same.

Afterwards the Lord Mayor of London commented: 'I can only observe one thing in this trial – the fixed resolution to get rid of the Queen at any price.' Even Chapuys agreed that the Queen had been a victim, not the Messalina whom Cromwell had described, condemned 'without valid proof or confession'.

Cromwell readily took full credit for Anne's condemnation, telling Chapuys, whom he knew would wholeheartedly approve, that, having received full authority from the King to discover the affairs of 'the King's concubine', he had taken a great deal of trouble in 'fabricating and plotting' the whole business.

The King was exposed as a tyrant, cold-bloodedly ready to sacrifice the woman he had claimed to love barely days before in a letter to his ambassador in Rome. The transcripts of the trials were bagged and removed to conceal the judicial murder.

Chapuys reported to the Emperor: 'I hear that, even before the arrest of the Concubine, the King, speaking with Mistress Jane Seymour of their future marriage ... To cover the affection he has for the said Seymour he has lodged her seven miles away in the house of a grand esquire and says publicly that he has no desire in the world to marry again.'

In fact, the King was openly celebrating, holding lavish banquets and going up and down the river by night in a barge with musicians singing and playing.

On 19 May 1536 Anne Boleyn was decapitated on Tower Green. John Hussey wrote straight to Calais: 'The Lord Rochford, Mr Norris, Brereton, Weston and Markes suffered with the axe upon the scaffold at Tower Hill on Wednesday the xvith of this instant, which died very charitably. And Anne the late Queen suffered with sword this day, within the Tower, upon a new scaffold; and died boldly. Jesu take them to his mercy if it be his will ...'

The following day, Henry was betrothed to Jane Seymour, and ten days after that the couple were married by that arch-conspirator, Bishop Gardiner. As Froude put it, 'the indecent haste' of the Seymour marriage followed 'the murder of Anne Boleyn' and Strickland describes Jane as a social climber who gave 'her hand to the regal ruffian before his wife's corpse was cold'.

The people watched these callous antics with growing fury. Public opinion swung in Anne's favour. Death was a daily occurrence and executions commonplace, but to behead a Queen was something beyond all comprehension and memory. The reaction in the country was divisive. Printed by underground presses, politically and religiously motivated ballads attacking the regime were passed from hand to hand, spreading dissent among the increasingly literate urban population.

Like ballads, libellous rhymes and verses were intended for circulation orally or in writing. Setting libels to tunes and posting printed or handwritten libels in public places would ensure wide-ranging transmission. In addition, libels were often set to familiar ballad tunes, relying on the associative meanings of the tune to heighten the defamatory effect of the abusive rhymes.

Jane Seymour was not popular and Henry hurriedly assured her that he was trying to crush the increasing number of scurrilous ballads against them. The King was called 'a tyrant more cruel than Nero' and 'a beast and worse than a beast'. It was said that if he knew the extent of the nation's loathing 'it would make his heart quake'.

The fall of Anne Boleyn was received with consternation in the Dowager's residence. There was a horrified reaction to the execution of a Queen of England, especially when that Queen was a Howard, the daughter of Norfolk's own sister Elizabeth.

Word soon filtered down to the Dowager's household about the King's callous behaviour, his dalliance with Jane Seymour, the unbelievable accusations against the Queen and the farce of the trials. They also learnt of the part played by the Duke of Norfolk in the Queen's downfall, how he had presided over her trial and pronounced the sentence of death upon her, his own niece.

What must have been Katherine's reaction to the news of her cousin's death? She had been brought up on stories of her cousin's astonishing success at court and would have admired her meteoric rise to fame, being eager to hear all the details of her sophisticated fashions, her grace, her style, her witty repartee and skill in composing music and playing the lute. To her younger cousin, Anne had been a role model to emulate, the living proof that even a country girl could come from relative obscurity to the very highest position in the land, to be Queen.

Then, almost overnight it seemed, all that had changed. Following the birth of Princess Elizabeth it was said that the King was angry, that he began to argue with Anne and started to pay attention to other women. Soon there were rumours of a rift, with the Duke of Norfolk turning from her, even cursing her, it was said.

To a nine- or ten-year-old girl this reversal was inexplicable and alarming. If someone as clever and accomplished as her cousin Anne could fall, then who among them would be safe?

The Dowager Duchess Agnes Tilney was a Howard only by marriage but she knew very well the nature and ambition of her stepson Norfolk. Like all men, he viewed woman as a marketable commodity, to be traded for profit. Anne Boleyn had been no exception.

When he first realised that the King was infatuated with Anne Boleyn, Norfolk had urged his niece to give in to Henry, becoming his mistress. As Head comments: 'Thomas Howard's loyalty to the crown was seldom more than a thin veil over his own deeper motives of self-interest, greed, ambition, and pride ... Norfolk saw no reason to change a system of government, a social order or a religious faith that tended to benefit his family and himself.'

When Anne rejected his pressure, he turned against her but bided his time as Henry grew ever more entrenched in his desire to make her his Queen. But Norfolk and the Boleyns were never close and religious differences had finally split the two families. With his crony Bishop Stephen Gardiner, Norfolk made an ally of Chapuys and the Emperor to work for the reversal of reforms, even if that meant relieving Henry of the throne in favour of his daughter Mary.

Norfolk had joined Anne's enemies, working behind the scenes to destroy her. He had not flinched at conducting her arrest or overseeing her mockery of a trial. There had never been any question that the verdict was already predetermined and his son Surrey even witnessed her execution. Norfolk had thrown his support behind the plot contrived by Thomas Cromwell, but there was little security for anyone under Henry VIII. Like the rest of the Catholic faction Norfolk aimed to overturn the Act of Succession and set Elizabeth aside for Mary, but Cromwell was no friend of his. There was no guarantee that he would not bend the King's ear to believe that the Howards were now a threat. Within just days of Queen Anne's judicial murder Cromwell's double-dealing was to be revealed.

Anne Boleyn was not the only participant in the dangerous

games that underpinned life at the Tudor court. The King's daughter Mary Tudor, now aged 20, was waiting in the wings.

With the cold-blooded removal of the Protestant Queen, the Catholic party in England were certain they now had Henry in their pocket. Mary had always been taught by her mother that the entire blame for their troubles was due to the 'heretic' and her influence. Now that Anne had been removed, Mary felt sure that she would soon be restored as princess and heir to the throne. [35] She was to be sorely disappointed.

Norfolk was sent to the King's daughter to repeat his threatening message that she must yield to the new order and accept her diminished position. Mary and Norfolk were natural allies, both enemies of the executed Queen through their loyalty to the memory of Catherine of Aragon and continued adherence to the Catholic faith, but Thomas Howard was far more of a political pragmatist. Although he could be equally stubborn in his opinions and ruthless in his actions, he never overstepped the boundary between safety and success.

When Mary refused to bend to her father's will, Norfolk was exasperated. He saw her resistance as due to woman's wayward and contradictory nature and lost all patience with her cause.

Henry reacted strongly when Norfolk informed him that Mary still refused to take the oath of succession. To be a Catholic was to owe allegiance to a foreign ruler, the Pope in Rome and his army of priests. To be a Protestant meant a conscious decision to put God first, but to this Henry had added an extra vital requirement – to acknowledge the King of England and not the Pope as God's regent here on earth. That was what Mary and many other Catholics refused to do. In a rage Henry told his Council that he would send his daughter to the Tower for high treason. Everyone around the King walked on eggshells.

Ambassador Chapuys continued to maintain his covert correspondence with Mary on behalf of the Emperor. The King's fury had convinced him that she must change tactics. He now advised her to submit and swear allegiance to her father the King. At a later date, he told her, she would be able to insist that her oath had only been made under duress and was therefore not binding.

Mary reluctantly took his advice and at last gave in, writing via Cromwell an abject letter of submission to her father in which she rejected 'the Bishop of Rome's pretended authority' and acknowledged the King as Supreme Head of the Church. She finally accepted that his marriage to her mother Catherine had always been null and void, 'by God's law and Man's law incestuous and unlawful', making her illegitimate.

On 6 July, Henry and his new wife rewarded Mary with a visit. For the first time in five years the King spoke to his daughter, testing her honesty. He demanded to know if her agreement had been sincere and asked whether she was receiving letters from Chapuys, which Mary denied. Henry then gave his daughter 1,000 crowns and Jane Seymour made her the gift of a diamond ring.

Cromwell also received his reward. He was granted a peerage and ennobled, becoming Baron Cromwell of Oakham. A year later he married his son, Gregory, to Elizabeth Seymour, the new Queen's sister.

After Anne's death, her child was neglected, if not forgotten. Lady Bryan wrote to Cromwell complaining that her charge had long outgrown her clothes and needed attention: 'Elizabeth is put from that degree she was afore and what degree she is at now, I know not ... For she is as toward a child, and as gentle of condition as ever I knew in my life. Jesu preserve her Grace.'

The death of Anne Boleyn without a son once again put Henry's son Richmond centre stage. The Act of Succession gave him precedence over Catherine's daughter Mary, but, as Robert Ratcliffe, Earl of Sussex, told the King at a Council meeting, now that Richmond and Mary were both of equal status – i.e., illegitimate – 'it was advisable to prefer the male to the female for the succession to the crown'.

But that summer of 1536 Henry's son suddenly died in mysterious circumstances just as an act was going through Parliament enabling the King to nominate him as heir to the throne.

Tradition says he died of tuberculosis, but for three weeks he had attended Parliament every day without any signs of illness. He was also present at the lavish triple wedding of the Neville sisters and Lady Anne Roos at which the King was guest of honour. Richmond had always been a robust young man, athletic, fond of physical sports and very far from an ailing consumptive.

What happened next is mysterious and baffling. Richmond missed the closing of Parliament due to a sudden illness and four days later he was dead. His death was immediately covered up. Henry sent Norfolk, Richmond's father-in-law, to remove the body in secret from St James's Palace. There would be no post-mortem investigation or the ceremonial funeral due to someone of such high rank and position.

Henry showed no interest in viewing his son's body or mourning his death. He moved back to London but ignored Richmond's widow, Mary Howard. Just days earlier the King had been urging legislation in Parliament to enable Richmond to be his heir. Now he ordered Norfolk to dispose of the corpse before it was barely cold.

Richmond's body was encased in lead before it was smuggled out of the palace under a cartload of straw. Norfolk took it to Thetford, where a rapid burial took place. His daughter, the widowed Mary Howard, followed with a wagon train of valuables, moving into the Howard family home at Kenninghall. She then wrote to the King asking for a pension as his son's widow but was curtly refused and told she would get nothing from him.

Having ordered the secret funeral, Henry now accused Norfolk of stealing his son's body away and burying it without proper regard for his royal status. Yet Henry ordered that all portraits of Richmond were to be destroyed. (The Holbein painting of Richmond as a child was taken to Basel and survived.)

Two years later Richmond's tomb, together with those of the Howard family ancestors at Thetford Priory, had to be rescued during the Dissolution and moved to St Michael's Church, Framlingham, in Suffolk, where they remain today. Curiously, his boyhood friend and brother-in-law Henry Howard, Earl of Surrey, had his portrait painted ten years later in which he leans on a broken pillar bearing Richmond's likeness. This was later blotted out, as if it was too dangerous to resurrect the dead boy's memory.

Cromwell had warned the King that if he made Richmond his heir the boy was 'very likely to fall into inobedience and rebellion'. He knew that Richmond and his mother's family had widespread support in Lincolnshire and East Anglia where there was growing opposition to the King.

In the north and rural areas, vast tracts of land were being enclosed to make estates for the new gentry under the King's direct patronage. In Lincolnshire, it was rumoured that everyone would be subject to taxation on income and property and 'think they shall be undone for ever'. The Duke of Richmond's mother, Elizabeth Blount, had remarried Lord Talboys and then Edward Fiennes, Lord Clinton, both influential figures in Lincolnshire. From his base at Collyweston, Stamford, Richmond, together with his mother's Lincolnshire relatives, had begun to gather what looked like an army of the disaffected from Yorkshire and all parts of the north. But the King's son conveniently died just weeks before a large popular uprising in that very region.

Unexpected death was commonplace in the period, but Richmond's sudden death led many to speculate that he had been murdered by his rivals. The speed with which the King had the corpse removed and buried struck many as unnatural and clearly suspicious.

One of the most overlooked causes of such sudden deaths was poisoning. Italian alchemists had a reputation for creating undetectable poisons and there existed a body of alchemists, known as the Council of Ten, which would eliminate anyone for a price. In France the Cardinal of Lorraine was murdered by handling coins spread with poison. It was said that Catherine de' Medici employed two poisoners, Bianco and Cosme Ruggieri.

The use of poison was considered by the English to be an alien way of acting against enemies. These 'eternity powders', which included herbs such as henbane, white water hemlock and mandragora, could kill over weeks rather than hours, being administered secretly in small doses that could pass undetected, giving the appearance of gastric problems. Arsenic became known as *poudre de sucession* ('inheritance powder'), the instrument of princes to remove rivals.

'He who drinks of the water in the Vatican will die soon', was a well-known warning, and the Borgia Pope Alexander VI and his son Cesare were notorious for their use of *La Cantarella*, whose secret has baffled experts in toxicology.

Ironically, in 1503 Alexander VI died when he drank the goblet of poisoned wine intended to murder Cardinal de Corneto, although another version has it that sweets were doctored. What is not in doubt is that the corpse soon became putrefied, horribly swollen and entirely black, so that 'many think that he died of poison'. The Venetian Ambassador recorded, 'it was the most loathsome, monstrous and frightful corpse that had ever been seen. It had neither the form nor the aspect of a human being.'

Perhaps this explains the secrecy surrounding the hasty removal of Richmond's body and why it needed to be encased in lead.

Ambassador Chapuys' reaction to Richmond's strange death is telling. He immediately reported back to his master the Emperor that 'the party of the Princess Mary is naturally jubilant at his death'. She and her mother Catherine had always seen Henry's natural son as a rival to their claim and Catherine had been in trouble for protesting against the many honours that the King had showered upon his natural son. His sudden death could only be seen as a victory for Mary's cause.

Who was responsible? Chapuys later suggested that the King had feared that Anne Boleyn was trying to poison Richmond, but was this suggestion a cover for the actions of his own agents? Was he reporting success in the venture when he wrote to the Emperor? His lack of surprise at Richmond's death is suspicious, but then so is the reaction of the King himself and his strange orders to Norfolk for secret burial.

Is it conceivable that Henry might have murdered his own son?

The King was actively pushing legislation through Parliament to make Richmond his heir when Cromwell whispered in his ear that the young man was gathering an army against him in Lincolnshire. It had been rumoured that Henry certainly intended to make him his successor, but Henry VIII was quite capable of switching from love to loathing in an instant, and highly susceptible to Cromwell's manipulation. His paranoia regarding the insecurity of his throne and the lack of a strong succession could easily have swayed him to take such a step. Nor was it as drastic as first appears, for Richmond was not Henry's only son.

There was still Henry Carey, the son of Mary Boleyn. The only reason that the King had never acknowledged this child and his sister Katherine Carey was because they were proof of his illicit relationship at a time when he had been struggling to marry Anne Boleyn. Although everyone at court knew of the liaison and that Mary Boleyn's marriage to William Carey had been purely a cover, the public declaration of their affair would have raised the suggestion of incest between the King and Mary's sister Anne. Mary Boleyn was simply paid off and her children became Careys, but remained close to the throne for they shared the same father as Mary and Elizabeth Tudor.

Henry had killed his wife and married Jane Seymour. He now anticipated her pregnancy and a legitimate heir at last. The possibility exists that he could have reacted impulsively against Richmond, lashing out in his anger, gambling on the hope of a future son to replace one who might plot rebellion against him.

Henry showed that he intended to concentrate power in himself. Although Jane Seymour had been proclaimed Queen of England on 4 June and her brother Edward was created Earl of Hertford, there was no coronation as there had been with Anne. Even if she could give him a son, Henry had no intention of raising another woman to the position he had given Anne. Nor was he willing to tolerate her interference in state affairs: when Jane attempted to give her opinion on the dissolution of the monasteries, her husband quickly reminded her of the fate that had befallen her predecessor, an ominous warning.

Jane suddenly realised that to be Queen was not the enviable position she had once assumed. Almost immediately she was aware of the change in Henry's attitude towards her. Becoming Queen had put her in the full glare of public interest, a position of great danger. Unless she soon became pregnant and could produce the longed-for son and heir, then even she would not be safe.

Chapter Six

The Music Master

KATHERINE HOWARD was still under her grandmother's care. Her father continued to endure a burden of debts, always seeking handouts. He had been forced to beg his elder brother Norfolk for help from the royal treasury. He had been told by his stepbrother, William Howard, that Cromwell had agreed to support him. Edmund wrote to thank him, complaining that he was so 'beaten in the world' and 'smally friended' that he needed all the help he could get. In fact, his friends had not fared too well by him; one proved to be too trusting when he made Edmund a loan and stood surety for his debts, later finding himself sent to jail by Edmund's creditors.

Katherine had been three years at the Dowager's house at Chesworth, being educated as befitted her station and prospects. In late 1536, when she was about ten or eleven years of age, it was arranged that she should start to receive music lessons. Dancing, singing and music were considered necessary social graces for girls of her class with any aspirations to appear at court. The King was a noted musician and composed his own songs, and Katherine must have been brought up hearing how accomplished her cousin Anne had been on the lute. Anne Boleyn was 'imbued with as many outward good qualities in playing on instruments, singing, and such other courtly graces, as few women were of her time'.

Anne could 'handle cleverly both flute and rebec' and would sing, accompanying herself on the virginals. Katherine now began lessons so that she might emulate her cousin's talents.

The young man chosen to be her tutor was Henry Manox or Monox, a cousin of Edward Waldgrave, one of the Dowager's gentlemen-in-waiting. Manox was brought in to teach Katherine to sing and to play, a requirement for any girl of her family's background and status, especially if she was to advance herself by a good marriage. However, Manox soon taught his pupil more than just music.

Very little is known about Henry Manox's background but it is possible that, as the son of a neighbour at Horsham, he was already familiar with the Dowager's household. Being Edward Waldegrave's cousin, he may have been one of the night visitors who were invited to join in the midnight picnics held in the women's dormitories. Waldegrave was born in Suffolk in 1514, making him about 20 when he was at Chesworth. He was later to marry one of Katherine's close friends and companions in the dormitory, Joan Bulmer, the daughter of George Acworth of Luton, Bedfordshire. Joan, born in 1519, was the heir of her mother Margaret Wilberforce and had married William Bulmer, son of Sir John Bulmer, but it was not a happy marriage and there were no children. She left her husband and joined the household of the Dowager Duchess, where she met Waldegrave. Their daughter Anne was later to marry one Humphrey Monox.

Over the years during which Katherine observed – and later participated in – these risky nighttime adventures there formed a tight clique of companions and friends who shared one another's beds and kept each other's secrets.

Joan Bulmer, Katherine and Malena Tilney, Alice Restwold and Margaret Benet were all among the Dowager's women. Edward Waldegrave, John Benet, Anthony Restwold, William Asheley, Henry Howard and Robert Damporte were among the men. All of these were later to be named and summoned to give evidence of what had actually taken place in the Dowager's houses. But at the time they were merely a group of carefree and lively young people who thought it great fun to fool around behind the Dowager's back and enjoy life.

The older women of the Dowager's household, such as Joan Bulmer, were often married and therefore sexually experienced. It was the example of women such as Joan that led the younger girls like Katherine to copy their antics. Acting as confidantes, Joan and her friends encouraged their virgin sisters into the world of adulthood by their own rash example.

Young lovers contrived to be together and in country areas the practice of allowing young couples to spend the night together was known as 'bundling' or 'courting in bed', a custom that continued in rural and colonial societies until the 19th century. 'Outercourse' or 'bundling' allowed a young woman to have sex while remaining technically a virgin.

Parents would permit or turn a blind eye to midnight visitors who were 'tested' by their daughters as prospective husbands, sleeping together without undressing, usually without full intercourse. Sometimes a board was placed between them or the girl was sewn into a 'bundling sack'. Often the nocturnal visitor would climb in through an upper window, as Romeo does in the Shakespeare play. He would leave by the same means before dawn, unseen and unheard by the sleeping household.

Bundling was an accepted part of 17th-century courting rituals. In Switzerland and Germany, it was known as *Kiltgang*, *Fensterln* or *Nachtfreien*. In colonial New England, outercourse was actively encouraged and still has support as 'a fine old Puritan practice'. Although accidents could happen, as a ballad warns: 'But bundlers clothes are no defence, unruly horses push the fence.'

The medieval Church banned all sexual relations outside marriage, although its own priests and nuns did not necessarily set a good example. Procreation was a duty but sexual pleasure was considered sinful. Church edicts actually forbade all sex for married couples for almost half the year – on Sundays, during penitential periods such as the 40 days of Lent or the four weeks of Advent, festivals such as Easter, on all fast-days and in the days before a penance or attending mass. In addition it was strictly prohibited when women were menstruating, pregnant or breast-feeding. Sex was hurriedly performed in darkness with some pious husbands even wearing the *chemise carouse*, a long nightshirt in which an opening permitted intercourse without sight or touch of naked flesh.

The Catholic Church saw sex as a necessary evil, particularly in order to control women whose nature was such that they developed hysteria when deprived. It was therefore necessary for all women to marry for their mental and physical well-being. Not only did a woman need the strong guidance and restraining control first of a father and then a husband, but the weaker feminine nature left to its own devices could lead to some form of dementia or sexual hysteria.

Virgins suffered from 'greensickness', a waning and wasting condition which signalled that she urgently needed to be found a husband and bedded.

Women were presented by society as dishonest and dangerous creatures who lusted after men and sought to entrap them in sin. Once they were no longer virgins and had experienced sex, women went 'mad for lust' and became uncontrollable: 'They follow men, and sollicite them for Copulation. Some will lie with any one they meet.'

A woman who acted independently was seen as wayward, sinful and against nature. An unmarried woman or a widow, even a noblewoman such as Webster's Duchess of Malfi who is used to managing a great household, could not be trusted to choose her own husband or lover. For love, the Duchess of Malfi takes someone 'beneath' her social status, thus disgracing her family. The same disgrace befell Mary, the elder sister of Queen Anne Boleyn. Mary had been the King's mistress, had borne him two children and was married off to William Carey, but when widowed after an outbreak of the sweating sickness, she then took it upon herself to find a new husband, William Stafford, explaining that 'love overcame reason; and for my part I saw so much honesty in him, that I loved him as well as he did me.'

Stafford was considered by her family too lowly a match for the Queen's sister and the couple were formally ostracised, although Anne sent them money in order to survive.

The Catholic Church had ecclesiastical or 'bawdy courts' to prosecute cases of 'uncleanness and wickedness of life' such as adultery, fornication and prostitution, which were punishable by public penance or the pillory. But in effect these ignored the majority of 'common-law' marriages and pre-nuptial rituals which flouted their rules.

A distinction was made between the acceptable 'bundling' of betrothed couples and the sinful behaviour of promiscuous wantons. The biblical example was given, where Ruth was advised to sleep next to Boaz during the harvest: 'Where it may seeme that Naomi counselleth her daughter an unlawfull thing, yea, rather to play the whoore, then to get her a husband by a lawfull meanes.' (Ruth 3.2) An engraving, *Bybel Printen*, by Dutch artist Matthew Merian, shows Ruth in a clinging gown lying beside Boaz ('The Original Bundlers'), under the caption: 'Bold daring Ruth ... touches fire.'

Sex could be the means to securing marriage. Many of the couples engaged in illicit encounters under the Dowager's roof were to marry – Joan Bulmer and Edward Waldegrave, Alice to Anthony Restwold and Margaret to John Benet. For a man of lower status like Manox, the seduction of a Howard girl could lead to a profitable match. An exchange of vows could ensure that the family confirmed a formal marriage between the two.

The promise to marry made the difference, as this was considered a binding precontract in canon law and just as valid as a ceremony in church, provided that the union had been consummated. Signs and tokens such as rings formed part of often-secret 'handfasting'. The Catholic Council of Trent later invalidated all marriages not performed before a parish priest but similar measures were not taken in Britain until the marriage act of 1753.

Katherine was no doubt flattered by the attentions of her music master. That they flirted is irrefutable, but Katherine always denied that he had seduced her, claiming that she was too conscious of the social divide between them. Manox was not deterred by the fact that she was of higher degree. His version was later forced from him and given in the hope of saving his life. Then he was finally to admit that in their meetings 'he felt more than was convenient' but vowed 'upon his damnation (he) never knew her carnally'.

Did Katherine and Manox have sex? She was later to confess, 'At the flattering and fair persuasions of Manox, being but a young girl, I suffered him at sundry times to handle and touch the secret parts of my body which neither became me with honesty to permit nor him to require.'

She was perhaps precocious enough to want to try out a little of what she had seen going on in the nightly encounters around her. According to tradition they met secretly in the Dowager's chapel.

Their relationship was no secret. Manox had bribed a maid to send Katherine love tokens, and rumours about them reached Mary Lascelles, the Dowager's chamberer (waiting woman), who was one of the girls sharing Katherine's dormitory. A member of the Nottinghamshire gentry, Mary was new to the household, having previously served Lord William Howard, the Dowager's son, as nursemaid. She was a girl of good morals, inclined to the reform religion, and the antics in the long room seem to have shocked her.

Mary was clearly worried about Katherine and later claimed that she had sought out Manox to berate him for his presumption in thinking of marriage with a Howard: 'She is come of a noble house and if thou should marry her some of her blood would kill thee.'

She later reported that Manox had boasted about his relationship with Katherine and declared that he would 'have her maidenhead'. He claimed that Katherine had promised that he would be the first, taking 'her maidenhead though it be painful to her'. She was 11 years old.

Today this would be a blatant case of child abuse but under the Tudors there was little sentimentality about childhood. The onset of puberty was regarded as an acceptable age for sexual and matrimonial consent. Records show that at this time the *menarche* occurred from the ages of 12 to 14, and that 'the widespread practice of child marriage at the highest levels of society' continued. The Church would sanction marriage for very young children, including babes in arms: 'little infants, in swaddling clouts, are often married by their ambitious friends, when they know neither good nor evil, and this is the origins of much wickedness'.

John Somerford, aged three, married Jane Brerton, aged two, in Chester as part of a land deal to stop the crown seizing an estate belonging to a minor. Such exceptional marriages awaited consummation at a suitable age, but child marriages were often consummated, as when Margaret Beaufort married Edmund Tudor at the age of 12, giving birth when she was barely 13. Henry VIII's sister Margaret had married James IV of Scotland at the age of 14. Katherine's own mother married when she was 12, but there are many examples of even earlier matches. In 1396, Richard II married Isabel of France, who was only seven years old.

Chaucer's Wife of Bath boasts that from the age of 12, 'Husbondes at churche dore have I had five.' In Shakespeare's *Romeo and Juliet* Lady Capulet married at an age younger than Juliet: 'By my count I was your mother much upon these years that you are now a maid.' (I.iii.73–75) Her husband remarks acidly, 'And too soon marred are those so early made.' Lady Capulet has not yet reached the ripe old age of 30 when her daughter Juliet is contracted to marry the Count of Paris but chooses to 'bundle' with Romeo on the promise of their marriage.

Thomas More advocated in his *Utopia* (1516) that women guilty of pre-marital sex should be forbidden to marry and made slaves, with extramarital sex punishable by death. The Catholic Church taught that Eve was the cause of original sin. Women were weak, untrustworthy, deceitful temptresses, morally inferior to men. This view has persisted. Katherine has been blamed for her naivety, with Alison Plowden even calling her a natural-born tart: 'Far from being the corrupted innocent she is sometimes depicted, Katherine Howard, it must be said, seems to have possessed all the instincts of a natural tart who knew exactly what she was doing.'

This assessment fails to take into consideration her very young age when she came, literally, into Manox's arms. The failure to deduce Katherine's true date of birth has presented her as a promiscuous and knowing girl in her later teens rather than the vulnerable and abused child of 11 or 12 that she more probably was in 1536.

The extent of abuse occurring in 16th-century England prompted lawmakers to pass a Bill in 1548 protecting boys from sodomy, and another in 1576 protecting girls under ten years from forcible rape, with both offences carrying the death penalty.

Yet there was little sympathy for an abused child. Courts focused attention on the sexual history of the girl, and having reached puberty they were considered accessories, not victims. Even today there remains this view that the child is an active agent and must carry some of the blame, but a child's lack of knowledge and issues of peer pressure from the other women could have influenced Katherine's behaviour. Even if both parties had given their consent, in the case of a girl as young as Katherine her consent cannot be considered relevant.

Nor can the effects upon her development be denied. An innocent child when she entered the Dowager's household, she was soon influenced by the conduct of the women who were her friends and tutors. From a modern perspective, it is hard to blame Katherine for succumbing to the flattery of her music master. An extrovert by nature, she longed to be accepted and admired. She wanted to be the centre of attention and accepted praise readily to bolster her confidence.

Eager to be part of their inner circle and to be included in their romantic adventures, she may have encouraged the much older Henry Manox, seeing nothing wrong in emulating and joining in the same activities as her close friends.

Studies conducted with children who have been initiated into sex at such an early age often show changes in character and behaviour, with dramatic effects upon their future lives. Is it any wonder that Katherine went on to demonstrate precocious sexual behaviour when she saw it among the other women around her night after night?

One of the poems of her contemporary John Skelton describes the forward girls and women that he knew:

> When we kisse and play in lust and liking,
> He calls me his whiting, his mulling and his mittine,
> His nobes and his conny, his sweeting and honny ...
> For, after all our sport, then will he rout and snort;
> Then sweetly together we lye as two pigges in a stye.

For a young girl like Katherine, deprived of her mother, brought up by nurses and servants among a large family of older sisters, it would have been natural to turn to these older women and girls for advice.

For some time the Dowager Duchess remained blithely unaware of her step-granddaughter's initiation. Events at court and the dangers threatening the Howard family preoccupied the matriarch right up to the moment when she walked in on an encounter and discovered the truth herself at first hand. She allegedly caught Manox and Katherine on the music room floor. Dowager Agnes handled the affair with brisk efficiency: 'She gave ... Mistress Katherine two or three blows and gave straight charge both to her and to ... Manox that they should never be alone together.'

Katherine's shame was concealed and Manox instantly dismissed from service. Katherine's father Edmund was still living in Calais, and it is possible the Dowager did not want to trouble him with news of his daughter's behaviour, perhaps because she knew him to be ineffectual or because he was often ill, nursed by an unsympathetic wife. Edmund suffered with gallstones, as a letter to Lady Lisle, the Governor of Calais' wife, shows:

Madame, so it is I have this night after midnight taken your medicine, for the which I heartily thank you, for it hath done me much good, and hath caused the stone to break, so that now I void much gravel.
But for all that, your said medicine hath done me little honesty, for

it made me piss my bed this night, for the which my wife hath sore beaten me, and saying it is children's parts to bepiss their bed.

Ye have made me such a pisser that I dare not this day go abroad, wherefore I beseech you to make mine excuse to my Lord and Master Treasurer, for that I shall not be with you this day at dinner. Madame, it is showed me that a wing or a leg of a stork, if I eat thereof, will make me that I shall never piss more in bed, and though my body be simple yet my tongue shall be ever good, and especially when it speaketh of women; and sithence such a medicine will do such a great cure God send me a piece thereof.

All youres,

Edmund Howard.

Lady Lisle's medicine may have been a remedy made of dried samphire (seaweed), white wine and oil with 'carp's eyes in powder with the bone in the carp's head'. For more stubborn cases there were recipes more reminiscent of the three witches: take the 'stone breaker', of saxifrage root steeped in the hare's blood and taken morning and night, but none of these seemed to have worked for Katherine's father.

The Dowager recruited her eldest son William Howard, Lord Effingham, to take his step-niece aside for a lecture and remind Katherine of the frailties of her sex. Twenty-six-year-old Lord William had recently married his second wife, Margaret Gamage, and, speaking like Polonius in Shakespeare's *Hamlet*, he warned Katherine bluntly not to embarrass her family any further by producing a bastard child. Ten years before, their relative Mary Boleyn had produced two children by the King and although a hasty marriage had been arranged, it was scarcely the great match that her family had hoped for. Now Katherine risked a similar fate.

Yet Lord William seemed less concerned with her morals than with the Howards' family reputation that had been put at risk by Mary Lascelles' denunciations, grumbling: 'What mad wenches! Can you not be merry amongst yourselves but you must thus fall out?'

Like the scholar Roger Ascham, Lord William perhaps regretted 'our time is so far from that old discipline and obedience' that
girls dared seek their own partners 'where they list and how they
list' without respect to 'father, mother, God, good order and all'.

The English were notorious for affording their women greater
freedom than those in the rest of Europe, where, in most Catholic
cultures, women were hidden away and even locked up to prevent
them from mixing with men outside the family. Jacob Rathgeb
reported, 'The women have much more liberty than perhaps in
any other place; they also know well how to make use of it.'

The Italian Francesco Ferretti thought English women were 'of
marvellous beauty and wonderfully clever'. They rode to hunt,
showing their legs, 'astoundingly impudent'.

Nicander Nucius reported 'the great simplicity and absence of
jealousy' of English men. Erasmus found such freedoms 'never to
be sufficiently recommended', noting 'You are received with a kiss
by all; when you take your leave, you are dismissed with kisses; you
return, kisses are repeated. They come to visit you, kisses again;
they leave you, you kiss them all round.'

Yet legally women were still subordinate to men, passing from
the jurisdiction of their fathers or brothers to husbands and even
later to their sons. Marriage was the means by which men
dominated women: 'The very being or legal existence of the
woman is suspended during the marriage ... for this reason a man
cannot grant anything to his wife or enter into any covenant with
her: for the grant would be to presuppose her separate existence.'

The consensus view was that 'Women and horses must be well
governed.' The Tudor family traditionally upheld a tyrannical
patriarchal authority, reflecting the all-powerful image of the King
himself: 'Woman in her greatest perfection was made to serve and
obey man.'

Women must be 'chaste, silent, and obedient'. Bishop Aylmer
placed them into two separate categories:

Women are of two sorts. Some of them are wiser, better learned,
discreeter and more constant than a number of men, but another

and a worse sort of them are fond, foolish, wanton, flibbergibs, tatlers, triflers, wavering, witless, without council, feeble, careless, rash, proud, dainty, tale-bearers, eavesdroppers, rumour-raisers, evil tongued, worse-minded and in every way doltified with the dregs of the devil's dung-hill.

Their natural instincts must be curbed, often by beating. The law permitted a husband to 'beat her violently with whips and sticks' but not an iron bar.

Young Katherine may have seemed contrite as she listened to Lord William's lecture.

She appeared demure and obedient enough to escape whipping but she was not ready to take his message to heart. The thrill of secret meetings and a hidden romance was to prove far more appealing to her self-destructive need for affection and excitement.

Chapter Seven

Dangerous Games

EVEN BEFORE RICHMOND's sudden demise, the King's fiery young niece Lady Margaret Douglas had been living at St James's Palace with her close friend Mary Howard, Richmond's duchess. During her time there, Margaret had fallen in love with Lord Thomas Howard, Norfolk's younger half-brother. He wrote poetry to Margaret, but their game of courtly love was soon to prove fatal.

They had secretly exchanged gifts and troths, promising marriage, but Margaret was to pay dearly for daring to play the game of romance at the expense of her status and relationship to the crown. When the King discovered what had been going on he immediately had the lovers arrested and sent to the Tower. Coming just two weeks after the execution of Queen Anne and the circle of Henry's close friends, this must have been a truly terrifying experience.

The King suspected that Norfolk was behind the match, still trying to manipulate his relatives into the royal family. Mary Howard had clearly known about it and it emerged that 'divers times' she had been the couple's only chaperone. Lord Thomas had apparently promised or made a secret precontract of marriage with the King's niece. This was binding in canon law.

In the Tower, Thomas confessed to his interrogator Wriothesley that his relationship with Margaret had been going on for a year. Wriothesley was Cromwell's most trusted assistant and everything he reported was passed directly to the King. He eventually persuaded Thomas to reveal that he and Margaret had been contracted to marry since Easter. It appeared that very few people at court knew it, 'only Lord William's wife that now is', and his mother's servant, a man named Hastings.

Wriothesley soon learnt that other retainers, John Ashley and Thomas Smith, had witnessed Thomas entering Margaret's chamber. This was not quite as damning as Wriothesley may have hoped, for his witnesses also confirmed that Mary, Duchess of Richmond had also been there, but denied they knew of any betrothal. Margaret heard that Thomas was being tortured and was horrified by the 'great pains he suffereth for my sake continually both night and day'.

Even within the confines of the Tower, the lovers continued to exchange poems clandestinely. Thomas wrote to reassure Margaret of his love for her, confirming their relationship:

> Of me which was your poor old friend,
> Your loving husband now to be;
> Since ye descend from your degree
> Take ye this unto your part,
> My faithful, true and loving heart.
> My love truly shall not decay
> For threatening nor for punishment
> For let them think and let them say
> T'word you alone I am full bent:
> Therefore I will be diligent
> Our faithful love for to renew,
> And still to keep me trusty and true. [4]

Mary Shelton, who acted as their go-between, seems to have copied their verses into the Devonshire Manuscript for the record as a kind of 'protest literature'.

Mary Shelton had suffered her own experience of tragedy. By 1536, she been betrothed for some time to the King's friend and companion Sir Henry Norris, a widower with a young son. He may have been alarmed by rumours of her flighty reputation, for he had postponed their marriage and when Queen Anne asked him the reason why, he allegedly suggested he was in love with her. This was the charge by which Cromwell fashioned Anne's downfall, a fiction that cost Anne and five other victims their heads.

It appears that Mary Shelton and her friends translated their own passions and fears into verse. The first poem in the Devonshire Manuscript warns of spies ready to betray the lovers. Secrecy was vital, for who could be trusted? Someone had betrayed Lady Margaret and Thomas to the King. The 'real character of the court' required the writers to remain anonymous. [6]

In much the same way, following Anne Boleyn's death Sir Thomas Wyatt had turned from writing elegant verses of courtly love to stinging political satire which warned the unwary against 'aspiring too high at court' and exposure to 'tyrants' like Henry.

Wyatt had been arrested on suspicion of his friendship with Queen Anne but was fortunate to escape with his head still attached to his shoulders, thanks to the support of Cromwell. He emerged from the Tower a changed man. From his prison in the Bell Tower he had witnessed the whole tragic finale. Later he wrote:

> These bloody days have broken my heart.
> My lust, my youth did them depart,
> And blind desire of estate.
> Who hastes to climb seeks to revert.
> Of truth, *circa Regna tonat*
> ['thunder rolls around the throne'].

Margaret Douglas was also to write down her thoughts and feelings following what had happened to her. She added a large number of poems to the Devonshire Manuscript, later taking firm possession of it and keeping it with her when she finally married the Earl of Lennox.

The King now moved to stop any marriage contracted with those of the blood royal without his direct approval. A Bill of Attainder went before the Parliament on 18 July 1536, was passed before noon and received the royal assent that afternoon. Henry found the use of attainder a useful tool against those he had determined to remove, as Katherine Howard would later discover.

Treason was no longer an act of opposition but the intent to act against the King's wishes or without his express consent. It now also became a crime for

> ... any man, of what estate, degree or condition so ever he be, at any time hereafter take upon him to espouse, marry or take to his wife any of the King's children [being lawfully born or otherwise commonly reputed or taken for his children] or any the King's sisters or aunts of the part of the father, [or any of the lawful children] of the King's brothers or sisters [not being married] or contract marriage with any of them without the special license, assent, and agreement first thereunto had and obtained of the King's Highness in writing under his great seal [or defile or deflower any of them not being married]. [Such a man] shall be deemed and adjudged a traitor to the King and his realm.

Any woman of the royal family who took it upon herself to choose her own lover or husband was under threat from this legislation. It was now a penal offence for anyone to indulge in a royal romance that had not been condoned by the King.

This law applied to Margaret and Thomas retroactively and Thomas Howard was sentenced to death. The Imperial Ambassador Chapuys had a certain sympathy for Margaret, reporting back to the Emperor that 'copulation had not taken place' and therefore '... in the present case the sentence will not be carried out on [Margaret Douglas], owing to the marriage not having been consummated, and to her having been pardoned since ... certainly if she had done much worse she deserved pardon, seeing the number of domestic examples she has seen and sees daily, and that she had been for eight years of age and capacity to marry'.

Disgraced, Margaret was moved on grounds of ill health to Syon Abbey near Windsor, still one of England's richest convents. The nuns here had lately been criticised by Queen Anne for their conduct, but the Abbess Agnes presided over a comfortable establishment and could offer Margaret Douglas a pampered shelter from the King's wrath. Soon she was running up bills for clothes, furniture of crimson velvet and paying the wages of her lover's servants.

In August she had written to Cromwell claiming she no longer cared for Thomas:

My Lord, what cause have I to give you thanks, and how much bound am I unto you, that by your means hath gotten me, as I trust, the King's grace his favour again, and besides that that it pleaseth you to write and to give me knowledge wherein I might have his Grace's displeasure again, which I pray our Lord sooner to send me death than that; I assure you, my Lord, I will never do that thing willingly that should offend his Grace. And my Lord, whereas it is informed you that I do charge the house with a greater number that is convenient, I assure you I have but two more than I had in the Court, which indeed were my Lord Thomas' servants; and the cause that I took them for was for the poverty that I saw them in and for no cause else. But seeing, my Lord, that it is your pleasure that I shall keep none that did belong unto my Lord Thomas, I will put them from me.

And I beseech you not think that any fancy doth remain in me touching him; but that all my study and care is how to please the King's grace and to continue in his favour ...

And my Lord, where it is your pleasure that I shall keep but a few here with me, I trust ye will think that I can have no fewer than I have; for I have but a gentleman and a groom that keeps my apparel, and another that keeps my chamber, and a chaplain that was with me always in the Court. Now, my Lord, I beseech you that I may know your pleasure if you would that I should keep any fewer. Howbeit, my Lord, my servants hath put the house to small charge, for they have nothing but the reversion of my board; nor I do call for nothing but that that is given me; howbeit I am very well intreated. And my Lord, as for resort, I promise you I have none, except it be gentlewomen that comes to see me, nor never had since I came hither; for if any resort of men had come it should neither have become me to have seen them, nor yet to have kept them company, being a maid as I am.

Now my Lord, I beseech you to be so good as to get my poor servants their wages; and thus I pray our Lord to preserve you both soul and body.

By her that has her trust in you,

Margaret Douglas.

Her mother the Dowager Queen of Scotland wrote to the King asking for her release but Henry did not reply to his sister before the end of the year: 'whereas you recommend unto us your daughter, although she has so lightly used herself, as was both to our dishonour and her own great hindrance, yet doubt you not, we shall for your sake, extend such goodness toward her, as you and she both shall have cause to be therewith satisfied, and for the same to give us condign thanks accordingly'.

In January 1535 Norfolk's brother had been sent on a secret mission to Scotland. It was later revealed that he was investigating the troublesome marriage and liaisons of the King's sister, questioning the legitimacy of her daughter Margaret Douglas, whose position was only clarified after the scandal in 1536, when she was formally declared illegitimate.

Although Lord Thomas had been sentenced to execution, he remained in the Tower for more than another year, dying in unexplained circumstances in October 1537 or possibly on All Hallows Eve, 1538.

Norfolk's son Henry, Earl of Surrey, wrote the following poem in memory of his great friend:

For you yourself have heard, it is not long ago
Sith that for love one of the race did end his life in woe.
In tower strong and high for his assured truth;
Whereas in tears he spent his breath, alas! the more the ruth.
This gentle beast so died, whom nothing could remove,
But willingly to lese his life for loss of his true love.

Margaret was freed from Syon in October 1539 and went to live with her friend Mary Howard, the newly widowed Duchess of Richmond, at Kenninghall in Norfolk. Mary's new interest in the reform religion had distanced her from the rest of her family, inciting fiery arguments with her brother Henry, Earl of Surrey. Ironically, later he too was to become an ardent Protestant.

The case of Margaret Douglas and her troubles was a warning to other women in the royal circle not to overstep the mark and seek to pick their own husbands without the King's consent. More crucially, it demonstrated the inherent dangers of being a member of the King's own family.

Margaret was not free to arrange her own marriage because of her status as the King's niece and the continuing uncertainty of the succession. As long as Margaret might be in line for the throne herself, then her marriage was the business of state. She could not be permitted to select a candidate of her own choice but would be forced to wait for the King to arrange a suitable match for her in his own time and to suit his own interests. This effectively warned off ambitious suitors such as the Howards who sought out marriages with those in close proximity to the throne.

England was now divided between two political factions reflecting religious divisions. The reform religion, which became known as Protestantism, had begun to produce radical changes in the country. Cromwell's *Acta in Consilio domini Regis* transferred the vast wealth of the Church, England's greatest landowner, to the Exchequer in order to make Henry the richest prince in Christendom. It has been estimated that the value of the property seized produced a revenue so immense that 'might, under judicious application, have extinguished all public burdens, both for the support of the state and the relief of the poor, and expectations of this kind were held out to the people'; however, 'they were soon undeceived; pauperism became more widespread than ever, and within one year from the period of the last appropriation, a subsidy of two-tenths, and another of two-fifteenths, were demanded by the King, and granted by parliament, to defray the expenses of reforming the religion of the state'. Not even Cromwell's best devices could supply Henry with the constant supply of revenue needed to carry out his grandiose schemes and dreams of conquest in France.

The dissolution of the monasteries took place over four years. Cromwell's men encouraged the voluntary retirement of monks and nuns, offering pensions from £266 for abbots to £2 per annum for monks. Many were glad to break out of religious orders, but some resisted. A register at Lambeth records 975 monks who left voluntarily without pensions.

Popular anticlericalism and the theological bankruptcy of late medieval Catholicism led to rapid expansion of Protestantism. In many cities, Protestants were gaining the majority, notably in the south and London. Catholics saw the rapid expansion of Protestantism as a threat. Traditional rituals and beliefs were now being challenged by direct reference to the Scriptures. But there were other reasons for discontent, especially in rural areas of East Anglia, Lincolnshire and the north. A series of bad harvests had provoked riots in Norfolk in 1527 and 1529.

The spread of enclosures converting arable farming land to pasture for sheep had boosted the lucrative wool trade but deprived increasing numbers of their common rights of grazing. Fencing or hedging of large tracts of common land for private use led to evictions, forcing people off the land to seek work or beg in the towns. Thomas More memorably described what the enclosures he witnessed meant for England:

For look in what parts of the realm doth grow the finest and therefore dearest wool, there noblemen and gentlemen, yea, and certain abbots, holy men no doubt, not contenting themselves with the yearly revenues and profits ... inclose all into pastures; they throw down houses; they pluck down towns and leave nothing standing but only the church to be made into a sheep fold ...They turn all dwelling-places and all glebe land into desolation and wilderness.

Those cast out were forced to 'depart away, men, women, husbands, wives, fatherless children, widows, mother with their young babies, and their whole household ... finding no place to rest in ... what can they then else do but steal, and then justly be hanged, or else go about a-begging'.

A 1531 Act of Parliament decreed whipping for all unlicensed beggars and by 1536 further punishments included mutilation and even hanging.

The general rising in Lincolnshire and the north in 1536 known as the 'Pilgrimage of Grace' was part of this land war, provoked by enclosures and the dissolution of the monasteries. In October a series of riots, led by 'Captain Cobbler', broke out in Louth and Horncastle against one of Cromwell's agents, John Heneage. The rioters took prisoners and forced Heneage to carry a letter to the King about their grievances. The spontaneous uprising soon took on a different character. A group of over 1,000 men headed by Sir Robert Dymoke and Sir Thomas Percy, both connected to the Talboys family, were joined by Edward Dymoke. Lord Hussey supported them but their leader was Lord Clinton who sought out the support of the Earl of Shrewsbury, while Sir John Russell and Sir William Parr blockaded the Great North Road with a force at Stamford. Thomas Moigne, MP for Lincoln, rode to join rebels who had gathered under Robert Aske, a solicitor, in Yorkshire.

When the King received the news, he sent the Duke of Suffolk north with an intimidating army, but on 13 October Aske and an army of 9,000 men marched on York. Within days the rebels had 20,000 men and York had opened its gates to them. By 23 October their numbers had risen to 30,000, Lincoln, Hull and Pontefract had joined them and the King faced the most dangerous rebellion of his reign.

In a 'Narrative to the King' Aske outlined his opposition to suppression of the monasteries and reformist 'heresy' and called for the dismissal of ministers like Thomas Cromwell. A number who joined his banner were Catholic zealots, but many were old Yorkists who bore an everlasting loathing for the Tudors. The de la Pole family were the last remnants of the Plantagenet claimants to the throne. They waited to see if the revolt prospered while Reginald Pole, who had narrowly escaped assassination by Henry's agents, now gained the backing of the Vatican. It rapidly seemed as if the popular protests were being turned into a conspiracy against England, designed to overthrow the Tudor dynasty and restore the country to the Catholic faith.

Chapuys reported to his master Charles V that the rebels 'counted in case of need' on Norfolk to 'support the cause of Faith and Church'. But Chapuys knew Norfolk's sense of self-preservation would never permit him to risk such rash action: 'owing to the said Duke's versatile and inconstant humour' no one could 'rely on him'.

Henry clearly shared the same opinion and therefore decided to put Norfolk to the test, summoning him from his estates and sending him north to deal with the rebels. With just 5,000 men, he confronted them at Doncaster. However, his artillery batteries controlled the main road and river crossing, forcing the rebels to halt. Norfolk addressed them: 'Alas, ye unhappy men! What fancy, what folly, hath led and seduced you to make this most shameful rebellion against our most noble and righteous king and sovereign?'

Aware that he did not have sufficient forces to fight them, he offered a truce and a royal pardon if they went home. They believed him. Norfolk could hardly contain his delight, writing to the Council: 'It is said in our army that I never served his grace so well as now as in dissolving the army of the enemy without loss of ours …Good my lords, it was not the fear of the enemy (that) hath caused us to (negotiate) but … foul weather and no housing for horse nor man …hunger both for men and horses of such sort that of truth I think never English man saw the like. Pestilence in the town marvellous fervent …'

Henry now played a close hand, offering to receive a delegation of his subjects. Aske accepted safe conduct and travelled south, leaving his supporters behind. He was warmly welcomed and put his case, reassured by Henry's proposal to call Parliament to discuss his complaints. In December Aske was pardoned and enjoyed Christmas as a guest of the King. The so-called 'Pilgrimage of Grace' was disbanded and the King now made his response, read out in the Chapter House of Lincoln Cathedral by Thomas Moigne. The royal message was far from conciliatory:

Concerning choosing of Councillors, I never have read, heard, nor known that Princes' Councillors and Prelates should be appointed by rude and ignorant common people; nor that they were persons ... of ability to discern and choose suitable Councillors for a Prince.

How presumptuous then are ye, the rude commons of one shire, and that one of the most brute and beastly of the whole realm, and of least experience, to find fault with your Prince, for the electing of his Councillors and Prelates; and to take upon you contrary to God's law, and man's law, to rule your Prince, whom ye are bound by all laws to obey, and serve, with ... your lives, lands, and goods ... you, like traitors and rebels have behaved, and not like true subjects, as ye name yourselves ...

We marvel what madness is in your brain, or upon what ground ye would take authority upon you, to cause Us to break those laws and statutes, which, by all the Nobles, Knights, and Gentlemen of this realm, whom the same chiefly toucheth, hath been granted and assented to; seeing in no manner of thing it toucheth you, the base commons of our realm ...

Think ye that We be so faint hearted, that, perforce, ye of one shire (were ye a great many more) could compel Us with your insurrections, and such rebellious demeanour, to remit the same? Or think ye that any man will or may take you to be true subjects ...

We may have cause to order you thereafter; and rather obediently to consent amongst you, to deliver into the hands of our Lieutenant 100 persons, to be ordered according to their transgressions at our will and pleasure rather than by your obstinacy and wilfulness to put yourselves, lives, wives, children, lands, goods, and chattels, besides the indignation of God, in the utter adventure of total destruction, and utter ruin by force and violence of the sword.

In Rome Reginald Pole had been created a cardinal by the Pope and sent with legatine powers to Flanders to await the rebels' victory, but it was already too late.

In the New Year Norfolk became the instrument of Henry's vengeance, implementing the King's orders to 'cause such dreadful execution upon a good number of the inhabitants, hanging them on trees, quartering them, and setting their heads and quarters in every town, as shall be a fearful warning'.

The rebellion was put down with punishing retribution and many executions. Lord Hussey was found guilty as an accomplice in the insurrection of Lincolnshire and was executed at Lincoln. Norfolk's reign of terror left the bodies of rebels hanging on gallows and rotting all over Yorkshire. Lord Darcy, who had handed Pontefract over to the rebels, was beheaded on Tower Hill. Before his execution, he accused Norfolk of having secretly encouraged the rebels.

If the King got to hear of this, he did not act upon the information. He had suspected Norfolk's motives before, but he needed his prowess as a soldier and enforcer to act against the rebels. He preferred to keep him busy, with spies close at hand to report his every move.

Sporadic resistance continued. In January 1537 Sir Francis Bigod of Settrington, Yorkshire, led an uprising at Beverley. Another revolt spread from Cumberland where rebels were repulsed from Carlisle. Robert Aske managed to evade capture until the following July, when he was found and hanged in chains from the gates of York. Norfolk reported to Cromwell, 'Now shall appear whether for favour of these countrymen I forbore to fight with them at Doncaster …. Never was gold tried better by fire and water.'

The King avenged himself with a series of massacres under martial law. Although Norfolk was always ready to decorate the walls of cities such as Carlisle with fresh corpses, he believed that the high rents and brutal enclosures of the Earl of Cumberland had caused the uprising and wrote as much to London, revealing a more understanding and even compassionate side to his nature.

> What with the spoiling of them now and the transgressing of them so marvellously sore in time past and with increasing of lords' rents by enclosing, and for lack of the persons of such as shall suffer, this border is sore weakened and especially Westmorland; the more pity they should so deserve, and also that they have been so sore handled in times past, which, as I and all other here think, was the only cause of the rebellion.

Rather than a great religious crusade, the revolt was a mass protest against harsh agrarian reforms that encapsulated the last desperate protest of the Plantagenet old guard against the Tudor usurper. Fifty years after Bosworth the White Rose of York was still a potent symbol.

Lacking planning, cohesion and leadership, the rebellion was always doomed. Norfolk would never have risked all to lead it, as Henry's own son Richmond appears to have considered when he collected 5,000 supporters at his base in Collyweston outside Stamford, a force capable of taking on his father's army had he dared. As Cromwell had warned Henry, Richmond had high ambitions of his own. Had he not died so abruptly, it was entirely possible that he might have led the rebellion now known as the 'Pilgrimage of Grace'.

The people had learnt the hard way that the King's word was worthless and that Norfolk would follow him in anything in order to keep in favour. Norfolk had increased his unpopularity by mercilessly quelling the uprising but Henry still proved ungrateful and he was refused permission to return to court, where his enemies took full advantage of his absence to denigrate his actions. Queen Jane's eldest brother Edward Seymour suggested, as Darcy had avowed and Henry had always suspected, that Norfolk and Surrey had secretly supported the northern revolt.

When the Seymours first came to Court they had been allies of the Howards. Tom Seymour had kept company with Norfolk's son Surrey and the son of Thomas Wyatt the poet, all three getting into trouble for their drunken rioting. Initially they shared the same objective, to remove the Boleyns, and the fortunes of the Seymour family had soared as the sly and acquiescent Jane became Queen. But months passed before she became pregnant and the Seymours were aware that if the King did not have a son, then Norfolk and Surrey were closer to the throne and therefore rivals to their interests.

It was not until February 1537 that it was confirmed Jane was finally expecting a child. Hall records the public rejoicing at the news:

> On 27 May 1537, Trinity Sunday, there was a Te Deum sung in St Paul's cathedral for joy at the queen's quickening of her child, my lord chancellor, lord privy seal and various other lords and bishops being then present; the mayor and aldermen with the best guilds of the city being there in their liveries, all giving laud and praise to God for joy about it. The bishop of Worcester, Dr Latimer, made an oration before all the lords and commons after the Te Deum was sung, explaining the reason for their assembly, which oration was marvelously fruitful to the hearers.
>
> And also the same night various great fires were made in London, with a hogshead of wine at every fire for the poor people to drink as long as it lasted. I pray Jesus, if it be his will, to send us a prince.

The King was ecstatic at the news, and no doubt relieved. He had been afraid that he was incapable and that the curse he had felt hanging over him had never been lifted, leaving him without a legitimate male heir. All that counted now was for his third wife to produce a son and not another girl.

There was considerable competition to find places at court. From Calais Lady Lisle desperately canvassed for her daughters, Anne and Katherine Basset, to be accepted in the Queen's household. Anne had finished her education with Madame de Riou, with £6. 13s. 4d. a year for her 'finding' and a marriage portion of 100 marks or £66.13s.4d.

But from London the Lisles' agent John Hussey reported, 'Madame … My lord showed me that the Queen had all her maidens' pointed already, and that at the next vacation he would cause my lady his mother to do her best for the preferment of your ladyship's daughter …' He promised to keep 'a vigilant eye' for an opening.

Hearing that Jane was finally pregnant, Lady Lisle judiciously sent her a gift of quails, for which she had expressed a craving. In July, the Queen enjoyed them at dinner and was reminded from whom the gift came. The ploy worked and Hussey wrote to Lady Lisle, telling her to send both girls for the Queen to choose one as her maid:

… for her Grace will first see them and know their manners, fashions and conditions, and take which of them shall like her Grace best …

But if honest changes they must have, the one of satin, the other of damask …But madam, the Queen will be at no more cost with her but wages and livery, and so I am commanded to write unto your ladyship.

And for as much as they shall now go upon making and marring, it shall please your ladyship to exhort them to be sober, sad, wise and discreet and lowly above all things, and to be obedient … and to serve God and to be virtuous, for that is much regarded, to serve God well and to be sober of tongue.

At no little expense, Lady Lisle equipped them in the latest French fashions. Unfortunately, Jane was reminded of Anne Boleyn's stylish French hood and gowns and insisted that they dress more conservatively. The faithful Hussey wrote 'Methought [the bonnet] became her nothing so well as the French hood, but the Queen's pleasure must needs be fulfilled.'

Jane eventually selected 16-year-old Anne Basset to join her household. She was 'a pretty young creature', 'fair, well-made, and behaveth her self so well that everybody praiseth her that seeth her'. The King had already noted that she was 'far fairer' than her rejected sister. It was obvious that one of the essential qualifications for the post of Maid of Honour to the Queen was good looks.

In the autumn of 1537 Jane Seymour chose Hampton Court Palace for her lying-in. After a long labour, she gave birth on 12 October to a long-awaited son and heir.

On 15 October the baby was christened Edward in the royal chapel, with Norfolk and Archbishop Cranmer as his godfathers and his half-sister Mary as godmother. The child was carried by Chapuys' spy, the Marchioness of Exeter, with the Duke of Norfolk 'staying his head, as she bare him'. The triumph of the Catholic party seemed complete.

Then on 23 October Jane became ill with 'an naturall laxe' or heavy bleeding. With all the fuss surrounding the new prince, no one had noticed any earlier sign of weakness until her condition rapidly grew much worse and she died suddenly in the night.

Yet very soon after her death rumours began to spread concerning the birth. A legend grew up that Jane had been sacrificed to provide the King with an heir by undergoing a Caesarean section.

'The Lamentation of Queen Jane' appeared in 1560, reprinted in *Old Ballads* (1723):

Queen Jane was in labour for six days or more,
Till her women got tired and wished it were o'er.
'Good women if you be, will you send for King Henry,
For King Henry I must see.'
King Henry was a-sent for, King Henry did come,
For to meet with Queen Jane:
'My love, your eyes do look so dim.'
'King Henry, King Henry, King Henry if you be,
If you have my right side open'd you will find my dear babye.'

The story had it that the doctors approached Henry asking whether they should save the boy or his mother. He immediately told them to have her 'side cut open to save his babye' and if Jane died he could 'easily provide himself with other wives'.

The facts do not support this story. Caesarean operations were remarkably rare in that period, only performed *in extremis* in order to baptise the infant before death or if the mother had already died. Not until the 20th century were such procedures usually successful thanks to better hygiene and the discovery of anaesthetic and antibiotics. Nor could there be a conflict of interest over the birth as no one could have known that the Queen's child would be a boy. There is no reference to Jane being ill when the baby was brought to her after the christening. She was soon sitting up and able to write letters. She lived for two weeks after the birth and appeared to be recovering well. More credible is Cromwell's explanation that Jane had died as a consequence of neglect. He later confirmed the Queen's death was 'the faulte of them that were about her, whiche suffred her to take greate cold and to eate such thinges that her fantazie in syknes called for'.

It is quite possible that with attention concentrated on her son, Jane's post-natal condition was neglected and she developed a puerperal infection, perhaps caused by retention of the placenta. The Queen was attended by the King's physicians, all male and hindered by decorum from an internal examination whereas, as Loach points out, an experienced midwife would have ensured the afterbirth was expelled. Even a broken placenta would have brought about septicaemia.

On 8 November the Queen's corpse was taken to Windsor and buried four days later in St George's Chapel. The Duke of Norfolk was in charge of the funeral, in which the King took no part. He remained at Whitehall, scarcely overcome with grief since it was reported he was 'in good health and merry as a widower may be'.

Chapter Eight

Wheel of Fortune

I N 1537 DOWAGER DUCHESS AGNES moved her household to London. Her large and imposing mansion, Norfolk House, was close to Lambeth Palace, the residence of the Archbishop of Canterbury sited on the banks of the River Thames opposite the Palace of Westminster.

Many members of the Howard family had been born at Lambeth and the local Church of St Mary contained the Howard family chapel, built in 1522. The Church was recorded in the Domesday Book, but its origins are Saxon, allegedly built by Goda, the sister of Edward the Confessor. Its distinctive tower dates from the 14th century.

For 12-year-old Katherine it was the most exciting period of her life. She was at last going to get her chance to see London, of which she had heard so much.

The Dowager's train travelled up from Horsham in a slow convoy of horsemen, ladies and wagons loaded with household goods and fresh food from her estate. It was unlikely they could travel more than ten miles a day, stopping overnight at the many great inns or taverns in market towns en route.

Duchess Agnes was now 61 and may have made the journey by litter, but Katherine was by now an expert horsewoman and would have ridden the whole way. Riding was a natural requirement for a girl of her status and upbringing and at Chesworth she would have learnt to hunt and hawk, the primary form of exercise and entertainment for men and women of the gentry.

Katherine was surely dazzled by her first sight of London sprawling out along the twisting opposite shore, dominated by the tower of St Paul's great cathedral. The city is described by William Dunbar (*c.* 1460–1520):

> London, thou art of Townes a per se Soveraign of cities,
> semeliest in sight of high renoun, riches and royaltie;
> Of Lordis, Barons, and many goodly Knyght;
> Of most delectable lusty ladies bright
> Of famous Prelatis, in habitis clericall,
> Of Merchauntis full of substance and might:
> London, thou art the flour of Cities all.

To the east lay the walled city with its imposing medieval wall some 22 feet high. It stretched around three sides of the city, circling the silhouette of the Tower of London with four great gates: Cripplegate, Moorgate, Bishopsgate and Aldgate. There were two further gates, Newgate and Ludgate, as it turned down to the river.

Behind these sturdy walls rose the whitewashed keep where all the Kings of England slept the night before their coronation. Here was also the great menagerie, where the public could view exotic wild animals from far-flung countries. Down at the bustling docks hundreds of ships unloaded exotic goods from distant lands.

The river was the life-blood of London. Sailboats used it as a highway, transporting goods and people by day and night according to the tides. It took but a short trip by barge or wherry to be translated to another world at the royal court. The city streets were so busy that those who could afford it travelled by river.

To travel to Greenwich cost 8 pence with the tide or 12 pence against, but you could catch a ride from Blackfriars to Westminster for just 3 pence. Only the brave dared shoot the fast-flowing weirs under the arches of the great bridge linking the city to the south bank. The bridge itself teemed with shops and tenements, even a fine chapel dedicated to St Thomas à Becket. In its centre was a drawbridge that could be raised in time of war and on its battlements were the rotting heads of traitors.

St Paul's Cathedral dominated the skyline with its great spire 489 feet high, the tallest in Europe. Although frequently struck by lightning, this had always been rebuilt and was a beacon on top of Ludgate Hill, visible for miles. The Norman structure was the greatest in London, with its famous nave and east-facing rose window. Outside was the open-air pulpit called Paul's Cross, where crowds gathered to hear the new evangelical sermons. The narrow streets all around were crammed with tottering houses and intersected by teeming alleys, dominated by a forest of steeples and towers, from which hundreds of church bells rang out across the river.

Within the walls of London, the rich merchants built themselves fine houses, controlled the craft and trade guilds, and decked themselves and their wives in rich velvets and gold chains in emulation of their betters. They had their shops on the wide cobblestone thoroughfare of Chepeside, where the Eleanor Cross of Purbeck marble commemorated a long-dead queen. The Great Conduit provided London's water supply from the Tyburn. On state occasions its brass taps ran with wine. Close by was the Standard, a tall stone where capital punishment was carried out in the shadow of St Mary-le-Bow. Every night at nine the famous Bow Bells rang the curfew hour.

London's population was rising dramatically, doubling from 50,000 early in the King's reign. Those displaced by the new enclosures in the countryside came to the capital in search of work, crowding the densely packed tenement houses in the east of the city. An overspill had spread beyond the city walls to merge with existing villages and form new suburbs. Rising prices and inflation made it hard to survive. Crime was on the increase, as was the number of women forced into prostitution and the number of beggars on the streets. St Martin-le-Grand, near Bladder Street, was the old sanctuary within the walls, crowded with debtors and criminals. The City Watch patrolled at night against crime after the curfew hour when the gates were shut.

On the south side of the river were the stews of Southwark Bankside, 'better termed a foule dene'. Here the last harlots plied their trade under licence from the Bishop of Winchester, Stephen Gardiner. The King had closed other houses of ill fame, but 'Winchester's geese' continued to thrive. Bishop Gardiner had his fine house nearby and clearly saw nothing wrong in collecting revenue from their immoral earnings. In 1546, because of the fear of the spread of syphilis, a new royal ban would close even these, as recorded in a popular ballad of the time:

> The Stewes in England bore a beastly sway,
>   Till the eight Henry banish'd them away:
> And since these common whores were quite put down,
>   A damned crue of private whores are grown,
>   So that the diuell will be doing still,
>   Either with publique or with private ill.

This was the breeding ground for summer outbreaks of 'the Sweat', a deadly fever which struck suddenly causing terrible stomach cramps, headaches and a rash of black spots. In just a few hours the victim was 'stiff as a wall'. In the great outbreak of 1528 Londoners fled in panic, blocking all the exit roads. Two thousand died. As a contemporary witness described it: 'People collapsed without warning, some in opening their windows, some in playing with children in their street doors, some in one hour, many in two, it destroyed ... some in sleep, some in wake, some in mirth, some in care, some fasting and some full, some busy and some idle; and in one house sometime three, sometime five, sometime more, sometime all.'

Mosquitoes carried malaria from infected sources of water. Consumption was endemic, worms, agues, palsy, dropsy and quinsy (tonsillitis) commonplace. Pockmarked faces were the legacy of scurvy, the pox (smallpox) or French pox (syphilis). Lice and nits were found even in the greatest houses. Erasmus had been shocked when he saw that English houses were 'strewed with rushes under which lie unmolested an ancient collection of beer, grease, fragments, bones, spittle, excrements of dogs and cats, and everything nasty'.

He added, 'It is impolite to greet someone who is urinating or defecating.' Men urinated anywhere, even in corridors or fireplaces. In royal palaces there were 'pissing areas' for members of the court. 'Some make the chimnie chamber pot to smell like filthie stink, Yet who so bold, so soone to say, fough, how these houses stink?'

Only the very wealthy had an inside toilet. The King had a close-stool or 'jordan' inside a box covered in black velvet and studded with over two thousand gilt studs, which cost an extravagant £4. Castles and great houses would have a *garderobe* or *jakes*, usually a communal arrangement of seats side by side over a strategic shaft to an outside cesspool. The Thames Long House could accommodate 64 men and women at a time.

When the foul odours of London became intolerable, the rich began to build their houses beyond the city walls. To the west, there were still orchards and pastures in open country. The great houses of courtiers and the nobility stretched out along the Strand, with beautiful gardens running down to the water and private jetties.

Then came the separate city of Westminster, clustered around the famous abbey church, with its sanctuary for criminals. The tall chapel of Whitehall was a landmark for the landing stage from the river, with the long roof of the great hall and palace beyond. Great changes were taking place as the King built himself new quarters, extending Whitehall Palace, and the government bureaucracy took over Westminster. From here, all the administration of the kingdom was carried out by flocks of black-suited clerks, lawyers and clergy. However, of far more interest to the Dowager and her 12-year-old step-granddaughter were the popinjay courtiers with all their trains of hangers-on and retainers, all eager to be close to the King.

King Henry was the centre of their universe. He was the sun to ambitious men – and women – who blossomed in his light or

shrivelled and died in the shadows. To be at court and in his presence was everything, whatever it might cost – and it cost a small
fortune which had bankrupted many men. To be dismissed and
sent away, as Norfolk and his sharp-tongued wife had been, was to
suffer exclusion and disgrace, wilting away in the provinces, out of
all influence.

For a Howard such a situation was not to be tolerated. If Norfolk could not be present in person, then at least Agnes would play
her part. Once it became known that the Dowager was again in
residence there was no shortage of visitors calling daily at Lambeth. Her house soon became a popular meeting place with many
ambitious young men set to make a mark on the world.

One such was Francis Dereham, a gentleman by birth, 'of a poor
house', employed by the Duke of Norfolk as a 'gentleman pen-
sioner', used to conduct business in England and abroad.

He soon became a favourite of the Dowager and was said to be
much taken by one of her married ladies, Katherine's friend Joan
Bulmer. It seems that the young ladies in the Dowager's London
household enjoyed the same freedom as at Horsham, perhaps even
more. Katherine soon discovered that what took place after night-
fall was of much more interest than the more sedate visits by day.

The door to their dormitory was always open to young men
like Waldgrave and Dereham, bearing 'wine, strawberries, apples
and other things to make good cheer' in their lovers' beds. There
was really no privacy, even with the bed curtains closed. The other
occupants of the dormitory knew exactly what was going on and
who was present; as one woman caustically remarked, 'Hark to
Dereham broken winded.'

Katherine was a witness and a confidante to Joan's affair with
Dereham, but at this time seems to have had no night visitors of
her own. It was not long, however, before Dereham's attention
began to turn from the older, married woman to that of her young
friend.

Dereham's age is unknown but he must have been many years
older than Katherine and well aware of the risks he was taking in
aiming at a girl of her status. As far as he knew she was an inexperi-

enced virgin, but he did not let that deter him from a calculated plan of seduction.

Dereham, like Henry Manox before him, clearly saw in Katherine an opportunity that could not be ignored. Even had Katherine not been a charming and biddable girl on the edge of womanhood, unprotected and brought up in a hothouse of promiscuity and deceit, she would still have been a magnet for such ambitious and ruthless men. Dereham saw his chance to advance himself by staking his claim to this Howard daughter. She might not be a great heiress, but she was the niece of the Duke of Norfolk, as Anne Boleyn had been.

Katherine was still just 12 or 13 years of age but already a precocious and knowing girl with an attractive figure. She never confessed to having sex with Manox, only fumblings, but Manox was to admit to heavy petting with her from the time she was just 11 years of age. He boasted that he knew an intimate mark on her body and asserted that he would take Katherine's virginity, but did this happen, given the timely intervention of Mary Lascelles?

Whatever kind of sexual initiation Katherine had undergone with her music master, two years later she was involved in an intense and ongoing affair with Francis Dereham which neither of them attempted to conceal from their friends. At 13 years of age, she was already a woman of experience.

Dereham had started out on the relationship with cold deliberation, passing over Joan Bulmer for her higher-born friend, daughter of the Howard house. He had wooed and seduced her, imagining her innocent.

As a gentleman serving the Duke of Norfolk, he had the means to buy Katherine expensive gifts, including a 'quilted cap of sarcenet', 'a heart's-ease of silk for a New Year's gift' as well as rich materials for a gown.

We have no record of Joan Bulmer's reaction to her lover's betrayal, but it must have soured the relationship between the two women and may have played a significant part in Joan's later actions.

Katherine 'was so far in love' with Dereham that from mere flirting they rapidly progressed to 'bundling' while still fully dressed. However, it was not long before Dereham abandoned his doublet and hose for 'naked bed', as Katherine herself expressed it later.

Before much longer the other women were reporting, 'I warrant you if you seek him in Katherine Howard's chamber ye shall find him there.' The lovers were seen 'after a wonderful manner, for they would kiss and hang by their bellies together as they were two sparrows'.

Not all the women condoned such behaviour. The pious Mary Lascelles formed the opinion that Katherine was 'light in both living and conditions'. Alice Restwold, who shared the same dormitory, was also critical of the young girl's behaviour with Dereham behind the bed-curtains. Alice was 'a married woman and wist what matrimony meant and what belonged to that puffing and blowing'. But almost everyone else around her was having illicit sex – with the exception of Mary Lascelles, whose views as a reformist believer were against the norm of the other 'ladies'.

We have on record Katherine's own view of their affair, albeit coloured by later events when she was forced to confess to their involvement. She admitted: 'Francis Dereham by many persuasions procured me to his vicious purpose and obtained first to lie upon my bed with his doublet and hose and after within the bed and finally he lay with me naked and used me in such sort as a man doth his wife many and sundry times but how often I know not.'

She confessed she had shared 'more than a hundred nights' with him.

Dereham was working hard to establish that he had a prior claim upon her, blatantly acting as though they were trothplight, or betrothed, to one another. By promising that they would marry, exchanging vows to one another and then indulging in a physical relationship, they were already married in the eyes of the Church. Such precontracts were commonplace, but binding. Later marriages could be dissolved to give precedence to an earlier affair such as Dereham shared with Katherine. He seems to have set out to confirm that they were a couple, calling her 'his own wife' in front of witnesses and telling Katherine to call him husband. When one of Katherine's friends asked whether 'Mr Dereham shall have Mrs Katherine Howard', his reply was 'By St John you may guess twice and guess worse.' He was already claiming to be her husband, establishing his right to be considered a member of the Howard dynasty.

Marriage was, first and foremost, a commercial undertaking. It was the duty of parents to arrange marriages for their children. Thomas Becon offered this advice:

> … it is the office and duty of good and godly parents to provide marriages for them, that they may marry in the Lord, and with the consent of their parents … Children in the state of matrimony ought not to follow their own blind judgement, foolish fancy, carnal appetite, sensual pleasure, but the grave, sage, prudent, and wise counsel of their parents … Those children, which of their own brain and fancy attempt marriage without the good-will and consent of their parents, do grievously offend; and seldom cometh to pass that such marriages come unto a fortunate and prosperous end.

Romance or lust was seen as a danger to the financial prospects of the entire family.

Women were not expected to think for themselves when it came to such a life-changing decision as choosing a husband. Arranged marriages were a business partnership, but that did not mean they were necessarily without love. The reformist Archbishop of Canterbury Thomas Cranmer judged that a bond of affection between husband and wife was 'a remedie against sinne', giving 'the mutuall societie, helpe, and coumfort, that the one oughte to have of thother, both in prosperitie and in adversitie'.

In many families coercion, such as that dealt out by the Pastons, was frowned upon but practised with the whip. Margaret Paston wrote about her wayward daughter Margery who had created an outrage when she dared to choose her own husband, the family's bailiff, Richard Calle, who was considered far beneath her in status:

On Friday the Bishop [of Norwich] sent for her ... and said to her right plainly and put her in remembrance how she was born, what kin and friends that she had ... and therefore he bade her be right well advised how she did, and said that he would understand the words that she had said to him, whether it made matrimony or not ... she said she thought in her conscience she was bound, whatsoever the words wern. These lewd words grieve me and her grandam as much as all the remnant. And the Bishop and the chancellor both said that there was neither I nor no friend of hers would receive her.

Margery Paston defied her family, declaring that she would marry Calle, even if it meant she had 'to sell kandyll and mustard in Framlyngham' town. Other men did not take well to women reversing traditional roles and proposing. When the merchant George Cely received a love letter from a mysterious Frenchwoman in Calais, 'Lady Clare', he was clearly swayed by her boldness in writing: 'If it please you to know, I have loved you a long time, but I dared not tell you so...And I let you know that my heart is set on no man but you ...'

George agreed to take her as his mistress, but she was apparently not suitable marriage material.

The age at which couples married was also on the increase, men sometimes delaying marriage into their late twenties, in order to establish some form of financial independence through inheritance, or apprenticeship to a trade, before having children. Margaret warns John Paston 'not to be too hasty to be married till ye were more sure of your livelode'. In *Measure for Measure*, Shakespeare's Claudio declares:

I got possession of Julietta's bed. You know the lady; she is fast my wife,
Save that we do the denunciation lack of outward order.
(I.II.146–52)

They delay their marriage 'for propagation of a dower', but not their 'mutual entertainment.' (I.I.139–143)

He is your husband on a pre-contract. To bring you thus together,
'tis no sin,
Sith that the justice of your title to him doth flourish the deceit.
(IV.1.71–5)

Katherine's supposed loss of virginity was a disgrace to the
Howard name and a marked depreciation of her value on the marriage market, but this loss allowed a gentleman of Dereham's rank
to take advantage, staking his claim to 'damaged goods'.

Dereham claimed Katherine as his wife and the women around
her reported that they were 'puffing and blowing' on a regular
basis. Her 'friends' were older and included far more experienced
married women who passed on their knowledge and advice to
her, tutoring her in taking necessary protection against the shame
of an illicit pregnancy. Bearing a child outside marriage was a great
disgrace and many an older and wiser woman had fallen into the
trap, including her own cousin Mary Boleyn.

Rates of illegitimacy were remarkably low, at just 2 per cent of
births. Although the medieval Church opposed any kind of contraception, women had always found means of avoiding conception. They knew enough to realise that an extensive period of
breast-feeding after childbirth could delay menstruation and
therefore prevent another pregnancy following on. In this way,
from early times women had succeeded in spacing their pregnancies and contraceptive methods had long been in use, whether it
was certain positions, herbs, or the popular but not very effective
rhythm method. *Coitus interruptus* or *coitus reservatus* had been
employed since biblical times. According to the Book of Genesis,
Onan 'spilled his seed on the ground' (Genesis 23). Ever since then,
many devout Jews and Christians have considered it a sin. The Tal-
mud recommends a sponge soaked in vinegar – *mokh* – for contraception if a woman was already pregnant or breast-feeding.
Dioscorides' *De Materia Medica* recommended many contraceptive
devices. Beeswax was used to seal the uterus. Many believed that
'hard pissing' after sex was the answer.

Condoms made of linen, animal gut or skin were first sold in the 16th century as protection against the epidemic of syphilis spreading through Europe. In France these were called *la redingote anglaise or la capote anglaise* (English cloak). In England they were known as 'Venus gloves'or 'quondam,' pronounced condom, after the hood or cowl worn by monks, playing on the sexual escapades in monasteries that were cited as the King's reason for closing them down. They were made by glovers such as the father of William Shakespeare, who wrote in one of his plays: 'Your quondam wife swears still by Venus Glove' (*Troilus and Cressida*, IV.v.179).

In Italy Gabrielle Fallopius developed a chemical solution that acted as a spermicide. There were also more extreme measures that might be employed, such as first placing a cockerel's testicles under the bed. Most women relied on potions and herbal concoctions. The old ballad 'Scarborough Fair' illustrates these 'womanly arts'. The traditional herbs 'parsley, sage, rosemary and thyme' were taken as herbal teas or used in a douche or sponge.

Rue was widely used for contraception and marigolds, savin, tansy, ivy, mandrake and the bark of white poplar for abortion. The use of abortion as a means of birth control may have been made more acceptable by the contemporary belief that the fetus did not acquire a soul until 80 days after conception. Such drug-induced abortions took place up to the fifth month of pregnancy, when the child first moved. It was believed that at the fifth month the soul entered the body. Later Katherine was to expose her secret knowledge when she remarked with naïve frankness that 'a woman might meddle with a man and yet conceive no child unless she herself would'.

No one chose to betray the lovers and no word of Katherine's antics appeared to reach the Dowager Duchess. And then a figure from the past suddenly returned to haunt Katherine.

Although the Manox affair had been discovered and the music master dismissed from service, he now contrived to follow the Duchess's household to London. In 1538 he succeeded in gaining employment in London with Lord Bayment. Somehow he heard that Katherine had become involved with Francis Dereham.

Later, Manox would insinuate that it was Katherine who first helped Dereham gain admittance to the women's chambers. He claimed she had forced Mary Lascelles, the Dowager's chamberer, 'to steal the key and bring it to her' so that the men could get in and out, 'into the little gallery' next door. Manox stated, 'They would commonly banquet and be merry there till two or three of the clock in the morning.'

Jealous and affronted, Manox clearly did not know that Dereham and other nocturnal visitors had been calling on Joan Bulmer and her friends long before he took an interest in Katherine. His report is clearly based on hearsay and rumour, with the name of Mary Lascelles added in spite for the lecture she had given him at Horsham. With her reformist religious beliefs, Mary Lascelles was the last person Katherine would have asked to help her in a promiscuous adventure.

The rejected Henry Manox sought revenge against the lovers by sending an anonymous note to the Dowager Duchess. In it, he informed her that her household was 'dishonoured' by the activities taking place under her roof: 'Your Grace, It shall be meet you take good heed to your gentlewomen for if it shall like you half an hour after you shall be a-bed to rise suddenly and visit their Chamber you shall see that which shall displease you. But if you make anybody of counsel you shall be deceived.'

The letter was laid in the Duchess's pew, where she found it and read it. Acting on his advice, 'when she came home she stormed with her women and declared how she was advertised ... of their misrule'. She apparently broke in on the antics in her women's dormitory one night, catching Katherine and Dereham in compromising postures.

Last time the Dowager had taken action against Manox, expelling him from employment but leaving her son, Lord William Howard, to try and explain to Katherine the damage she had done to her own reputation. Clearly his lecture had failed. According to Manox's later story, Katherine wanted to find out who had betrayed her and 'stole the letter out of my Lady's gilt coffer and showed it to Dereham who copied it and thereupon it was laid in the coffer again'.

Manox alleged that Dereham sought him out, called him insulting names, suggesting he 'neither loved (her) nor him'.

Young Katherine once more found herself in disgrace. Virginity was regarded as an asset, to be bartered in the marriage negotiations. A young girl was foolish to throw this away on a whim of 'romantic love' when she could use it as a bargaining counter to get herself a wealthy husband. A woman's honour was based upon her virginity. As part of traditional wedding celebrations, the bride and groom would be escorted to bed by a raucous procession of relatives and friends. Part of the ritual the next morning was the demonstration of the bride's virginity when the bloodstained sheets from the wedding night were hung out in the street for everyone to see. For an unmarried girl her virginity was considered a vital asset and its loss was a disaster, not only for herself but for her entire family. If exposed to public knowledge, she would face humiliation and her chances of making a good marriage would be ruined. In Shakespeare's *Much Ado About Nothing*, the wronged Hero is publicly shamed for falling 'into a pit of ink' and derided as 'smirched' and 'mired'. She is rejected by her future husband because of the loss of her maidenhead, but the blame extends to her father who has not kept her pure: 'There, Leonato, take her back again, Give not this rotten orange to your friend.'

Katherine has been described by some writers as 'a juvenile delinquent', but even now she was not yet 14 years old. A correct reading of her age is crucial to the perception and understanding of the young girl caught in the maelstrom of ambition and intrigue.

At the hands of two men twice her age, Katherine had been subjected to persistent child abuse, although she seemed blithely unaware of the fact. Katherine's rash and foolish conduct was a disgrace to the Howard name, but the Dowager had no wish for the news to become public. It would ruin her step-grandaughter's marriage prospects and make the Dowager the butt of bawdy jokes. Shortly afterwards Francis Dereham was sent away to Ireland on business. This suggests that his master, the Duke of Norfolk, had some knowledge of the affair. At the very least, he appears to have been asked by his stepmother to remove the gentleman in question as far away as possible from his vulnerable and wayward niece.

Dereham departed but continued to treat Katherine as his wife, leaving behind all his savings, £100, in her safekeeping. He clearly intended to return to claim his prize.

Did Katherine consider herself betrothed? She was no longer an innocent, but she was still young and naïve. Francis Dereham may have been handsome, but he was her inferior in status and she must have been told in no uncertain terms by her grandmother that her family would not look favourably on such a match for the Duke of Norfolk's own niece.

Katherine was apparently out of danger. She made no effort to communicate with Dereham and chose not to succumb to his fantasy of marriage. She seems to have behaved with perfect obedience, turning her back on the affair, certain that she would hear no more of him.

She was looking to her own future. Now that she was in London and knew so much more of the world, her sights were beginning to be set far higher.

Across the river, the court was a savage arena in which ambition and greed dominated. The Seymour brothers had survived the temporary setback of their sister Jane's death, maintaining their influence with the King. Now, in the absence of a queen, the court was once more a man's world, ruled by client–patron relationships, the life-blood of Tudor society.

Since the break with Rome and the many new powers that he had accrued, Henry had recreated himself. Now everyone had to kneel at his approach as though he was imbued with some kind of quasi-religious mystical aura. His vanity and arrogance knew no bounds and he would brook no opposition. Henry blamed his ministers for his own faults, but as Cardinal Pole noted: 'Who will tell the prince his fault? And if one such be found, where is the prince that will hear him?' The King was surrounded by fawning sycophants who 'doff off with their bonnets to you that gladly would see your head off by the shoulders', as Sir Francis Bryan remarked in his 1548 *Dispraise of the Life of a Courtier.*

Henry could be malicious, treating those closest to him with open contempt. He insulted his servants, called Wriothesley, Cromwell's assistant, 'my pig' and often struck Cromwell in public:

> The King beknaveth him twice a week and sometimes knocks him well about the pate; and yet when that he hath been well pummelled about the head and shaken up as it were a dog, he will come out of the Great Chamber shaking off the bush with as merry a countenance as though he might rule all the roost ... [he] hath called my Lord Privy Seal villain, knave, bobbed him about the head and thrust him from the Privy Chamber.

The King's moods took violent swings so that no one knew which way he would turn from one day to the next. Under his boisterous public face, Henry was stubborn, cold and peevishly unpredictable. He could change his opinion in a second. He was plagued with constipation, haemorrhoids and a suppurating leg ulcer that refused to heal. This was the result of a jousting accident and meant that he could no longer exercise. In May 1538, when the King was 46, his leg ulcer induced a septic infection and sudden fever. He was 'without speaking, black in the face, and in great danger'. He suffered severe headaches, which, together with the pain from his leg, drove him into terrifying rages against whoever was near.

It was suggested that a new queen might be a calming influence. It had not escaped anyone's attention – least of all that of the Duke of Norfolk – that the King was already casting eyes at the young women at court. The idea that he might be considering taking another wife provoked a flurry of activity among the Howard family.

The marriage market was, after all, the key to gaining allies but since the callous execution of Anne Boleyn, Henry was regarded as the most dangerous match in Europe.

Christina, the 16-year-old widowed Duchess of Milan, had 'a good personage of body' suitable for breeding, but when Wriothesley went to woo her, Christina rejected Henry out of hand, retorting that she wanted 'not to be wife to such a husband that either putteth away or killeth his wives', but that 'If I had two heads, one should be at his Grace's service.' Wriothesley's answer, according to his own version, was the perfect diplomat's speech:

Oh, Madam, how happy shall you be if it be your chance to be matched with my master. If God send you that hap, you shall be matched with the most gentle gentleman that liveth; his nature so benign and pleasant that I think to this day no man hath heard many angry words pass his lips. As God shall help me, if he were no King, I think, an you saw him, you would say that for his virtue, gentleness, wisdom, experience, goodliness of person, and all other qualities meet to be in a Prince, he were worthy before all others to be made a King.

Wriothesley thought she would have laughed 'had not her gravity forbidden it'. Baldassare Castiglione, visiting England in the reign of Henry VII, noted that there was 'a most wanton life in every kinde of vice: the women enticefull ... and the men womanish'. Foreign ambassadors reported that every woman at court was seen as a whore, every man a pimp: 'King Henry gave his mind to three notorious vices – lechery, covetousness and cruelty, but the two latter issued and sprang out of the former.'

The English royal court was a place where corruption and vice flourished. 'That great courtesan, the court' was a jungle with 'nothing but every man for himself'. The poet Sir Thomas Wyatt's comparison of the country mouse and town mouse exposes the abuses of power and sordid sexuality of court intrigue. The 'sely mouse' is betrayed by the 'traytour Catt' in an intrinsically shallow world where women are degraded and despised.

As Wyatt cynically observed, it was profitable to act as the King's procurer. His poem 'A spending Hand' is addressed to Sir Francis Bryan, ironically advising him how to succeed at court, working his way into the King's favour by providing 'the vilest of services for one old or oldish man, Henry VIII', prostituting sisters or daughters.

> In this also se thou be not idle:
> Thy niece, thy cousin, thy sister, or thy daughter,
> If she be fair: if handsome be her middle:
> If thy better hath her love besought her:
> Advance his cause, and he shall help thy need.
> But ware I say, so gold thee help and speed:
> That in this case thou be not so unwise,
> As Pandar was in such a like deed.
> For he the fool of conscience was so nice:
> That he no gain would have for all his pain.
> Be next thy self for friendship bears no price.

The thought had certainly not escaped Thomas Howard, Duke of Norfolk. A Howard queen would be an influential asset for the entire clan. There were sufficient Howard daughters, nieces and cousins to provide a suitable candidate to satisfy the King.

Dynastic politics had pushed Mary Howard into marriage with the King's bastard son, allegedly leaving her a virgin aged 17. In 'A face that shuld content me' Wyatt describes her as 'Maiden-wife, and widow'. Her grace and strength of character may have been admired but they brought her into bitter conflict with her own brother.

Surrey and his companions, Wyatt's son and Tom Seymour, were the 'roaring boys' of London, who had scandalised the capital late at night with their 'racketty life'. Such rowdy youths were the original 'street walkers', out on the prowl at night with friends, looking for trouble. They were punished by Tom's unyielding elder brother Edward Seymour, Earl of Hertford, with a few days in jail to cool their heels. He had already clashed with Surrey over his sympathies for the northern rebels and considered Norfolk's son to be 'the most relish prowde boye that ys in England'.

Surrey never forgave Edward Seymour. This time in jail he took the opportunity to write his 'Satire on the Citizens of London'. A feud had developed between the Howards and Seymours that would not die away.

Mary Howard had many suitors. First it was Cromwell, then it was Tom Seymour, but Surrey furiously opposed that, saying the Seymours were 'those saucy fellows that had crept into Court under their sister's petticoats'. Now Surrey came up with the idea of another suitor: the King himself. Mary had been married to Henry's bastard son, but that did not prevent her brother from suggesting that if she could not become Queen she should try to become the King's mistress.

Mary understandably told him exactly what she thought of this proposal, adding that she would rather die than find herself in the King's bed.

As a result, relations between brother and sister continued to be poor. Mary had broken with family tradition and her Catholic roots to become a reform believer while Surrey and his father remained tied to the old faith. But Mary had befriended her father's mistress Bess Holland, and both children supported their father in his very public rift with their mother, who complained bitterly that 'Never [were] so ungracious an eldest son and so ungracious a daughter and so unnatural.'

It was then rumoured that the sparkling Mary (Madge) Shelton might be a candidate, but she finally managed to escape this fate by marrying Sir Anthony Heveningham. However, the suggestion that the King might take another wife of English blood soon motivated the Howards. Their patriarch Norfolk recognised an opportunity when he saw one and determined to find the right instrument for Howard glory.

The search for a new Queen had begun.

Chapter Nine

Pawn for a King

IN THIS UNSTABLE WORLD of shifting alliances, of covert and backroom deals, trust was unknown. A new treason law had been enacted in 1534, based on the 'intent' or the presumption to commit treason; no action was necessary. It was the thought or aim that counted, not the fulfilment of the deed itself, and those who wished death or harm to the King were held guilty. Sir Edward Neville had been reported by an informer for criticism of the King's advisers: 'The King keepeth a sort of knaves here, that we dare neither look nor speak, and if I were able, I would rather live any life in the world than tarry in the Privy Chamber.'

In November 1538 Cromwell turned against his former Catholic allies, striking down that residue of the Yorkist nobility, the de la Pole family. He claimed to have discovered a conspiracy even worse than the Pilgrimage of Grace.

Margaret Plantagenet, Countess of Salisbury, the aged daughter of the Yorkist Duke of Clarence, was living peacefully in Hampshire when she was arrested by the Earl of Southampton. She and her son Lord Montague were revealed by Sir Geoffrey Pole to be trafficking with Cardinal Pole in exile. Lady Salisbury was transferred to the Tower, where for two years she suffered from the cold and neglect. The Marquis of Exeter, his wife and young sons were also imprisoned in the Tower, accused of plotting to usurp the throne and carrying on a treasonable correspondence with the Imperial Ambassador Chapuys.

In June 1540 Cardinal Pole heard that his mother had been found guilty:

> You have heard, I believe, of my mother being condemned by pub-lic Council to death, or rather to eternal life. Not only has he who condemned her, condemned to death a woman of seventy – than whom he has no nearer relative, except his daughter, and of whom he used to say there was no holier woman in his kingdom – but at the same time her grandson, son of my brother, a child, the remain-ing hope of our race. See how far this tyranny has gone, which began with priests, in whose order it only consumed the best, then [went on] to nobles, and there, too, destroyed the best.

Exeter, Montague and Sir Edward Neville were beheaded on 9 December. The rest languished in captivity while the entire de la Pole family was attainted for treason.

The Countess of Salisbury, as niece of both Edward IV and Richard III, was the surviving heiress of the Plantagenet kings. She was also the mother of Cardinal Pole and for that, aged 68, she was still seen as a threat to the Tudor King.

Henry's agents abroad tried to assassinate Cardinal Pole, but he survived to revenge his family by organising European opposition to Henry with the Pope's support. While Gertrude Blount, Mar-chioness of Exeter, received a pardon and was set free, her son Edward Courtenay was not released for another 15 years. Just 12 years old when arrested, he spent most of that time in solitary con-finement. His plaintive cry was carved into the wall of his prison: '*Ubi lapsus quid feci? Quod verum tutum.*' (What have I done? What is true is safe.)

One of his visitors was the arch-conservative Stephen Gardiner, Bishop of Winchester, who entertained hopes that Courtney might one day marry the King's Catholic daughter Mary, although she was considerably older. The Catholic faction at court did not disappear but simply bided their time.

Gardiner had been packed off to France, marginalised by his enemy Cromwell, who kept him away from the King by arranging for diplomatic missions abroad. The bishop was angry and frustrated. Known to be as irascible and as bad-tempered as the King, often beside himself with rage, he became a target for the educated reformists: 'There was at that tyme in authoritye amongst the kinges counsellors one Steven Gardener, Byshop of Winchester, who as he was in those daies most cruell, so was he also of a mooste subtile and craftye witte ... gropynge rounde aboute to get occasion to let and hinder the Gospell ...'

Gardiner sought to undermine Cromwell's influence at every opportunity, joining his old master Norfolk in a clandestine alliance to bring about his downfall. Norfolk made no secret of his resentment at the advance of men like Cromwell, ill-born upstarts, 'thieves and murderers' who sought to replace the nobility in office.

After many requests for a recall Gardiner was at last allowed home in July 1538, alarmed to discover how quickly reform had spread throughout England. Norfolk and Gardiner sought to reverse the trend but the Liber Regis shows just how much the Crown had gained from the dissolution of the monasteries. More than 600 religious houses and over 2,000 chapels and chantries for the dead had been closed. The royal exchequer profited from the seizure of church lands and goods, much of which was sold on to favoured members of the nobility, buying their support. While some abbeys were converted into cathedrals or colleges, others were turned into hospitals or grammar schools and many smaller establishments became manor houses for the King's personal friends.

Religious division was at the heart of court and society. Archbishop Cranmer's reforms depended upon the continuing goodwill of the King, but in his royal supremacy Henry was, as ever, unpredictable, regarding his will as that of God.

In 1537 Cranmer had given him a new English translation of the Bible in the hope that it 'may be sold, and read of every person, without danger of any Act, proclamation, or ordinance, heretofore granted to the contrary'.

In 1539 the Great Bible was produced under the King's seal. Every church was to 'provide one book of the whole Bible of the largest volume in English and the same set up in some convenient place within the said Church that ye have care of, whereas your parishioners may most commodiously resort to the same and read it'.

Cranmer wrote to Cromwell: 'I rejoice to see this day of reformation now risen in England, since the light of God's Word doth shine over it without a cloud.'

Yet that same year the Catholic party succeeded in winning the King's assent to the draconian Act of Six Articles which effectively outlawed the majority of Protestant beliefs. The Duke of Norfolk and Bishop Gardiner were rightly blamed for influencing the King to agree to extreme measures: '... while this [godly] council was about him, and could be heard, he did much good, so again when sinister and wicked councillors under subtle and crafty pretences had gotten ever the foot in, thrusting truth and verity out of the prince's ears, how much religion and all good things went prosperously forward before, so much on the contrary side all revolted backwards again'.

The day after the Act was passed, Norfolk was seen having a terrible row with Cromwell at Archbishop Cranmer's house. Not long before, Norfolk had learnt that Cromwell was protecting more than 60 Protestants in the English enclave of Calais who had been hunted down and denounced as 'heretics' by Lord Lisle. Very likely Norfolk suspected Cromwell of giving them his support.

Bishop Gardiner now launched a ferocious attack on his enemy Cranmer. He had become so confident that he dared to accuse the Archbishop of Canterbury openly of 'heresy'. Cranmer was saved only thanks to the King's personal intervention. His opinion might have changed had he known that Cranmer had a wife, Margaret, niece of the Lutheran theologian Osiander. The Six Articles had re-imposed the vow of celibacy upon all priests. That meant that married Protestant clergy were now forced to part from their wives and families, causing much distress. Cranmer himself was obliged to send away his German wife.

The jails of London were overflowing. Reform leaders like Robert Barnes, Jerome, and Thomas Garret were sent to the stake. This was the nation under 'Bluff King Hal'. More than 50,000 were to suffer execution at his hands and everyone remembered that his own Queen had been one of them.

Two years after the demise of Jane Seymour, the King was eager to take a fourth wife. After France and Spain signed a temporary peace at the Treaty of Toledo, Henry needed to show that he was still orthodox in his theology despite the break with Rome. In this he found Gardiner a willing ally.

The Elector of Saxony expressed his astonishment to King Henry that he had allowed himself to be taken in 'by the conspiracy and craftiness of certain bishops, in whose mind the veneration and worshipping of Roman ungodliness is rooted'.

But Henry feared a Catholic invasion and determined to put on a show, as John Hussey described to Lord Lisle:

And they that be in the King's chapel shewed me … that upon Good Friday last past the King's grace crept to the cross from the chapel door upward, devoutly, and so served the priest to mass that same day, his own person, kneeling on his grace his knees … And his grace every Sunday doth receive holy bread and holy water, and doth daily use all other laudable ceremonies, and in all London no man upon pain of death to speak against them.

All this was meant to reassure Catholic Europe. With foreign markets closed to English goods, Henry needed an ally, but the alliance Thomas Cromwell suggested was with the leader of the German Protestant states, William, Duke of Cleves, who just happened to have an unmarried sister called Anne.

A marriage with Anne of Cleves could protect England from the threat of invasion by the Holy Roman Empire. It would provide a Protestant bastion in northern Europe against the Catholic south. It would also strengthen Cromwell's hand against his political enemies at home, namely Gardiner, Bishop of Winchester, and Thomas Howard of Norfolk. Cromwell reported: 'Every man praiseth the beauty of the said Lady Anne, as well for her face as for her person, above all the ladies excellent. She as far excelleth the Dutchess of Saxony as the golden sun excelleth the silver moon. Every man praiseth the good virtues and honesty with shamefacedness which plainly appeareth in the gravity of her countence.'

In March 1539 Nicholas Wotton and Robert Barnes had been sent as envoys to Cleves.

The King's favourite artist Hans Holbein, himself a fervent Protestant, was dispatched to paint the prospective bride's portrait. Reports of her bearing and beauty had already swayed Henry and the likeness that Master Holbein produced only seemed to confirm his decision to take her. By autumn the marriage treaty was signed and the princess of Cleves prepared for her destiny as England's new Queen.

There was already much competition for places at court. In Calais Lady Lisle was anxious that her daughter Katherine Basset should join her sister Anne as a lady of the future Queen's household. She surely knew of the rumours that Anne Basset had caught the King's attention and been sent the gift of a horse and fine saddle. Was she his mistress? Probably not, for she had been ill and had been sent out of London to recover at Westminster, as a letter home reported:

Madam, My duty done, I humbly recommend me unto your Ladyship, desiring you of your daily blessing. The cause of my writing unto you at this time is, that I am now with my cousin, at the King's grace's commandment: for whereas Mistress Mewtas doth lie in London there are no walks but a little garden, wherefore it was the King's grace's pleasure that I should be with my Cousin Denny; for where as she lieth there are fair walks and a good open air; for the physician doth say that there is nothing better for my disease than walking; and I thank God I am a great deal better than I was … I trust to God that we shall have a mistress shortly, and then I trust I

shall see you here when she comes over, which I hope to God will
not be long. No more to you at this time, but I pray God send your
Ladyship long life, to the pleasure of God.
From Westminster, the Sunday after Michaelmas day.
By your humbell dowter
An Basset.

Her mother still seemed to think that she had sufficient influence
with the King to arrange the posting for her sister. She hoped the
King's new wife would be 'good and gentle to serve and please'.
Those chosen to serve Anne of Cleves must all be 'fair, and meet
for the room'. The princess of Cleves was bringing with her a retinue of 350 Germans.

The Catholic party at court, piqued to have been overtaken by
events, determined to go ahead with their plans to promote alter-
native candidates for the King's attention. In late 1539 Norfolk
secured three of the appointments of new ladies-in-waiting to the
future queen for his great-niece, Katherine Carey, Henry's daughter by Mary Boleyn, and his nieces, Mary Norris and Katherine
Howard.

Norfolk's search for suitable young women had borne fruit. The
ideal candidate had been right there all this time, hidden away in
the house of his stepmother Agnes, Dowager Duchess of Norfolk.

He had forgotten his brother's children, much as he had tired of
Edmund himself.

Katherine's father had died only in March that year, as he was
approaching the age of 60. Edmund Howard had lived and died an
embarrassment to his family. Looking at his daughter, Norfolk
could only hope that she would make up for all his shortcomings.

Katherine was summoned to her uncle's presence and examined with just one thing in mind. She was now aged about 14,
short of stature but already pert and nubile in figure, well able to
take a pretty compliment and to attract any man's attention. Norfolk himself was of the opinion that the girl 'who strikes the fire of
full 14' was ripe for a husband.

Katherine aspired and longed for all the things she had never known – warmth and affection, financial security and status. Ever since she had first arrived in the Dowager's household she had been taught that the royal court was the centre of the universe. Now she was being offered a place as one of the future Queen's ladies-in-waiting. She would be content to be rewarded with material pleasures, a good Catholic girl, bending to the wisdom of her elders. As Katherine herself was later to say, 'All that knew me, and kept my company, know how glad and desirous I was to come to the Court.'

Now Anne of Cleves, the mail-order bride, was on her way. She had set off with her retinue from Cleves in November 1539 but by the time she reached Calais the onset of winter storms in the Channel prevented a crossing. Lord Lisle was obliged to entertain the future Queen of England over Christmas with impromptu celebrations until the weather improved, not an easy task considering that the princess did not speak a word of English.

A high-powered delegation eventually braved the tempestuous waters of 'the Sleeve', led by the Seymour brothers and the Earl of Southampton. They had strict instructions to 'cheer my lady and her train so they think the time short'. Fortunately, the weather broke and the wedding party resumed their passage, reaching Kent on 27 December. Wriothesley reported the scene:

This year on St John's Day, 27 December, Lady Anne, daughter of the duke of Cleves in Germany, landed at Dover at 5 o'clock at night, and there was honourably received by the duke of Suffolk and other great lords, and so lodged in the castle. And on the following Monday she rode to Canterbury where she was honourably received by the archbishop of Canterbury and other great men, and lodged at the king's palace at St Austin's, and there highly feasted. On Tuesday she came to Sittingbourne ... On New Year's Eve the duke of Norfolk with other knights and the barons of the exchequer received her grace on the heath, two miles beyond Rochester, and so brought her to the abbey of Rochester where she stayed that night and all New Year's Day.

They prepared for the journey to Greenwich to meet the King early in January. Henry, however, had other ideas. Like some greedy schoolboy he could not wait for his surprise, but what a surprise it turned out to be.

Having hurried down to Rochester in disguise to gain an unscheduled look at his future bride, he burst into her rooms unannounced and caught her totally unprepared. At first he could not tell the princess from her bevy of German ladies. Their heavy ornate fashions were alien and unbecoming while their lack of English added to the confusion. When at last he realised which one of them was Anne, he apparently panicked and lost all restraint. Wriothesley described what happened next:

> ... suddenly he embraced and kissed her, and showed her a token which the King had sent her for New Year's gift, and she being abashed and not knowing who it was thanked him, and so he spoke with her. But she regarded him little, but always looked out the window ... and when the King saw that she took so little notice of his coming he went into another chamber and took off his cloak and came in again in a coat of purple velvet. And when the lords and knights saw his grace they did him reverence ... and then her grace humbled herself lowly to the King's Majesty, and his grace saluted her again, and they talked together lovingly, and afterwards he took her by the hand and led her to another chamber where their graces amused themselves that night and on Friday until the afternoon.

Wriothesley was being diplomatic.

Sir Anthony Browne, who was present, later stated that Anne clearly had no idea of the identity of her visitor, nor was Henry impressed. Lord Russell later remarked, 'he never saw His Highness so marvellously astonished and abashed as on that occasion'. The King mumbled a greeting and immediately fled the scene, declaring emphatically once he was outside, 'I like her not.'

What had gone wrong? Henry told Cromwell that she was pitted with smallpox scars and was 'nothing fair and have very evil smells about her'. He warned that he could 'have none appetite for displeasant airs'.

Marillac, the French Ambassador, confirmed her 'want of beauty', her 'determined and resolute countenance' and came finally to the conclusion that she was 'not so young as at first thought, nor so handsome as people affirmed'. Although she was 24, she looked more than 30. Some writers claim she was actually 34.

Yet Holbein, surely the greatest and most realistic of portrait painters, had captured the likeness of a perfectly pleasant-looking woman with a demure expression and a rather heavy nose, but hardly a 'Flanders mare'.

One wonders did Holbein deliberately flatter his sitter, anxious to please Cromwell and promote this alliance with the Protestant states? Curiously, the King did not vent his anger on Holbein at all, as might be expected if he had tricked or deceived the King. Henry appeared to blame no one, hurrying straight back to Greenwich, grumbling that the princess was 'nothing so fair as she had been reported' and that had he known the truth he would never have let her 'come within the kingdom'. He demanded that some remedy be found.

But it was too late now to cancel the lavish welcome which had been organised to greet the princess of Cleves. At Shooter's Hill a great tented village had been set up, with tourney pavilions heated by charcoal braziers. The German retinue attended, escorted by the Duke of Norfolk. Welcome speeches were made and then the King himself came to meet his intended for the second time, on this occasion surrounded by his court and dressed in all his bejewelled splendour. At Blackheath the royal couple met and exchanged greetings, closely scrutinised on every side.

Over 60 'great ladies of the household' would become the Queen's attendants, including 'Mabyell Sowthampton, Margaret Taylebois, Alys Browne, Anne Knevyrt, Jane Meows, Elizabeth Tyrwhyt, Margrett Howarde, Jane Lady Denny, Elsabeth Harvy, Anne Basset', Jane Lady Rochford and the King's former mistress Elizabeth Blount, now Lady Clinton. Among those presented to their new queen were her new ladies. Anne of Cleves was less delighted to see them when she learnt they were to replace 15 of her German attendants.

The new ladies included the King's wayward niece Lady Margaret Douglas and Norfolk's daughter Mary, the widowed Duchess of Richmond. Among the younger women were Norfolk's three candidates, Katherine Carey, Mary Norris — and Katherine Howard.

Chapter Ten

The Bartered Bride

'THE COURT' WAS EVERYTHING within a ten-mile radius of wherever the monarch was living. Henry VIII spent lavishly on rebuilding and refurbishing new residences such as Hampton Court Palace and Whitehall, both taken from Cardinal Wolsey. At these larger palaces there were as many as 1,000 or 1,500 courtiers and servants in residence, housed and kept at the royal expense. The King was constantly on the move between palaces as the seasons changed, and moving involved all the upheaval of transporting between 400 and 800 courtiers and retainers who accompanied the monarch, many with servants of their own.

The royal household was governed by a comprehensive set of regulations laid down by Edward IV and revised by Cardinal Wolsey, known as the Eltham Ordinances. The Board of the Greencloth checked on the number of servants at court '... to see if there be any Strangers eating in the said offices or chamber at the meal times, or at any other time, contrary to the King's Ordinance'.

The Queen had her own household, with well-born ladies of the nobility chosen to serve in her privy chamber and at her beck and call by day and night. These ladies-in-waiting 'received not only room and dining privileges, but also shared daily with the other maids two loaves of coarse bread and three of white, four gallons of ale, and a half pitcher of wine. From the last day of October to the first day of April, the maids were issued three torches a week, six candles a day, six talshides [pieces] of wood and six bundles of faggots, amounting in value to over £24 a year.' A Duchess at court might receive 'one torch, one pricket, two sises, one pound of white lights, ten talshides, eight faggotts'. Complaints were made about people using fires to cook in their private rooms, taking food for illicit guests smuggled into court.

Katherine was in the second rank of the Queen's ladies, sharing quarters with the younger women. Some of these, such as Mary Howard, had served other queens and were therefore able to advise and instruct her in the complex etiquette of the court. Much of her service was to attend the Queen, to entertain her with conversation and music in private and to accompany her on state occasions, and for this an extravagant wardrobe was required.

The cost of a wardrobe lavish enough for attendance at court was enough to ruin some gentry. Queen Anne's former chaplain and almoner John Skip, Bishop of Hereford, warned that many a courtier had ended up in debtors' prison or worse for their folly in trying to keep up with court fashions. Sumptuous, jewel-encrusted clothes flaunted their wearers' wealth and status. 'Whole estates' were worn at court as dandies competed to outshine one another in ostentation. Thousands of pounds were gambled on the effect of high fashion, houses mortgaged, families plunged into debt just to create the impression of prosperity in the King's sight. There was such 'excess of apparel' at the royal court, Skip complained, that 'a man cannot well discern a gentleman from a yeoman, a lord from a gentleman, a prince from a lord'.

To separate the classes the King introduced his Sumptuary Laws, defining what fabrics could be worn by each class within the social hierarchy. People had to know their place and heavy fines were imposed on those who defied the regulations.

Katherine's family now saw her as an investment, representing the Howard name in the full glare of public scrutiny. She was equipped with the wardrobe suitable for her new status, regardless of cost, and found herself outfitted with gowns made of rich velvets and silk such as she had never had before.

A court dress was made up of composite parts, fitting together to make different combinations of styles and colours. Gowns had separate bodices, skirts, underskirts and sleeves, of various designs and fashions, which were attached by laces or with a myriad of pins. Necklines were low and square. Women traditionally bound up their breasts with long strips of cloth, flattened by a long triangular stomacher made of stiff brocade. Married women concealed their cleavage with a *partlet* showing the thin lawn shift that was worn underneath and regularly changed as underwear. Less modest women used fur trimmings around the neckline or jewellery that scarcely concealed the nipples.

Bodices were tightly laced to make an elegant waist. The farthingale gave the skirt its distinctive silhouette, held in place by a construction of willow canes or even ropes. Even less wealthy women aped this fashion on special occasions, wearing 'bum-rolls' of cloth which were tied around the waist under the gown. The outer material of the gown contrasted with the underskirt or 'forepart' of a different material and colour.

Sleeves were long and tight-fitting underneath, often with a wide hanging cuff of contrasting velvet. They were secured by ribbons or laces at the shoulder. Bell-shaped over-sleeves are clearly seen in Holbein's portraits of the King's daughters in the late 1530s and 40s.

Together with continental fashions, Anne Boleyn introduced the stylish French hood into England. This revealed a woman's hair for the first time, sitting towards the back of the head and decorated with 'billiments' or bejewelled edges. A black veil fell below the shoulders from the back of the hood. It was both elegant and flattering compared with the more matronly fashions of Catherine of Aragon or Jane Seymour. Young Elizabeth followed her mother in her preference. The style evolved from the 1540s, sitting further and further back on the head so that it required a strap worn beneath the chin to keep it on.

Alleged miniature of
Katherine by Hans Holbein,
c.1540. Royal Collection,
St James' Palace.

Katherine's uncle,
Thomas Howard,
3rd Duke of Norfolk.
He holds the Earl
Marshall's baton and
the Lord Treasurer's
stave. By Hans
Holbein in 1539,
Royal Collection,
St James' Palace.

Henry VIII in his prime.
By Hans Holbein, National
Portrait Gallery, London.

Henry VIII in old age.
Sketch by Cornelius
Matsys, National Portrait
Gallery, London.

Anne Boleyn, Katherine's cousin, executed by Henry in 1536. National Portrait Gallery, London.

Henry VIII's third wife Jane Seymour, mother of his only legitimate son Edward, Prince of Wales. By Hans Holbein, Kunsthistorisches Museum, Vienna.

EARL OF ESSEX.

Henry VIII's chief minister Thomas Cromwell who engineered the disastrous marriage to Anne of Cleves. After Holbein, National Portrait Gallery, London.

Anne of Cleves, Henry's hapless fourth wife – the controversial portrait by Hans Holbein which convinced Henry of her charms.

Henry Fitzroy, Duke of Richmond, Henry's VIII's illegitimate son by Elizabeth Blount, who died in mysterious circumstances in 1536.

HENRY FITZROY.
DUKE of RICHMOND.

From a Miniature Picture in the Collection of the Earl of Orford. Strawberry Hill.

Edward Prince of Wales, Henry VIII's only legitimate son, who succeeded him upon his death in 1547. By Holbein.

Thomas Cranmer, first Protestant Archbishop of Canterbury, was instrumental in Katherine's downfall by revealing her past to the King. By Holbein, National Portrait Gallery, London.

Stephen Gardiner, Bishop of Winchester, was the shrewd leader of the Catholic faction and close ally of his mentor, the Duke of Norfolk. Their brazen promotion of Katherine to seduce the King was designed to increase their own influence and ultimately restore the Catholic faith in England.

Katherine's only surviving, handwritten letter to Thomas Culpeper, in which she wrote: 'I never longed so much for a thing as I do to see you and to speak with you, the which I trust shall be shortly now.' National Archives.

Henry Howard, Earl of Surrey, son and heir of the Duke of Norfolk, the poet; executed by Henry VIII in 1547, just before Henry's own death. National Portrait Gallery, London.

The Haunted Gallery, Hampton Court Palace, where the ghost of Katherine is reported to have been sighted.

Katherine would have been pleased to show off her golden hair. While in the Dowager's house, she probably wore a simple cap or 'biggin'. In the sketch by Holbein said to be Katherine, she is shown very simply and modestly dressed, with her dark blonde hair worn under a plainer version of the French hood. The plainness of her dress in this sketch suggests that this must have been made before she became Queen, perhaps on her appointment as a lady-in-waiting to Anne of Cleves. The image on the cover of this book is from a print of 1800 after the drawing by Holbein in the Royal Collection, traditionally held to be of Katherine. Her fresh face and vitality make her seem very young. She was probably then just 14 years of age.

On their return to London, the court learnt that the royal wedding was to be postponed. Cromwell was under no illusion that his career was on the line. Just looking at the delight on his enemies' faces would have convinced him of that. Norfolk in particular must have observed the King's reaction with elation, with his three well-chosen alternatives just waiting in the wings. If Henry disliked his intended bride, he would surely turn to one of these young Howard girls.

In the past Cromwell had sought a solution to the King's disaffected marriage with Anne Boleyn through the device of a pre-contract. While Queen Anne was in the Tower, he had done his utmost to persuade her earlier suitor Henry Percy of Northumberland to confess to a liaison with the Queen. Although Percy had rejected the very suggestion out of hand, Archbishop Cranmer later announced that a contract had existed between them, thus making Henry's marriage to Anne Boleyn invalid. However, this made no difference whatsoever to Henry's decision to have her executed for treason and adultery. Cranmer's offer of a reprieve was all deceit: he had been used by the unscrupulous King and Cromwell.

It was therefore no great surprise that now Cromwell immediately raised the question of an earlier betrothal between the Princess of Cleves and Francis of Lorraine. During negotiations for the marriage the past autumn he had been reassured that no precontract existed because the couple had been too young to consummate the marriage, but he now demanded to see a dispensation. As Anne of Cleves had been fully 20 in 1535, there was good cause to doubt the official explanation.

On 5 January the Princess herself declared that there had been no consummation and suddenly Henry was faced with the ghost of Catherine of Aragon and a repeat of the protracted legal wrangle over his first wife's virginity. Short of calling his new bride a liar, there was really no option but to go through with the wedding.

'Against my will,' he declared he would 'put my neck in the yoke'. He feared that to break their agreement and send her home now in disgrace would force Cleves into the camp of his Catholic enemies. Yet he told Cromwell: 'My Lord, if it were not to satisfy the world, and my Realm, I would not do that I must do this day for none earthly thing.'

They were married the next day, Twelfth Night, 6 January 1540. The wedding night remains, mercifully, a mystery but when Cromwell made the error of enquiring, Henry retorted, 'I liked her before not well, but now I like her much worse.'

He later divulged his true feelings to one of his closest favourites, Sir Anthony Denny, the 'servant whom he used secretly about him'. Denny had been promoted and was now the King's closest personal servant and confidante. Born in 1501, he was discreet, cultured and something of an intellectual, being a devout believer in the reform Protestant faith and therefore hopeful that the Cleves marriage would succeed. He listened patiently to the King's complaints, how he was 'struck to the heart' by disgust at the sight of his bride, how she was 'not as she was reported, but had breasts so slack and other parts of body in such sort that [he] somewhat suspected her virginity'.

Henry insisted that he had 'left her as good a maid as he found her'. He was offended by her body odour, a common enough problem of the times. Bathing was not yet a ritual even in wealthy families. Few houses had piped water, so filling and heating a wooden bath was a long process requiring a good fire and a fleet of servants ferrying buckets. Those concerned with personal hygiene made an effort to wash regularly, using concoctions of vinegar and camomile to sponge down and disguise the worst smells. Working people had little time for such niceties.

Those at court were anxious to protect their expensive clothes, which could not be washed or cleaned. Undergarments were worn by both sexes, linen and fine lawn shifts that absorbed sweat and odours from wearing the formal and heavy gowns and doublets of the period.

Bad breath was a constant problem. Many people had lost their teeth by their twenties, including the King's daughter Mary. A mixture of vinegar and honey did more harm than good, and the rich wore perfume or carried pomanders of sweet-smelling herbs.

Clearly the customs of Cleves did not match up to the King's exacting standards.

He confided to Sir Anthony Denny that he could not bring himself to have sex with the Princess as 'he could never in her company be provoked and steered to know her carnally'. He hastened to add that 'he thought himself able to do the act with other but not with her'. As Sir Anthony sympathetically commented: 'The state of princes in matters of marriage is far of worse sort than the conditions of poor men. For princes take as is brought them by others, and poor men be commonly at their own choice and liberty.'

Nothing had changed by February. Anne herself was said to have spoken about her concerns to two of her new ladies, Eleanor Paston, the Countess of Rutland, wife of her own chamberlain Sir Thomas Manners, and Jane Lady Rochford, the enigmatic widow of George Boleyn and sister-in-law of Queen Anne, whom she had betrayed.

Anne of Cleves confided in these two experienced women, though in what language is unknown. She could not speak anything but the Oesterse dialect, an early form of Dutch, although she was rapidly picking up some English, but surely not enough for such a complex conversation. Her ladies reported her account of what had so far taken place in the royal bedchamber: 'He kisses me and taketh me by the hand and biddeth me "Goodnight, sweetheart"; and in the morning kisses me and biddeth me "Farewell, darling"', adding, 'Is not this enough? I am contented with this, for I know no more.'

For one whose grandfather had earned the name 'The Baby-maker', Anne was astonishingly naïve and ill-informed. Perhaps it was all part of the ruse to conceal her earlier precontract, conceal-ing her sexual experience just as Catherine of Aragon had done after her first marriage. Did Anne want to be Henry's wife? Even if she did not want the marriage to continue at this time, it was later evident that she wanted to be Queen, with all the status and financial security it offered.

Cromwell must have heard a report of the conversations with her ladies, perhaps from his ally Lady Rochford, whom he had provided with funds after the death of her husband. Cromwell later confirmed to the Duke of Suffolk that the King's marriage remained unconsummated and that Anne of Cleves 'was still as good a Maid ... as ever her Mother bare her'.

The King hotly denied that the fault was his, claiming that he was perfectly capable. He told his doctors that he had recently had '*duas pollutiones nocturnas in somno*' (two nocturnal ejaculations) during the same period but that 'her body [was] in such a sort dis-ordered and indisposed' it filled him with loathing, because of the 'hanging of her breasts and looseness of her flesh'. She simply did not 'excite and provoke any lust in him'.

No one asked the Queen her opinion of Henry.

He was now nearly 49, unable and unwilling to consummate the marriage, but eager to find a way out of his humiliation and seeking an opportunity for revenge.

Norfolk was confident that Cromwell would never recover from this failure. He even referred to the prospect of his removal while on mission to the French court in February. He convinced King Francis that this 'wicked and unhappy instrument' must be eliminated.

Cromwell may well have suspected some machination by his enemies, for in March he wined and dined Bishop Gardiner in the hope of a reconciliation to set aside 'not only all displeasures' but to 'be perfect entire friends'.

It was a vain hope. Cromwell knew very well the part the bishop had played in the downfall of Anne Boleyn, ruthlessly destroying a good woman without a scruple, while Cromwell himself, claiming to share the same reform faith as Anne, appears to have developed a conscience as his own position grew ever more precarious. He even sought the help of reformist friends such as Hubertus Leodius of Heidelberg to plan his escape abroad.

It was the perfect moment for the Howards to play their trump card. Norfolk looked on his niece as a sexual commodity. Women were mere chattels to be traded for the best advantage. In a family like the Howards, girls served only one purpose: to make profitable marriages arranged by their fathers. Now that Katherine was an orphan, that duty fell to Norfolk as her uncle. And what better match to aspire to than the King himself? The Duke of Norfolk and Bishop Gardiner now made certain that Katherine was fully aware of the great honour that was open to her. If she seemed somewhat overwhelmed, that was only natural. She was, after all, an innocent in these matters, as any virgin should be.

Did Norfolk know anything of her past? He had agreed to send Francis Dereham away at a most convenient time, but had the Dowager, his stepmother, risked his anger by telling him the entire truth about Katherine's affair? That would have been a confession that she could not control the activities of the young women in her own household.

The loss of such a valuable asset as the marketable value of the Duke's own niece was not something to be taken lightly. Norfolk made much of the fact that his own daughter Mary, although a widow, was still a virgin and therefore highly to be desired. It seems incredible that the Dowager would have told him of Katherine's loss of virginity after she and her son Lord William had gone to all the trouble of covering the matter up.

From the older, more experienced women about her Katherine may have learnt there were methods in use to conceal the loss of virginity. A bride might try and fake her virginity by substituting animal blood, as well as less scrupulous ways even to 'restore' it, 'using an ointment or another medicine so that she would be thought a virgin'. Other recipes included 'take nutmeg and grind to a powder; put it in that place' or 'take myrtle leaves and boil them well with water until only a third part remains; then, take nettles without prickles and boil them in this water until a third remains. She must wash her secret parts with this water in the morning and at bedtime, up to nine days.'

Norfolk was quite ready to use Katherine to further his own political agenda. He had no moral scruples about using his own brother's child as a pawn to secure the King's support and an alliance with the crown. He no doubt reminded Katherine of the successes and faults of her cousin Anne. As her family saw it, Anne Boleyn had captured and held the King's interest for years, using her virginity as a bargaining card. Unlike her sister Mary, she had dangled her virtue in front of the King with the promise that submission would surely bring him his desired son and heir.

That was the pattern that Norfolk pressed Katherine to emulate. Only marriage could achieve it and it was an astonishing seven long years before Anne had finally surrendered to the King. She had won through, becoming Henry's wife and Queen of England. The fact that she was dead just three years later was best forgotten.

Katherine was no Anne Boleyn. She was, in fact, her exact opposite: fair where Anne was dark, short and plump where Anne was tall and thin, Catholic while Anne was a Protestant reformer. Katherine was no intellectual, although bright and impulsive, fully capable of charming a King. She would not tie Henry up with heated theological arguments, passing him illegal and heretical books to read. Katherine would flatter and praise where Anne had dared to point out his mistakes. In short, Norfolk must have judged, Katherine would do as she was told.

If, as her uncle Norfolk clearly believed, her presence as one of the Queen's ladies could lead to greater things, then she was willing to go along with whatever hand Fate dealt her. She was a Howard by birth and she knew her destiny.

Did she protest? Did it even occur to her that she had any choice in the matter?

Katherine had heard all about Anne Boleyn, conflicting tales that appeared to contradict one another. Some said she was a saint, others a strumpet who had divided the realm. What Katherine knew for sure was that cousin Anne had been clever, too clever for her own good. She had not settled for attracting a King, but had held out for the crown itself, gambling everything on becoming pregnant with a son. And she had lost, lost it all. That was the one overriding lesson Katherine remembered. That and the fact that it was Norfolk, her own uncle, who had supervised her trial and execution.

She must have known of his reputation for violence. News of the harsh penalties enacted upon the northern rebels had surely reached the Dowager's London household. Norfolk had beaten his own wife and thrown her bodily out of the house. He had been sent to make Mary, the King's daughter, sign the oath of submission, threatening that he would knock her head against the wall if she did not sign.

Knowing all this about her uncle's character, Katherine had no option but to agree to his plans, to offer herself up to advance her scheming family and serve her King and religion.

Katherine had been raised as a traditional Catholic, in awe of the rituals, swayed by the mysticism and unquestioning theological doctrines. She lit candles for her dead parents, ate fish on Fridays and said her prayers by rote in the happy assurance that whatever she did would be forgiven in the confessional. For the Catholic party at court, she was the key to regaining the King's favour and reversing the tide of religious reform.

Tradition has it that this was the way that Anne Boleyn became Queen, manipulated into the King's bed by her ambitious, scheming father. In reality, this was the story of her young cousin, the victim of a conspiracy between their uncle Thomas Howard, Duke of Norfolk, and Stephen Gardiner, Bishop of Winchester, the very men who had been Anne's great enemies and who supervised her defamation and execution.

Bishop Gardiner had recently been readmitted to the Privy Council. The bishop had a colourful personal reputation and was not opposed to acting as pander for the King, nor shocked by Norfolk's manipulation of a young girl if it would further the interests of his church.

From her relative obscurity in the Dowager's household, Katherine was now fussed over and feted. Attention and money were showered on her as her family rushed to prepare her for sacrifice. A fortune was spent on her clothes. Norfolk was willing to finance her presentation in the very latest French fashions, certain that the girl was worth the risk. With her long dark blonde hair and wide green eyes, she was the picture of innocence. She was their tool, the pretty little doll dressed to provoke an ageing lecher to lust after her.

Norfolk and Gardiner now planned a banquet to try and cheer the King. It was to be held at the Bishop of Winchester's palace, 'a very fair house, well repaired, and hath a large wharf and landing-place, called the bishop of Winchester's stairs'. It was no accident that among the guests should appear Mistress Katherine Howard.

Henry himself became a willing accomplice to Norfolk's scheme. If he could not abide his 24-year-old wife, then surely he could be tempted by a vivacious 14-year-old. She was the ideal bait to whet his appetite and seduce a king. Desperate to prove that he was still virile and capable, his roving eye soon fell upon the youthful and assuredly pure young creature dangled before him.

And what did Katherine see?

In his prime, Henry had been a fine figure of a man, but by 1539 there was no disguising his decline. 'If a man may approach to forty or sixty years, men repute him happy and fortunate, wrote Thomas Paynel in 1541. It was believed that 40 'begins the first part of the old man's age'.

The spectacular display of fine clothes and jewels was dazzling, but even they could not conceal the King's bulk and the difficulty with which he now walked. In a lavish court, no one dressed more extravagantly, casting a giant shadow over the lives of his fellow men and women. As Henry's silhouette expanded, so the men at court aped the new look. Shoulders grew impossibly broad, padded, with great puffed sleeves. Flared doublets exposed the legs and extravagant codpieces, highly padded pouches to cover the penis, often strangely shaped and elaborately decorated, secured with points or laces were worn.

Thanks to his insatiable appetite Henry's waistline had increased to overtake his age, now measuring a massive 54 inches, although he still clung to his youthful image of the handsome rake. He was now so obese that he often had to be carried in a chair. According to Fuller, he 'had a body and a half, very abdominous and unwieldy with fat. And it was death to him to be dieted, so great his appetite, and death to him not to be dieted, so great his corpulency.'

He was going bald and his red face and venal piggish eyes were sunk into folds of flesh over-spilling his collar.

The King set the style for beards but his, once so fiery, was now sparse and grey. His sight was increasingly bad and he had spectacles especially made for him to use in private. He wore corsets and creaked as he moved, stiff with cloth of gold and rustling satin, his huge podgy fingers clustered with jewels.

He still chose to see himself as vigorous and potent, writing songs that rejected the reality facing him in the mirror:

> Though some saith that youth ruleth me,
> I trust in age to tarry . . .
> Though some say that youth ruleth me.
> I pray you all that aged be,
> How well did ye your youth carry?
> I hurt no man, I do no wrong,
> I love true where I did marry,
> Though some saith that youth ruleth me.
> Then soon discuss that hence we must.
> Pray we to God and Saint Mary
> That all amend, and here an end,
> Thus saith the king, the eighth Harry.

Observing that Henry was reluctant to acknowledge his decline, the poet Sir Thomas Wyatt dared to satirise his vanity in this most scathing poem:

> Ye old mule that think yourself so fair,
> Leave off with craft your beauty to repair,
> For it is true, without any fable,
> No man setteth more by riding in your saddle.
> Too much travail so do your train appair, Ye old mule.
> With false savour though you deceive th'air,
> Whoso taste you shall well perceive your lair
> Savoureth somewhat of a Kappurs stable.
> Ye old mule, Ye must now serve to market and to fair,
> All for the burden, for panniers a pair.
> For since gray hairs been powdered in your sable,
> The thing ye seek for, you must yourself enable
> To purchase it by payment and by prayer,
> Ye old mule.

A drawing by Matsys (see plate section) shows that the handsome and athletic golden King had long since disappeared.

Henry had been King for 30 years and his reputation went before him. Courtiers dropped in obeisance to him as if he were some exotic deity. They fought one another to be close to him, to attract his attention and favour, manoeuvring their daughters, cousins and sisters into his presence, just as the Howards had contrived with Katherine.

Competition was fierce, but she was small, dainty, laughing prettily as she danced before him, sure to catch his jaundiced eye. After a long procession of worldly-wise women, her very child-like simplicity was irresistible.

It was little wonder that it was reported the 'King's Highness did cast a fantasy to Katherine Howard the first time that ever his Grace saw her'.

While the King ignored his wife, he began to visit the Dowager's house in Lambeth almost every day and every night.

Duchess Agnes had never known such favour, casting caution to the winds as she entertained her sovereign, acting hostess and bawd together.

Great hopes were pinned upon Katherine and she had been especially coached and primed how to behave, taught 'in what sort to entertain the King's Highness and how often'. If Duchess Agnes recalled the Manox and Dereham affairs she now prepared to suggest that Katherine put those experiences to good practice.

Given that Henry was barely capable he could have been easily satisfied by a cleverly instructed girl. To the King, however, the Dowager was eager to 'commend and praise Katherine for her pure and honest condition'. Henry expected nothing else from a girl of her tender years – little Katherine Howard, fresh and pure like a breath of spring from the country. Her very youth and simplicity were what attracted him.

Contemporaries record the great difference in their ages, some 35 years. They noted that Katherine was unusually young. She was fully nine years younger than the King's elder daughter Mary and just eight years older than his daughter by Anne Boleyn, Elizabeth.

She had been brought up in the country, unsullied by the ways of city life, nor ruined by an excess of education. She could read and write, which was more than the late Jane Seymour, but she was very far from the outspoken intellectual Queen Anne, whose ability to outwit and outface Henry had killed his love for her. Katherine Howard was naïve, romantic, child-like, unsophisticated and the tool of her ambitious Catholic family.

Katherine's success was immediate and her new status was flaunted before the country. The King had chosen her from among all others. Great changes were in the air as Marillac noted on 10 April: 'There will be seen in the country a great change in many things; which this King begins to make in his ministers, recalling those he had rejected and degrading those he had raised.'

Yet exactly a week later on 17 April the King appointed Cromwell to become Lord Great Chamberlain of England and created him Earl of Essex.

If Cromwell had lost the King's confidence over the failure of

Henry's marriage why did the King promote him and make him an earl? Did he not blame Cromwell for the Cleves fiasco after all? Master Holbein had not felt the fallout from Henry's wrath over his portrait of the bride, nor was the marriage one of the issues that were later laid at Cromwell's door at his fall. It appears that the King was either concealing his wrath, playing a cruel game, or that he was perfectly satisfied with Cromwell's services.

Those who were not satisfied were Norfolk and Gardiner. They realised that the man who knew most of Cromwell's secrets was his ambitious secretary, Thomas Wriothesley. He had been raised as one of a generation of 'coming men' favoured for their intelligence and lack of scruples, evident during the dissolution of the monasteries when he made a small fortune. He was seen as 'an earnest follower of whatsoever he took in hand and did very seldom miss, where either wit or travail were able to bring his purpose to pass'.

Wriothesley had studied law with Stephen Gardiner while a student at Cambridge and was married to Jane Cheney, one of the bishop's relatives. In the end it was these ties of family and patronage which were to carry greater weight with a man of ambition than his loyalty to Cromwell.

By April the royal marriage was exposed as a spectacular and humiliating failure. Impatient to be rid of his unwanted wife, Henry 'lamented his fate that he should never have any more children if he so continued, declaring that before God he thought she was not his lawful wife'.

The delegation from Cleves had failed to produce any evidence that Anne's earlier betrothal with Lorraine was null and void. Fearing that the King was fast losing patience with his marital situation, Wriothesley 'asked lord Cromwell to devise some way for the relief of the King, for if he remained in this grief and trouble, they should all one day smart for it'.

On May Day the King hosted a great tournament in the company of his neglected new Queen, but this show deceived no one about his new relationship with Katherine: 'It is a certain fact that about the same time many citizens of London saw the king very frequently in the daytime, and sometimes at midnight, pass over to her on the river Thames in a little boat ... The citizens regarded all this not as a sign of divorcing the queen, but of adultery.' The merchant Richard Hilles wrote to the Protestant theologian Bullinger in Zurich that 'the King's affections were alienated from the lady Anna to that young girl Katherine Howard'.

Cromwell was far from blind. As he saw the King fall headlong for the charms of Katherine, he knew it was the handiwork of Norfolk and Gardiner. He could be in no doubts that his enemies were plotting to bring him down over the disastrous Cleves marriage, even to the point of providing the King with their own replacement, the pretty little Catholic doll, Katherine Howard.

Cromwell now discovered that Bishop Gardiner had been in contact with Lord Lisle to implicate him with the so-called 'sacramentarians' of Calais who denied the Catholic doctrine of the 'Real Presence' in the mass, the 'burning issue' which brought many to the stake. This charge was intended to associate Cromwell with some kind of extremist Protestant sect that refused to acknowledge the draconian Act of Six Articles. [37] But then, as Cromwell was struggling to keep his head above water, Lisle's aide, Sir Gregory Botolf, defected to Rome to join the exiled enemy of the state, Cardinal Pole. Suddenly Cromwell was granted an opportunity to turn the tables on his deadly enemies and he took it, arresting Lord Lisle on 19 May for plotting with Botolf to surrender the English enclave of Calais to the Vatican.

The shock of Lord Lisle's arrest sent his wife 'almost out of her mind'. Lisle remained in the Tower for 18 months and all his plate, goods and documents were seized.

On 30 May Norfolk and Gardiner's ally Richard Sampson, Bishop of Chichester and Dean of St Paul's, was elevated to become Bishop of Westminster, but now Cromwell counter-attacked. He arrested a coterie of his enemies including Sir Nicholas Carew and Bishop Sampson, whom Marillac reported 'two hours later was led to the Tower as accused of treason'. The French Ambassador suspected Cromwell was aiming at Gardiner himself, suppressing 'the old preachers' to bring in 'new doctrines ... even by arms', but dared not move against him. He concluded

'Things are brought to such a pass that either Cromwell's party or that of the Bishop of Winchester must succumb.'

He backed Cromwell to win: 'things seem to incline to Cromwell's side'. Cromwell himself understood the gravity of the situation, writing to Richard Pate that 'the whole of Christendom hangs in the balance'.

When the end came it was swift and unexpected. On Saturday 10 June 1540 in the middle of the afternoon the King's guard interrupted a meeting of the Privy Council. They had come for Cromwell and he knew it, rising instinctively to meet them and looking desperately around at Norfolk.

Now the Catholic party turned like a pack of hounds on a wounded stag: Norfolk tore the collar of office from about his neck and Wriothsley seized the insignia of his Order of the Garter. Sir Edward Knyvet crowed 'Nowe is that foul churl dead so ambitious of others blode; nowe is he stricken by his owne staffe.'

The man who had ruled in everything but name for the past ten years was then hauled out to the river and taken by barge to his final destination – the dreaded Tower of London.

Chapter Eleven

The Sacrifice

THE ABSENCE OF A QUEEN, with Jane Seymour's death and Anne of Cleves' failure, had left a vacuum at the very heart of the close social circle that revolved around the King, which Katherine Howard had now filled.

'The King's affection was so marvelously set upon that gentle-woman, as it was never known that he had the like to any woman.' Such was the warning that Ralph Morice sent to his master, Archbishop Cranmer.

Katherine Howard had stepped out from the shadows onto centre stage, from a childhood of obscurity into the brilliant glare of public scrutiny at the side of the King. At 15 years of age, she was everything that the King's wife Anne of Cleves was not. She wore her hair long as a maiden should, a rich dark blonde that tumbled down her back, and her hazel-green eyes were bright and innocent. She danced with 'superlative grace'. Of a 'very diminutive stature', she was already precociously developed, displaying her figure to its best advantage '*vestue à la française*,' that is, dressed in the latest French fashion, in stark contrast to the unfashionable Germanic costumes favoured by Anne of Cleves or the stiff and uncomfortable Spanish corsets and farthingales. Apart from the French hood, French style called for small bodices and low necklines, lifting and often exposing the breasts. Surely this was a reason why Katherine drew Henry's attention.

If there were whispers of earlier suitors, these were soon quashed by the Howards themselves. Any suggestions that there was an 'understanding' between Norfolk's niece and a certain Francis Dereham were explained away by the Dowager Duchess herself who later claimed that Katherine had turned him away with a broken heart. However, Dereham returned from Ireland in late spring.

When the lovers parted Katherine had been just another of the vast brood of Howard girls enjoying a carefree adolescence under her grandmother's roof. Now Dereham found a very different young woman at court – polished, pampered and richly dressed, wearing her family's fortunes on her back. Gone was the natural, mischievous and delightful girl on whom he had pinned his future hopes. In her place, he saw a worldly and more sophisticated young woman flattering the ageing King while her uncle Norfolk and Bishop Gardiner observed all from the wings.

Katherine must have been alarmed when Dereham confronted her in private. Here was a ghost from her past that she had been told to forget. Francis Dereham and their history together could only pose a threat to the plans her family had for her and to the great destiny within her reach. Katherine was later to explain how she told him brutally to keep silent and leave her alone: 'Why should you trouble me therewith, for you know I will not have you.'

But Dereham was an adventurer and he had staked a great deal on his relationship with Katherine to secure his alliance with the Howards, boasting that 'I could be sure if I would, but I dare not' and ignoring the danger posed by the fact that his rival was no ordinary man but the King himself. He was rashly heard to declare that, were the King removed from the equation, 'I am sure I might marry her.'

It was the hottest summer for years with widespread drought and losses to agriculture and livestock. In the increasing heat there was more than a lustful atmosphere at court as plague threatened

London. The King lost no time in using the danger of an epidemic to force his rejected wife away to Richmond in Surrey so that he could devote himself to young Katherine. No one was fooled by this ploy. Ambassador Marillac reported cynically that Henry had sent Anne of Cleves away because of plague but he had stayed behind in London although 'he is the most timid person in the world in such cases'.

There was no doubt of the King's infatuation with little Katherine Howard. While there was comment on the great difference in their ages, it was not unique. Henry's own sister Mary had been married against her will as a young girl to the King of France, then in his fifties. One month after their wedding night, King Louis died and she was free to marry the man of her choice – Charles Brandon, her brother's hunting and whoring companion.

Brandon, Duke of Suffolk, was something of an example for Henry. A widower at 49 he shocked the court by stealing his son's intended fiancée, the 14-year-old heiress Catherine Willoughby. She was the same age as his youngest child but she brought him a fortune. His jilted son and heir, Henry Brandon, Earl of Lincoln, shortly died, but his betrothed's marriage to his father was apparently a success. Catherine produced two sons, Charles and Henry, the first born when she was just 15.

The King may well have taken heart from Brandon's lead, hoping himself for more sons from a young wife. But his powers were very much in question. As Henry had confessed to his closest advisers, he had been quite unable to fulfil his duties as bridegroom to Anne of Cleves. With a complete lack of gallantry, he blamed the ill-favoured bride, but everyone around the King still remembered the trial of Queen Anne Boleyn, and the sensation when the Queen's brother George Boleyn, accused on a ludicrous charge of incest with his sister, had bravely voiced in open court that the King was often incapable of making love: '*Le Roy n'estoit habile en cas de soy copuler avec femme et qu'il n'avoit ne vertu ne puissance.*' Henry lacked both skill (*vertu*) and power (*puissance*).

This doubt is sustained by recalling that in 1532 the King told Parliament that he was not marrying Anne simply out of passion, 'for I am 41 years old, at which age the lust of man is not so quick as in lusty youth'. But when, in 1533 Chapuys had rashly told him that, although he was marrying Anne Boleyn, he had no guarantee that he would have a son, Henry took this to be an insult, a slur on his virility, and he raged indignantly, 'Am I not a man like other men? Am I not? Am I not?'

Anne Boleyn's failure to produce a living son only served to confirm increasing doubts about the King's capacity. When, after all his trouble to free himself, Anne's successor Jane Seymour did not immediately become pregnant, Henry 'doubted whether he should have any child by the Queen (Jane)'.

Henry was, as we would say nowadays, in denial, but he was an obsessive hypochondriac, always anxious about his health and that of those around him. When he was a child, his elder brother Arthur and his mother, Elizabeth of York, had died suddenly, leaving him with a morbid and even paranoid fear of sickness and death. His household accounts list a constant supply of pills, potions and enemas provided by an army of apothecaries and he was always interested in new-fangled cures, even recommending his own remedy of 1528 '*pro tumore testiculorum*'.

Did he have a tumour? He was certainly troubled about his sexual abilities for many years. It has been suggested that he had 'the pox', '*verole*' (smallpox) or '*roniole*' (syphilis) having nearly died from an outbreak at Christmas 1513 when he was only 22, although this may actually have been a severe attack of measles. The 'French pox', or syphilis, had been imported to England by troops returning from war. This new and frightening disease spread rapidly throughout mainland Europe, though its origins were uncertain. Some said it came from the Spanish who had found the 'New World'; others believed it came from the Moslem East.

The first warning signs were bad breath and small lesions over the face and body. Migraines, intense fevers and pains in the joints were all symptoms. Fits of insanity and sterility soon followed. There were many suggested cures, including an ointment concocted of 'oldbane, oil of roses, quicksilver, bitterage of gold and turpentine'. But by far the most drastic treatment was to swallow a draught of mercury. It was said that the fashion for codpieces was devised to conceal heavy bandages and protect outer garments from balms and medication for the disease.

Prostitution was blamed for the spread of syphilis. As the royal barber-surgeon William Clowes wrote in 1579: 'This pestilent infection of filthy lust is a sickness very loathsome, odious, troublesome and dangerous, which spreadeth itself throughout all England and overfloweth as I think the whole world. It is testimony of the just wrath of God against that filthy sin of fornication.'

In 1546 Henry ordered that all brothels should be closed, although this did not solve the problem. Henry may well have contracted syphilis from his many mistresses, including Mary Boleyn whom he had shared with the King of France, Francis I, who eventually died of syphilis, his body being so contaminated and rotting that it exploded in his coffin.

It is possible that if Henry had developed syphilis, it would have affected his fertility. John Erley, secretary of the Bishop of Bath, suggested that the King was impotent and incapable of fathering sons. Yet he had earlier produced many children with Catherine of Aragon, although all but Mary died, and had one thriving son with Bessie Blount, Richmond, another with Jane Seymour and a healthy son and daughter by Mary Boleyn, Henry and Katherine Carey.

Henry had to consult his doctors after marrying Anne of Cleves because he never 'took any [pleasure] from her by true carnal copulation'. Dr Chamber 'counselled his majesty not to enforce himself, for eschewing such inconveniences as by debility ensuing in that case were to be feared'. He reported that Henry could not 'be provoked or stirred to that act'.

Henry may not have been put to the test by Anne of Cleves but the youth and unmarred beauty of young Katherine Howard was too great a temptation. She was barely 15 years old and, he believed, the epitome of innocence and virtue. If he could not perform with her, he could not do it with anyone.

Aphrodisiacs were widely sought after. There were many advice manuals with recipes for a 16th-century form of Viagra. The powers of *mandragora* or mandrake were derived from its appearance. A blend of chestnuts, pistachios and pine nuts could be boiled down in ragwort and sugar. The Renaissance doctor Leonardo Fioravanti recommended any man to 'Drink this and go to it.'

Other remedies included attaching a tourniquet to the left testicle, or taking large-winged ants together with the testicles of a quail and mixing them with bark oil and amber, then applying the concoction. Giovanni Marinello, provider of this recipe, continues, 'The man who will have healthy boys is strong of body himself, with hard and bulging muscles, hot sperm, large testicles, spermatic veins, and an ardent sexual appetite that does not diminish after intercourse.'

To bear sons a woman must have 'a rosy complexion and a pretty visage: her body is neither heavy nor flabby ... she is neither constipated nor does she have diarrhoea; her eyes are white not yellowish; and she is young'.

The King had little time to waste. With summer came an urgency, not only of Henry's desire for Katherine, but to be rid of Anne of Cleves in order to make way for her and the possibility of a child.

On the very night that Cromwell was arrested, his offices and house were ransacked and papers seized. Norfolk claimed that many incriminating letters were found, which were proof of high treason.

The day after his arrest Cromwell was confronted with the charges brought against him. Curiously, the King's failed Cleves marriage featured nowhere. His enemies accused him of 'heresy', referring back to March 1539 when he had defended Robert Barnes and other reformers, saying that they taught the truth and pledging he would remain a Protestant against all odds: 'Yet I would not turn, and if the king did turn, and all his people, I would fight in this field in mine own person, with my sword in my hand *against him* and all other.'

If true, this last rash boast was tantamount to an admission of treason.

Norfolk and Gardiner had concocted a reformist conspiracy.

Because he was of the reform faith, Cromwell had protected those 'sacramentaries' who denied the mass, spread 'heretical literature', licensed 'heretics' to preach and released them from prison. Regrettably, Cromwell could do nothing to save Robert Barnes, Thomas Garret and William Jerome, who were denied a trial and executed soon after. They were all condemned by Act of Attainder, which allowed the accused no recourse to defence.

This was potentially a dramatic change to the country's judicial system. As Katherine was to find out, the Bill of Attainder became the principal weapon against the crown's opponents, although denounced even by Catholics as 'a most iniquitous measure'.

Just seven days after his arrest, while the King was obsessed with his new love, Cromwell was indicted before Parliament in an Act of Attainder. This was 'a tissue of half-truths and lies', claiming he had sold export licences illegally, granted passports and commissions without royal knowledge. Above all, he had misused his powers. Although the Bill met with some opposition in the House of Commons and received some amendments, it was rushed through by the Lords with three readings in one day. Cromwell was denied a trial for fear of what he might say in his defence.

In Richmond Palace, the neglected Queen was also placed in an invidious position.

Anne of Cleves was officially informed that her marriage was in question because of her earlier precontract with the heir of the Duke of Lorraine. The aquiescent Parliament sent a delegation to the King with the very welcome suggestion that his marriage was illegal. They recommended an enquiry into the status of the Queen and whether her earlier precontract made their marriage null and void. Henry gratefully accepted this advice and sent Bishop Gardiner to Richmond to negotiate some kind of deal for an annulment.

Anne now showed herself to be very far from the dumb and rather comic provincial of tradition. With a shrewd awareness of the fate of her predecessor, the other ill-starred Queen Anne, the princess of Cleves determined to take Henry for all he was worth.

She cannot have been unaware of the stories circulating of the

King's passion for little Katherine Howard; far from envying her former lady-in-waiting's situation, she seems to have been relieved and even grateful to her for luring Henry away. Furthermore, his good humour distracted him from all thought of dispatching her in a similar manner to Anne Boleyn, while his sense of urgency meant that he was willing to pay anything to be a free man.

While 200 clerics argued the validity of the marriage in canon law, Anne of Cleves and her advisers milked Henry and the exchequer in perhaps the greatest divorce settlement ever concluded. Besides a vast annual income, Anne would keep all her royal jewels, plate and goods to furnish properties now transferred to her, which included Bletchingley, Richmond and Hever Castle, her unfortunate predecessor's family home. She was to be known as 'the King's sister' and would be welcome at court as the fourth lady in the royal family, after any new queen and Henry's two daughters, the Ladies Mary and Elizabeth.

On 9 July the Convocations of Canterbury and York pronounced the marriage invalid and next day Bishop Gardiner, with a straight face, led a delegation to implore the King 'to frame his most noble heart to love whom his Majesty might have some more store of fruit and succession to the comfort of his realm'.

Anne's part was to sit down and – clearly with help – write to her husband the King in perfect English:

Pleaseth your most excellent majesty to understand that, whereas, at sundry times heretofore, I have been informed and perceived by certain lords and others your grace's council, of the doubts and questions which have been moved and found in our marriage; and how hath petition thereupon been made to your highness by your nobles and commons, that the same might be examined and determined by the holy clergy of this realm ....

She agrees to have the validity of their marriage examined:

though this case must needs be most hard and sorrowful unto me, for the great love which I bear to your most noble person, yet, having more regard to God and his truth than to any worldly affection, as it beseemed me, at the beginning, to submit me to such examination and determination of the said clergy, whom I have and do accept for judges competent in that behalf.

In other words she agrees to go along with Henry's ploy to end their marriage.

But at a price:

... entirely putting myself, for my state and condition, to your highness' goodness and pleasure; most humbly beseeching your majesty that, though it be determined that the pretended matrimony between us is void and of none effect, whereby I neither can nor will repute myself for your grace's wife, considering this sentence (whereunto I stand) and your majesty's clean and pure living with me, yet it will please you to take me for one of your humble servants ... for your sister; for the which I most humbly thank you accordingly.

Thus, most gracious prince, I beseech our Lord God to send your majesty long life and good health, to God's glory, your own honour, and the wealth of this noble realm.

From Richmond, the 11th day of July, the 32nd year of your majesty's most
noble reign.

Your majesty's most humble sister and servant,

Anne the daughter of Cleves.

On 12 July the marriage was annulled by Act of Parliament, and Henry was free to remarry.

Why was there such urgency for the King to find a new wife? The King was making an exhibition of himself, besotted with a girl young enough to be his granddaughter. He made her lavish gifts of rich materials with which to make even more extravagant gowns, besides jewellery and even, on 24 April, land that had been declared forfeit from a prisoner. Such gifts were a demonstration of his very public desire for Katherine, the 'jewel of womanhood'.

Clearly they were a reward in return for her services, which no one doubted. In July Ambassador Marillac stated that she was 'already *enceinte*' (pregnant).

Once Katherine's good fortune became public knowledge, she received a letter of congratulations from Joan Bulmer, one of many ghosts from her past who returned to haunt her. It seemed that there were many old faces who saw in Katherine's rapid rise an opportunity for themselves.

The poet Thomas Wyatt's critiques reflect the dangerous political undercurrents, satirising the cynical social climber who is coldly prepared to deceive in order to advance: 'It is necessary to deceive in order to live … My wit is nought, I cannot learn the way. Never let friendship get in the way of advantage – this is the only recipe.'

Joan Bulmer was Katherine's former rival for the affections of Francis Dereham at Lambeth, the young married woman who had left her husband to serve the Dowager Duchess. She had been put 'into the utmost misery of the world and most wretched life' and now wrote at length to her former 'friend' seeking a share of that golden future which awaited Katherine as Queen.

Joan began by warmly congratulating Katherine on her good fortune. Her sycophantic words barely conceal her haste in driving home the point that she wants something from her former friend: 'If I could wish you all the honour and good fortune you could desire, you would never lack health, wealth, long life, nor yet prosperity. I know no remedy without your goodness. You could find the means to get me to London. If you could write to my husband and command him to bring me to you, he would not dare disobey.'

Her tone soon turns to desperation and a wheedling flattery that should have set Katherine immediately on her guard: 'I beseech you to find a place for me. The nearer I were to you, the gladder I would be of it. I would write more unto you, but I would not be so bold for considering the great honour you are toward, it did not become me to put myself in presence: but the remembrance of the perfect honesty that I have always known in you hath encouraged me to do this …'

Playing upon their friendship, Joan concluded with a flourish of pathetic fawning, elevating Katherine to a position so exalted that it did not then exist: 'To have in your remembrance the unfeigned love that my heart hath always borne towards you not to be forgetful of this my request, for if you do not help me, I am not like to have worldly joys. Desiring you, if you can, to let me have some answer of this for the satisfying of my mind; for I know the Queen of Britain will not forget her secretary, and favour you will show. Your humble servant with heart unfeigned, Joan Bulmer.'

The presumptuous letter was an appeal to Katherine's better nature from a woman who had been one of her older and more experienced companions in the Dowager's household. Withdrawing from an unhappy marriage, Joan found life difficult trying to survive in a society where she was something of an outcast. She may have had hopes of Francis Dereham until his interest transferred to her 12-year-old friend. Her letter was surely a far from subtle form of blackmail, reminding Katherine of secrets shared that were now best forgotten.

Katherine took the hint. Whether out of a desire to share something of her success with old friends or an acceptance that it was safer to give Joan Bulmer what she wanted, Katherine rewarded her with a place in her household once she married the King.

At about the same time, from Lambeth Palace the Archbishop of Canterbury, Thomas Cranmer, wrote to the King on behalf of his fellow reformer still waiting in the Tower for his fate to be determined. Cranmer claimed that Thomas Cromwell 'was such a servant, in my judgement, in wisdom, diligence, faithfulness, and experience, as no prince in this realm ever had'.

Yet this defence was tinged with his usual caution, always conscious of his own precarious position and his enemies watching in the wings. He added, 'I loved him as my friend, for so I took him to be; but I chiefly loved him for the love which I thought I saw him bear ever towards your grace, singularly above all other. But now, if he be a traitor, I am sorry that ever I loved him or trusted him, and I am very glad that his treason is discovered in time; but again I am very sorrowful; for who shall your grace trust hereafter if you might not trust him?'

Cromwell's fall remains a mystery. As in the trumped-up case against Queen Anne, the King seemed oblivious to the absurdity of the evidence. His mind was fixed and he would not shift his ground. If it was not the Cleves marriage that had triggered this desire to be rid of such an excellent servant, it may have been the charge that the lowborn Cromwell had usurped royal authority. As Niccolò Machiavelli writes in *The Prince*: 'It is always possible to find pretexts for confiscating property…On the other hand, pretexts for executing someone are harder to find.'

Unable to defend himself in public, 'with heavy heart and trembling hand' Cromwell wrote from his prison two letters to the King declaring his innocence. 'It much grieved me that I should be noted a traitor when always I had your laws in my breast; and that I should be a sacramentary, God he knoweth the truth and that I am of the one and the other guiltless.'

He chose his words with care, knowing the character of the King probably better than anyone, and using all his skill and experience to try and sway Henry's favour: 'I have after my wit, power and knowledge travailed therein, having had no respect to persons (your Majesty only excepted and my duty to the same), but that I have done any injustice or wrong wilfully I trust God shall bear me witness and the world not able justly to accuse me.'

Without recourse to a public platform, he then poured out his most fervent plea for mercy to his former master:

And this is all that I know, most gracious and most merciful sovereign lord, beseeching Almighty God … to counsel you, preserve you, maintain you, remedy you, relieve and defend you, as may be most to your honour, with prosperity, health and comfort of your heart's desire … I am a most woeful prisoner, ready to take the death, when it shall please God and your Majesty; and yet the frail flesh inciteth me continually to call to your Grace for mercy and grace for mine offences: and thus Christ save, preserve, and keep you.

Written at the Tower this Wednesday, the last day of June, with the
heavy heart and trembling hand of your Highness' most heavy and
most miserable prisoner and poor slave,
Thomas Cromwell.
Most gracious prince, I cry for mercy, mercy, mercy.

The second letter has suffered some damage, being burnt as someone attempted to destroy it. What remains, however, is enough to
provide a harrowing picture of a man only too conscious that his
fate has already been decided: 'First, where I have been accused to
your Majesty of treason, to that I say, I never in all my life thought
willingly to do that thing that might or should displease your
Majesty ...'

Cromwell then reminds the King of all he has achieved for him
as his servant: 'What labours, pains, and travails I have taken,
according to my most bounden duty God also knoweth ... If it
had been or were in my power, to make your Majesty so puissant,
as all the world should be compelled to obey you, Christ He
knoweth I would ... for your Majesty hath been ... more like a
dear father ... than a master.'

Even for Cromwell, this is surely pressing too much. Henry a
father to him? He had treated him at times with open contempt,
beating and degrading him before the court. If this was fatherly
behaviour, then it was a harsh and brutal example. Now, however,
he gets to the real point of the letter, shifting blame to his enemies
who have maligned and borne false witness against him. He
means, of course, the Catholic faction under Norfolk and Gardiner. 'Should any faction or any affection to any point make me
a traitor to your Majesty, then all the devils in hell confound me,
and the vengeance of God light upon me ...'

He points to the biblical example of Susannah to plead his
innocence: 'Yet our Lord, if it be His will, can do with me as he
did with Susan, who was falsely accused ... Other hope than in
God and your Majesty I have not.'

He confesses to passing secret information, which he had shared
to persuade Anne of Cleves to try and coax the King back to her bed:

… I spake privily with her lord chamberlain … desiring him … to find some means that the queen might be induced to order your Grace pleasantly in her behaviour towards you … If I have offended your Majesty therein, prostrate at your Majesty's feet I most lowly ask mercy and pardon of your Highness … Written with the quaking hand and most sorrowful heart of your most sorrowful subject and most humble servant and prisoner, this Saturday at the Tower of London.

Thomas Cromwell.

When no reply came from the King, Cromwell seemed to resign himself to his fate, no doubt all too aware that Henry never changed his mind when it came to removing those who had offended him. Recognising that the game was up and he was to die, he wrote again, seeking Henry's help for his family, notably for his son Gregory, who was married to a sister of the late queen Jane Seymour: 'Sir, upon my knees, I most humbly beseech your gracious Majesty to be a good and gracious lord to my poor son, the good and virtuous woman his wife, and their poor and also to my servants. And this I desire of you for Christ's sake.'

The King certainly received these desperately pathetic appeals and apparently took Cromwell's last request very seriously, commanding 'it thrice to be read to him' [37] but in the end it failed to prevent the sentence of death from being carried out on the man who had been his most loyal and ruthless servant.

Henry was a lonely and damaged man who had a gift for destroying every one of his relationships, both personal and professional, by his suspicion and paranoia. Moreover, he was skilled at representing himself as much misunderstood. In the words of Francis Hackett:

Even those who felt he was a fox, secretive, dexterous, canny, false and mischievous, a fox alert and twisting, never to be understood by mere intelligence but only by getting inside his red temper and his verminous soul – even they, plumbing his nature, sure of his inconstancy, could at any moment, just by listening to his own account of his large motives and simple attachments and genuine impulses, begin to feel shaken in their judgment and see in him an easy, great-natured and miscomprehended man.

On 28 July 1540 Cromwell was taken out and executed on Tower Hill. He died with dignity, making the traditional last speech from the scaffold to the gathered crowd of onlookers:'I am come hither to die, and not to purge myself … I have been a great travailler in this world, and being but of a base degree, was called to high estate; and since the time I came thereunto I have offended my prince, for the which I ask him heartily forgiveness, and beseech you all to pray to God with me, that He will forgive me … I die in the catholic faith.'

This does not mean Cromwell died a Catholic; he simply uses the word to mean wide-ranging and inclusive, 'not doubting in any article of my faith, no, nor doubting in any sacrament of the Church'. He went on to justify himself, claiming once more that 'many have slandered me, and reported that I have been a bearer of such as have maintained evil opinions; which is untrue'.

On his way to the scaffold his path had crossed with that of Walter, Lord Hungerford, who was also facing execution on charges of witchcraft and buggery, being the first man sentenced for violating the new statute on homosexuality, denounced as that 'abhomynable vice… comytted with mankinde or beast'. Understandably, Hungerford was looking 'all heavy and doleful' and Cromwell stopped to speak to him, telling him 'with cheerful countenance and comfortable words, "there is no cause for you to fear, for if you repent and be heartily sorry for that you have done, there is for you mercy enough with the Lord who, for Christ's sake, will forgive you; and therefore be not dismayed. And though the breakfast which we are going to be sharp, yet trusting to the mercy of the Lord, we shall have a joyful dinner." '

It is hard to find sympathy for the man who so cold-bloodedly disposed of innocent men in order to trap Queen Anne Boleyn. He had at first supported the Boleyns as fellow reformers against the Catholic party at court, only to turn savagely against them later. He had been prepared to sacrifice Anne to save himself, abandoning any last vestiges of integrity he may have had. He then went on to secure his own position by enforcing the dissolution of the monasteries, creating a revolution in government that would destroy the old order and promote men of similar backgrounds and ambitions to himself. As Machiavelli says, 'He who, blinded by ambition, raises himself to a position whence he cannot mount higher, must thereafter fall with the greatest loss.'

Walter Raleigh was later to recognise Henry as the 'merciless prince': 'For how many servants did he advance in haste and with the change of his fancy ruined again, no man knowing for what offence?'

What Cromwell achieved was the transformation of the nation state within five years. The split with Rome launched England as an independent power in the world, financed the treasury, created a new class of gentry, a more centralised system of government and a stronger, more tyrannical monarchy. He had created a monster that soon grew out of control. He had steered the Reformation beyond the point the King could accept and became more a liability than an asset. Like Wolsey before him, Henry VIII demonstrated his power by throwing his trusted minister to the wolves.

The poet Sir Thomas Wyatt owed his own life to Cromwell who had rescued him from the 'bloody days' of Anne Boleyn's downfall. Wyatt witnessed Cromwell's death and later wrote this lament:

> The pillar perished is whereto I leant,
> The strongest stay of mine unquiet mind;
> The like of it no man again can find.

Chapter Twelve

The Fifth Queen

ON THE VERY DAY of Cromwell's execution, 28 July 1540, Henry married Katherine secretly at the newly rebuilt Oatlands Palace near Weybridge in Surrey, which he had bought and expanded from a late medieval manor house three years before. The quiet ceremony was performed by Bishop Bonner and not revealed for the ten days of the royal couple's honeymoon idyll.

Henry was besotted, transformed by the youth, vitality and charm of his pretty little toy, who pandered to his every need. But how much of an idyll was it for the teenage bride married to the 49-year-old King?

Katherine was dazzled by the prospect of glory with which her family had enticed her to the task. For once in her life she was the centre of her family's attention, she was flattered, pampered, bribed and praised. She was made aware of her great name and the heritage of being a Howard at such a time in England's history.

No doubt the sly Bishop Gardiner reinforced her sense of destiny by reminding her of her Catholic faith and her future salvation, her role in luring the King to return to orthodoxy and perhaps even to restore the ties with Rome.

She would be Queen. It was far beyond anything that

Katherine in her wildest dreams had ever envisaged. Yet her cousin had achieved the very same; it was not impossible. Her family told her it would happen, it *must* happen, for the good of the country and the benefit of the Howards.

If she had qualms, these were soon pacified. An elderly husband was not unusual for the time. Henry had forced his own sister Mary, aged 18, to marry the ailing King Louis XII of France, 'so feeble, old and pocky a man' – actually 52 – who barely survived the honeymoon.

Was the King's marriage to Katherine consummated? The evidence comes from Henry himself. His whole demeanour and attitude point to his immense self-satisfaction, his brief new-found energy and almost boyish pride. The French Ambassador Marillac had remarked in July that he suspected Katherine was 'already *enceinte*'. Later he added, 'The King is so amorous of her that he cannot treat her well enough, and caresses her more than he did the others.'

On 6 August the King made a surprise visit to his discarded wife, Anne of Cleves, at Richmond. This courtesy call was a signal of their new relationship to the curious foreign diplomats at court, who now heard that the King had remarried.

Henry personally chose the motto for his new wife: '*Non autre volonte que lasienne*' ('No other will than his'). The new Queen appeared in public for the first time at mass in the chapel royal at Hampton Court. The handsomely rebuilt and refurbished palace Henry had taken from Cardinal Wolsey was now even more spectacular than ever and he showed it off with pride.

Wolsey's palace had been inspired by Renaissance Italy but much had been changed and extended since the Cardinal's fall. Henry's new palace was more of a throwback to the best in English Gothic style. The immense Great Hall was the centre of the festivities to welcome the newly wed couple. Its ornately carved hammerbeam roof was painted in vivid blue, red and gold and a new oriel window had been installed on one side. The walls were adorned with priceless Flemish tapestries woven to order for the King by Wilhelm Pannemaker. They told the story of

Abraham in six great scenes, each worked in gold and silver thread.

The palace's living accommodation centred around two large courtyards, one for the courtiers, the other for the King's family. Henry must have been eager to show Katherine his new astronomical clock showing the sun revolving around the earth. It was possible to tell the month, hour and phases of the moon as well as time of high tide at London Bridge.

Nothing was too much for Queen Katherine. Throughout August she was on display to foreign ambassadors who reported back to their masters that 'she reigns supreme'. She was dressed lavishly in the very latest fashion and every day the King brought her fresh gifts, as Marillac noted: 'The King had no wife who made him spend so much money in dresses and jewels as she did, who every day had some fresh caprice.'

Katherine let her new position and influence over the King go to her head. She was a proud Howard and had now reached her destiny as England's Queen and wanted this recognised. Her jewels included the parure of royal rubies belonging to the Queens of England, as seen in the Holbein portrait of Jane Seymour. This has helped to identify a portrait of Katherine wearing the jewels, a watercolour miniature by Holbein on vellum, very likely painted during her first winter as Queen. This portrait has also been identified as Lady Margaret Douglas, but this does not explain why she is wearing the royal jewels. The jewels in the miniature appear to be exactly the same parure as worn by Jane Seymour in Holbein's portraits of her – and they also match an inventory of Katherine's jewels. It is highly likely, therefore, that this miniature does provide an image of Henry VIII's fifth queen.

For years another portrait was assumed to be that of Katherine, although the sitter is clearly dressed in widow's weeds. She also has dark brown hair and seems to be considerably older than Katherine would ever be. This is now assumed to be Lady Elizabeth Cromwell, who married Cromwell's son Gregory. She was one of the Seymour sisters, as can clearly be seen from the marked similarity in expression to Jane Seymour.

The summer heat brought the plague and 300 people were dying each week in London. The royal couple left Hampton Court for the safety of the countryside, hunting their way through the Home Counties until the worst was past. Hunting was seen as a noble pastime for the King and his courtiers, providing vigorous exercise. An anonymous enthusiast wrote to Richard Pace:

> By God's Body I would rather that my son should hang than study literature. It behoves the sons of gentlemen to blow horn calls correctly, to hunt skillfully, to train a hawk well and carry it elegantly. But the study of literature should be left to clodhoppers.

Ambassador Marillac was amazed by Henry's energy and had 'never seen the King in such good spirits or in so good a humour'. He reported that the King 'has taken a new mode of living, to rise between 5 and 6 am, hear mass at 7 and then ride until dinner time, which is 10 am. He says he feels much better thus in the country than when he resides all winter in London.'

Henry seemed revived by Katherine's youthful enthusiasm, attempting to keep up with her, unaware that his antics made him ridiculous in the eyes of many.

One who took a jaundiced view of the young bride was Henry's daughter, the Lady Mary. She was now 24, ten years older than her new stepmother. They were both Catholics, but Mary was a world removed from Katherine in her strict upbringing and unbending faith. Her open disapproval of her father's new wife and criticism of Katherine's spontaneous gaiety only served to alienate the two women.

Katherine had been prepared to welcome both Henry's daughters, but after her rude reception the Spanish Ambassador reported that she complained how Mary did not treat her 'with the same respect as her two predecessors'. As a result the King punished Mary by dismissing two of her favourite waiting women.

Katherine continued to show her preference for her cousin Anne Boleyn's child, taking a great interest in her new little stepdaughter, who was now seven years old. She often played with her and gave her trinkets of jewellery, 'little thing worth'. When she first dined in public, she gave Elizabeth the privileged seat opposite her. To the young Elizabeth, this must have been a great moment and she was to remember Katherine's kindness.

Henry indulged his new bride with a continuous round of entertainments, dancing and banquets. He was seeking to regain his lost youth, re-enacting the heyday of his reign with obscene extravagance. The King's kitchens worked round the clock to prepare vast quantities of meat and fish to feed a court that often numbered 1,000 people. Henry spent the astonishing amount of £1,520 a year on food. It was recorded that 8,200 sheep, 2,330 deer, 2,870 pigs, 1,240 oxen and 33,000 chickens were consumed at the King's table in just one year. As Marillac recorded, 'nothing being spoken of here but the chase and the banquets to the new Queen'.

The King ate with a voracious appetite, working his way through three courses of roasted meats that would provide complete meals to us today. Whole sheep and sides of beef were cooked on the spits in the vast kitchens at Hampton Court Palace. Hundreds of courtiers, retainers and servants ate at the King's expense every day. Dinner was served early, often between ten and midday. Supper was taken about dusk, but was a far lighter meal. Great festivals and banquets could last all day and far into the night.

There were numerous options at each course, and with a minimum of three courses, this could often mean 30 to 40 different dishes. Each separate course was a parade of savoury, fish, meat and sweet dishes. Soups were followed by brawn, egg fritters and a variety of poultry, including pheasant, swans and peacocks, down to the smallest birds like sparrows and blackbirds baked in 'coffins' or pies. Curious combinations were created, from rabbit and crawfish, oysters, baked fruit and lamb.

The Tudor diet was chiefly meat: roast beef, boiled beef, lamb, mutton, pork, veal, capons, rabbits, and wild fowl such as geese, larks and swan. Thomas Nashe noted, 'We eat more meat at one meal than the Spaniard or Italian do in a month.' Meat was salted for the winter, but often turned rancid. Those who could afford to import expensive spices disguised the taste with rich sauces. As Philip Stubbs recorded: 'Nowadays, if the table be not covered from the one end to the other with delicate meats of sundry sorts, and to every dish a sauce appropriate to its kind, it is thought unworthy of the name of a dinner.'

The King's sweet tooth was catered for with subtleties, exotically carved concoctions, rich custard pies and tansy cakes. Wine and sack (sherry) were imported, but ale and cider were the staple beverages, with women and small children drinking 'small beer'. Hippocras or hot spiced wine was served in winter and on special occasions. Water was far too dangerous to drink.

When one course was over there was the chance to relax, go out to relieve oneself or even vomit in order to make room for the next one. Drunkenness was common and banquets could get raucous, but children of the nobility were taught table manners, learning to limit their wine, to pick only two or three dishes from each course and never to pick their nose, belch or fart at table.

The hope that Katherine might already be pregnant was put to rest as she continued to ride and dance, wearing her poor husband down as he struggled desperately to keep up with her. By October Henry became ill with a fever, perhaps even a recurrence of the malaria from which he suffered intermittently. His legs began to trouble him once again and by 22 October the court had returned to Windsor. After just four months of marriage to his young bride, he was obliged to realise his own limitations.

The Howards now achieved prominence. Lord William Howard became ambassador to France while the Queen's brother Charles found a place in the King's Privy Chamber. When it came to the establishment of the new Queen's private household, Norfolk's widowed daughter Mary, Duchess of Richmond, aged 21, and Lady William Howard, daughter-in-law of the Dowager Agnes, were among Katherine's ladies. Another was her sister Isabel, Lady Baynton, whose husband Sir Edward Baynton remained governor of the household (a position he held under five of Henry's queens). The Queen's other ladies included the King's once disgraced niece Lady Margaret Douglas, Katherine's aunt

Lady Arundel, the Countess of Sussex, and Joan Champernowne, Lady Denny, the wife of Sir Anthony Denny.

Chief of her Privy Chamber was Jane Parker, Lady Rochford. Norfolk-born and some 15 years older than the Queen, Jane Parker was the daughter of Henry, Lord Morley, a noted scholar and translator. She had been married at 16 to George, the brother of Anne Boleyn. The marriage was not a success, but they had one son, also called George, the future Dean of Lichfield Cathedral.

The Boleyn family, with the exception perhaps of Mary, were all devoted to the reform faith, whereas the Parkers were Catholics. When Anne became Queen, they continued to support the rejected Catherine of Aragon and her daughter Mary, and in 1534 Anne sent Jane away from court. Whether from revenge, jealousy or some political or religious motive, Jane played along with the plot concocted by the Chapuys with Cromwell to destroy the Boleyn faction. Her testimony against her own husband sent him to the block and ensured the judicial murder of a Queen.

The widowed Lady Rochford was granted a pension by Cromwell, restored as Lady of the Privy Chamber to Queen Anne's successors and in 1539 received the manor of Loxley in Warwickshire. Now aged 30, she was placed at Katherine's side, in charge of the Queen's private chamber and the bevy of royal chamberers drawn from the Queen's old companions from her past: Katherine Tylney, Alice Restwold, Margaret Morton and the impudent Joan Bulmer.

Had Katherine merely been eager to have familiar faces around her, pleased to advance old friends, or was there something more to the inclusion of these women who knew all the secrets of her past at Lambeth and Horsham?

Very likely she felt alone, even abandoned. At barely 15 she had been prepared like a sacrificial gift for an ageing and infirm king, taught how to please him in order to secure favours for her extended family. The Howards were once more in the ascendant, with the Catholic party at court, and Bishop Gardiner in particular, riding high. But Katherine was all alone at night in the bedchamber with the King and only she knew whether he was actually capable of giving her the son who would ensure Howard glory.

A second son was Henry's dearest wish. Pampered and protected, Prince Edward had survived his first years of life when half the children born in England routinely died of poverty or sickness. He appeared to be healthy and thriving, but Henry himself had been a second son, inheriting the throne from his elder brother Arthur. A 'spare' was the key to success, as Norfolk and Gardiner knew very well, and they were looking to Katherine to provide him for the King.

Katherine obliged her uncle in his schemes and was ready to listen to the requests of the Dowager Duchess to offer places to some of her favourites from Lambeth. These not only included the chamberers about her but, unbelievably, a position for the errant Francis Dereham.

There is some confusion over who promoted Dereham to the Queen. Duchess Agnes later reported that 'Lady Bridgewater and Lady (William) Howard sued to speak to the Queen for Dereham.' But Katherine herself later contradicted this: 'My lady of Norfolk hath desired me to be good unto him, and so I will.'

Was this appointment sheer naiveté on Katherine's part or was she forced to try and counter the hidden threat of blackmail? Surely she was in a state of panic because of Dereham's return. She was now surrounded by a group who knew all her intimate secrets, including an ex-lover who clearly saw fresh opportunities in taking full advantage of her position as Queen. Once at court, Dereham bragged rashly of his superiority to one of Katherine's ushers, Mr Johns: 'I was of the Queen's council before he [Johns] knew her and shall be when she hath forgotten him.'

Surely Katherine must have thought it wiser and safer to do as she was requested and reward Dereham and her childhood friends rather than risk antagonising such an ambitious and potentially dangerous group. By keeping their favour, she thought to silence any gossip, while at the same time being able to relax in their company without having to keep up the pretence of the innocent bride.

Another of this clique was Lady Margaret Douglas, herself no stranger to romantic intrigue. While the King and Queen had been occupied on their hunting honeymoon, Margaret had become involved with Katherine's own brother, Charles Howard. He and his brother George had been granted a lucrative licence to import 1,000 tuns of wine from Gascony and timber from Toulouse, but he was still not an appropriate suitor for the King's niece, who was in the line of succession to the throne.

It might have been expected that Margaret had learnt her lesson after the dangers of her ill-fated relationship with Lord Thomas Howard, son of the Dowager Agnes. Their arrest and confinement in the Tower should have been sufficient to put anyone else off romance for life, but not so Margaret Douglas. She had clearly inherited her mother's arrogant and passionate Tudor temperament, indulging herself in a new affair while her uncle was preoccupied with his new Queen. She was no longer an immature girl and, like Charles Howard, had become subject to an older and more powerful relative who controlled all marriage prospects.

According to law, Margaret could not chose her own husband, while Charles was obliged to please his uncle Norfolk. And here, surely, was the perfect match to suit Howard ambitions! Margaret was of the blood royal, the granddaughter of Henry VII. There was always the possibility that she or her future children would inherit the crown, which was why the King kept her single.

Unfortunately for the lovers, their secret was betrayed on the King's return and while Charles fled abroad for his life, Margaret was packed back to the nuns of Syon to cool her ardour for a year. She was warned to 'wholly apply herself to please the King's Highness' and abandon 'overmuch lightness'.

Norfolk's ploy had failed but the head of the Howard clan was very much in favour as Lord Treasurer, soon to be the new Lord Lieutenant of the North. His supporter Robert Ratcliffe, Earl of Sussex, was appointed Great Chamberlain, while William Fitzwilliam, Earl of Southampton, took Cromwell's key post of Lord Privy Seal.

Since Cromwell's fall the King had been obliged to pay more

attention to the administration of the state, scrutinising documents himself rather than leaving it all to the one man who had been capable of taking on this burden of work. He attended the Council, scribbling notes in the margins of papers. His paranoia led him to be suspicious of everyone around him and his unpredictable outbursts of temper caused every man to be afraid of him. He denounced his Privy Council, claiming that they were flatterers and deceivers but he would catch them out.

It was a wonder that men like Sir Anthony Denny survived the tempestuous rollercoaster ride of the King's moods. He was the rising star of the Privy Chamber, 'the hub of the whole court'. Keeper of the Palace of Westminster, Yeoman of the Robes and eventually Keeper of the Privy Purse, Denny had learnt to keep his head down when his master lashed out, but was still open about his reformist beliefs and friendship with Archbishop Cranmer. John Leland recorded that 'the whole court bore testimony to his *gratia flagrans*' or his high reputation with the King – what we might translate as his blazing repute with the King.

He acted as confidante for his master's secrets while managing to retain his good humour in the eye of the storm.

Henry's bad leg caused him considerable pain and he took more and more to his privy chamber. In new plans for his palaces at Hampton Court and Whitehall these 'secret lodgings' were enlarged and connected by discreet entrances. Only his most trusted and confidential servants had access to these apartments, with men like Denny acting as effective 'gate-keepers' to the King's presence.

Christmas 1540 surpassed those of recent years. The King was feeling better and took the opportunity to show off his new wife in the magnificence of the newly completed palace of Hampton Court. On New Year's Day it was traditional to present gifts to the King. But that January Henry's New Year gifts to Katherine included a brooch with 33 diamonds and 60 rubies, a square of 27 'fair table diamonds' and 26 clusters of pearls, a rope of 200 large pearls, a collection of some 158 pearls ready for setting and a 'muffler of black velvet furred with sables containing 38 rubies and 572 pearls'. Pearls had to be fetched at great cost from the Far East or the new world of the Americas. They were enormously expensive and therefore highly fashionable, but Henry chose them for his new bride because they symbolised purity.

On 3 January Anne of Cleves arrived to deliver her New Year gift to the royal couple in person. This was a handsome pair of horses richly turned out in purple velvet, which the 'King's sister' knew would assure her welcome.

Six months before Katherine had been simply an unknown member of her train, one of her waiting women. Anne could have been resentful and bitter at the girl who had displaced her as Queen, or perhaps envious of Katherine's success at winning Henry where she had failed, but she was a shrewd woman who recognised her fortunate escape. According to the Spanish Ambassador, she seemed eager to show that she was perfectly content with her new life and paid homage to her successor, making a deep curtsey to the ground. Chapuys described the encounter: 'Lady Anne approached the Queen with as much reverence and punctilious ceremony as if she herself was the most insignificant damsel about court … addressing the Queen on her knees.'

Katherine raised her to the feet and Henry kissed her cheek. She gave Anne in return a ring and two little lap-dogs.

The night was merry and the two queens stayed up long after Henry had gone to bed, talking and dancing. Anne had picked up enough English to carry on a conversation and perhaps they shared some confidences about their experiences in the King's bedchamber.

Surely Anne must have pitied the young girl who had usurped her place. For all her fine clothes and jewels, Katherine was still the one who had to prepare herself each night to sleep with the King.

Katherine was conscious that her new status was totally dependent upon Henry's goodwill. She was Queen but her future hung on a knife-edge. Before her she had the example of her cousin, Anne Boleyn, who had been too clever for her own good.

Katherine devoted herself to keeping the King content. Her girlish pleasure in material things led Henry to assume that she was nothing but an empty-headed and pretty toy for his pleasure. When the King was satisfied, then Katherine was able to plead for her own particular causes. Among these were her cousin John Legh and a certain Helen Page, whose lives had been at risk under suspicion of treason.

In February she intervened in the case of Sir Edmund Knyvet, who was involved in a quarrel with Thomas Clere, one of Surrey's men, on the royal tennis court. Clere was injured and Knyvet was sentenced before the Court of the Verge to have his right hand amputated. A team was immediately summoned, comprising the sergeant surgeon, the sergeant of the woodyard, the sergeant farrier, the sergeant of the poultry and even the cook who supplied the knife. 'Thus every man in his office ready to do the execution.' When Katherine heard that the King had approved the sentence, she dared to speak up on Knyvet's behalf and the barbarous ceremony was stopped just in time. Sir Edmund was apparently more frightened than hurt.

Katherine also spoke up for a former admirer of her cousin, Anne Boleyn. The new political order continued to take effect with a series of arrests among former Cromwell supporters and in January Sir Thomas Wyatt was one of several ambassadors arrested abroad while on diplomatic missions and brought back to the Tower as suspects. Sir Richard Southwell was sent to the Wyatt home, Allington Castle in Kent, to confiscate all his goods and weapons.

Wyatt was reported by an informer for making treasonable statements, although he had no idea what they could be: 'God knoweth what restless torment it hath been … perusing all my deeds to my remembrance, whereby a malicious enemy might take advantage by evil interpretation.'

For the second time in four years the poet feared that his life hung in the balance at the King's whim. In 1536 Thomas Cromwell had rescued him, but now Cromwell himself was gone and Protestants were once again persecuted. Many chose to flee abroad, but although Wyatt had been on a mission for the King in Spain, this did not save him from being thrown into the Tower.

Katherine came to his rescue when, on 19 March, she made her first entrance to London as Queen. At the King's side she travelled in the royal barge downstream as the cannons of the Tower of London saluted her with 'a great shot of guns'. They were greeted by a delegation of the Lord Mayor and his Aldermen who sailed out to escort her in a fleet of barges dressed overall. Ambassador Chapuys records, 'The people of this City honoured her with a most splendid reception ... the Queen took courage to beg and entreat the King for the release of Mr Wyatt, a prisoner in the Tower.'

Henry succumbed to Katherine's charm and vivacity and agreed, yet with a condition. The King required Wyatt to acknowledge his faults and reform his life by giving up his affair with Elizabeth Darrell and returning to his estranged wife, Elizabeth Brooke. The King seemed unaware or uninterested in the fact that the poet had originally left her because of her adultery.

Wyatt had little choice but to do as Henry commanded. He had come too close to death twice to risk another confrontation, but he felt that he lost 'the last vestiges of his self respect' in making the false confession.

A letter to Sir William Howard from the King's Council on 26 March reported that Wyatt had confessed

> ... in a like lamentable and pitifull sorte ... declaring thole history of his offences, but with a like protestation, that the same proceeded from him in his rage and folishe vaynglorios fantazie without spott of malice; yelding himself only to his majesties mercy, without whiche he sawe he might and must needes be justely condemned. And the contemplation of which submission, and at the greate and contynual sute of the Quenes Majestie, His Highnes, being of his owne most godly nature enclyned to pitie and mercy, hathe given him his pardon in as large and ample sorte as his grace gave thother to Sir John Wallop.

Wyatt gave up Elizabeth Darrell and returned to his wife, turning to religion. He became inclined to a 'Lutheran influence', as his dear friend Anne Boleyn had been, and found 'peace of mind' reading the Psalms. In his reworking of Psalm 51, Wyatt saw his lost mistress as Bathsheba and repented of their affair.

The intervention of the Queen was to become a talking point. Another prisoner in the Tower who drew her sympathy was Margaret Pole, the aged Countess of Salisbury, regarded as a living saint and martyr by many Catholics. Hearing of the Countess's suffering in her prison through the cold winter, Katherine had sent her a gift of blankets and even paid her own dressmaker to provide her with warm clothes and slippers. When, however, Katherine tried to plead for the Plantagenet heiress's life, Henry soon showed that he was not about to give way to her on everything; later in the year he found an excuse to send the old lady to the executioner's block.

Katherine had acted out of compassion and generosity to save these supplicants, but could she save herself? Becoming Queen had placed her in a position of great danger. She was soon to realise that she would not survive for long if she could not produce another son for Henry.

Chapter Thirteen

The Queen's Progress

THE SUIT OF ARMOUR made for Henry in 1540 (now in the Tower of London) shows he was by then a barrel of a man, with a 54-inch waist and 57-inch chest. He suffered from a number of recurring illnesses, from malaria, which he had contracted in 1524, to the ulcerous condition of his leg brought on by a heavy fall when jousting in the same year. The development of varicose ulcers inflamed by additional knocks and falls – notably that in January 1536 when the King lay unconscious for two hours – led to thrombosis. Both legs became swollen due to his weight and every year he fell victim to pain and fever when his ulcer troubled him again.

In 'The Diagnosis of King Henry's "Sorre Legge"', Sir Arthur MacNalty denies the theory that Henry suffered from a syphilitic ulcer, as there is no record that his surgeons used mercury to treat him. MacNalty's credible opinion is that Henry developed osteomyelitis – a chronic septic infection that could not be cured by the primitive medical practices of the day. Although his doctors worked to drain the suppurating pus and fluid from the ulcer, the application of strange balms and lead poultices only exacerbated his condition, and the leg required frequent dressing and bandaging.

The infection flared up in February 1541, sending the King into unpredictable and violent moods. He lashed at all around him, announcing that he was worn out governing an ungrateful nation, 'he had an unhappy people to govern whom he would shortly make so poor that they would not have the boldness nor the power to oppose him'.

He now regretted the loss of Cromwell, complaining that 'on light pretexts, by false accusations, they made me put to death the most faithful servant I ever had!' He would not listen to his advisers, warning them that 'he knew the good servants from the flatterers, and, if God lent him health, he would take care that their projects should not succeed'.

He and Katherine were back at Hampton Court to spend the Shrovetide festival. This was the last opportunity to feast before the 40-day period of Lent, when it was forbidden to eat meat and abstinence was strictly observed. On Shrove Tuesday there were usually cockfights and sport, with great banquets at court followed by masques and dancing. This year, however, the King spent the festival 'without recreation, even of music'. Henry was in a foul temper and in no mood to listen to anyone, not even Katherine.

By the end of the month he was too ill to attend several court functions. His face turned black and in 'great alarm' surgeons worked for ten days to release the dangerous blockage of his ulcer.

For the first time Katherine was kept out of his presence. Whether this was because he was simply too sick to see her or whether he was too vain to have her see him in such poor condition is hard to say. But suddenly she was kept out of the picture with no influence at all on the outcome of events. There were even some malicious rumours circulating about the court that the King had tired of her.

Among those attending the King's Privy Chamber was a distant relative of the Queen, Thomas Culpeper. Katherine's own mother Jocasta had been a Culpeper, making her daughter and Thomas sixth cousins, once removed. At some stage, as the Howard family moved from house to house when Katherine was a child, she may have encountered this distant cousin, although she would have been less than seven and Thomas was probably ten years older. A meeting seems unlikely as, like Katherine, he had been sent away from home at an early age, fortunate enough to be 'placed out' at court as a page. He had been serving the King for several years before Katherine met him.

His elder brother, also called Thomas, served Thomas Cromwell. Probably the older boy had been sickly as a child and not expected to live, so that his parents gave both boys the same name. With almost half of children dying young, it was quite common for families to give two children the same name in the hope that at least one would survive to continue the family name. In the event, both Thomases survived to make careers in high places.

The Culpeper family was notorious for a great scandal in which two younger sons of the family without prospects, Nicholas and Richard, abducted the two heiresses of the Wakehurst fortune to Bobbing in Kent and married them. Their grandmother Elizabeth claimed that they were 'with force and armes, riotously agense the Kinges peas, arayed in the manner of warre ... toke and caried away (... with) grete and pittious lamentacion and weping'.

The girls were not the main concern but the property and wealth that came with them, but both marriages went ahead. A brass in Ardingly church commemorates Nicholas and his wife Elizabeth with all their 18 children, while Richard Culpeper and his wife had 11 children.

The Thomas Culpeper brothers were by all accounts equally ambitious and not too particular about the way in which they operated to advance at court. They were very active in the grab for property and pensions after the dissolution of the monasteries. But as the Rev. Williams had found out, it was dangerous to challenge the Culpepers. The elder Thomas suddenly pulled a knife on him in a dispute over land:

> ... the said Thomas Culpeper broke the brow of the said William, clerk, with the shaft of a knife so that the blade ran down his face in the presence of this deponent ... then the said Culpeper gave the said William, clerk, a blow or two with a staff for he was not able to

sing mass for a fortnight after, and thereupon the said clerk plucked the said Culpeper down by the beard in the sight of the wife of the said Culpeper who with one or two of her servants came running to help to beat the said William clerk, so that he was forced to cry to the said William Playce and Robert Fulcher for aid ... and by report the said Culpeper drew his dagger at another time to strike the said William, clerk, and more he cannot depose.

In the same year, 1539, it seems that the swaggering younger Thomas attacked and raped the wife of a park-keeper while three or four of his followers held her down. As a merchant in London later mentioned in a letter to Germany, Culpeper 'had violated the wife of a certain park-keeper in a woody thicket, while, horrid to relate! three or four of his most profligate attendants were holding her at his bidding'.

When one of her neighbours tried to rescue the woman, he was promptly murdered. Although the villagers later seized Culpeper and his men, when the case was brought for justice, the King himself pardoned him. Clearly the rape of a peasant woman counted for very little. In *The Art of Courtly Love*, Andreas Cappellanus counselled that a knight should have no qualms about taking any woman he came across working in the fields.

The younger Thomas won the King's favour with his good looks and by his skill at dressing Henry's ulcer. He was apparently on call day or night and used to sleep in the King's chamber, possibly even in the King's bed, as the French Ambassador reported.

Culpeper's proximity to and influence with the King was widely recognised. He was also very attractive to women. In 1537 Lady Lisle had ordered her agent John Hussey to cultivate the good offices of the King's favourite: 'There is no remedy; Culpeper must have a hawk.' She also sent him little admiring notes and presents, including bracelets, claiming 'they are the first that ever I sent to any man'.

The new Queen was surely aware of him, knowing the family connection. During the period when the King had been taken ill and locked himself away in his private apartments, she may have contacted her cousin in order to learn how he was recovering. By Easter Culpeper could report that the King's leg was beginning to heal and his temper had improved.

According to his later version of events, Katherine summoned him to her presence chamber on Maundy Thursday, which fell on 14 April in 1541. Here she gave him the gift of a cap made of velvet adorned with a jewelled brooch. Culpeper claims he was surprised, exclaiming, 'Alas, Madam, why did not you this when you were a maid?' She replied that had she 'tarried still in the maidens' chamber' then she 'would have tried' him.

How much of this is credible? Given the atmosphere of 'courtly love' that had flourished at the royal court in Henry's heyday, pretty compliments and flattery, love tokens and poetry were all part of the 'game of love' recorded in the Devonshire Manuscript by Anne Boleyn's ladies. But the game had turned sour. The shadow of the Tower had destroyed romance, with imprisonment and executions to dampen the ardour of young women like Mary Howard and Margaret Douglas. But Katherine, experienced in the games played at Horsham and Lambeth, did not learn this lesson.

According to Culpeper, Katherine was the motivator, summoning him to her presence, giving him gifts and flirting with him. She was conscious of the danger they were running, allegedly telling him to hide her gift under his cloak in order 'that nobody see it'. [12] She was the Queen; how could he refuse her?

In April Culpeper was taken ill at Greenwich Palace. Katherine was anxious enough about him to send some special food to aid his recovery. She also took the time to sit down and write him a letter, although this was clearly an effort for a girl unused to writing.

The letter shows that the Queen could not visit Culpeper in person. This would have been against all protocol and would have exposed their friendship, raising instant suspicions about the nature of their relationship. At court there were always those ready to inform upon secret meetings and liaisons for their own advancement. Although Katherine and Culpeper were distant cousins, any private association between them would have provoked gossip.

When Anne Boleyn had been visited by her own brother in her chamber during a pregnancy, their meeting was reported as suspicious by his scurrilously minded wife Jane, Lady Rochford. Ironically, that lady was now in the service of Katherine.

Katherine's letter began:

> Master Culpeper, I heartily recommend me unto you, praying you to send me word how that you do. It was showed me that you was sick, the which thing troubled me very much till such time that I hear from you praying you to send me word how that you do, for I never longed so much for a thing as I do to see you and to speak with you, the which I trust shall be shortly now.

She then bluntly reveals the true depth of her feelings for him:

> That which doth comfortly me very much when I think of it, and when I think again that you shall depart from me again it makes my heart die to think what fortune I have that I cannot be always in your company.

Until this point we have no indication whether her love has been requited, but the next line shows that their secret relationship is already well advanced:

> It my trust is always in you that you will be as you have promised me, and in that hope I trust upon still, praying you that you will come when my Lady Rochford is here for then I shall be best at leisure to be at your commandment.

It appears that Jane Parker, Lady Rochford, was already active in the role of accomplice. But Katherine was worried about keeping their contact a secret and went on to warn Culpeper to be cautious for:

> I do know no one that I dare trust to send to you, and therefore I pray you take him to be with you that I may sometime hear from you one thing. I pray you to give me a horse for my man for I had

much ado to get one and therefore I pray send me one by him and in so doing I am as I said afor, and thus I take my leave of you, trusting to see you shortly again and I would you was with me now that you might see what pain I take in writing to you.

Yours as long as life endures,

Katheryn.

She then hastily scribbles another reminder to look after their messenger: 'One thing I had forgotten and that is to instruct my man to tarry here with me still for he says whatsomever you bid him he will do it.'

That she should involve a number of her servants in the intrigue shows that this was already a highly dangerous affair for all involved. Culpeper chose to keep the letter at great risk.

Wiser men than he knew the dangers of holding onto letters of a sensitive nature. Lord Lisle had gone to the Tower and yet he had routinely warned that secret matters should never be put to paper but spoken by a trusted messenger: 'Touching news, this bearer will inform your lordship.' Sir William Wentworth warned that letters may be intercepted and used by enemies: 'It is common custom to keep letters and years later produce them for evidence against you in court or elsewhere.'

Like Polonius giving advice to his son Laertes, Wentworth taught the evil nature of men and women: 'Ever fear the worst … Suspect everyone, trust no one, beware of false friends, flatterers and dissemblers. Never trust any friend or servant … Your friend today, your enemy tomorrow.'

Others would agree, for the 'men among whom we be born be of so evil disposition, the world with whom we live so fierce and cruel … that they hurt us'.

Should we assume that Katherine was a flighty and rather stupid young woman who was now sexually frustrated by her marriage to an ageing, tyrannical husband? Her earlier promiscuity has been seen as proof of baser instincts that now led her into a rash and heady affair with the dashing Thomas Culpeper. But this is far too simplistic.

Katherine was not a woman of 20 but a young girl who had been abused since the age of 11 under her own grandmother's roof. Her innocence had been traded for food and lodging from the age of seven thanks to a wastrel father and a callous family. Deprived of love and security, she had turned to the women in her peer group for friendship and support. She used these mentors as role models, eager to join their inner circle and share in their secrets.

Whereas her cousin Anne had been sent to France for her sophisticated education, returning as an object of fascination but maintaining her piety and virginity, little Katherine had been 'finished' in a far more earthy and basic school.

Her letter clearly took some effort and is full of errors, exactly as Katherine had struggled to write it. The result gives a picture of a charming, light-hearted young girl who took pleasure in flattery, flirting, secret messages and hidden fumblings.

Culpeper chose to keep the letter at great risk. Starkey insists that his relationship with Katherine remained unconsummated. It was 'like stuff out of a Shakespearean comedy. They don't actually do anything but they spend hours talking about it, from midnight to three in the morning in this wonderful figurative language – it is absolutely delightful.'

But how likely is that Culpeper the rapist would have settled for a juvenile romance of whispered endearments and pretty promises?

Culpeper and Katherine's story is not a great romance – there is nothing romantic about this grasping trickster and murderer. He was not a callow boy but at least ten years Katherine's senior and surely knew what he was getting into. Like Francis Dereham before him, he must have seen in Katherine an amazing opportunity, not just to take advantage of a neglected young wife but to carve out a future for himself.

Was his rash involvement with this woman motivated by more than mere desire? Were Katherine and Culpeper meeting secretly behind the King's back for a great deal more than an exchange of love-tokens and letters?

Katherine had been married for nine months with several false alarms of pregnancy. Even as Queen, she was granted little privacy regarding her health and was fully aware that enquiries were made of the ladies in her household of the details of her menstrual cycle. Not only the King himself, but foreign ambassadors sought the latest information concerning her fertility. Ambassador Marillac had reported on 10 April that, for the second time in less than a year, 'this Queen is thought to be with child, which would be a very great joy to this King, who, it seems, believes it, and intends if it be found true, to have (her) crowned at Whitsuntide'.

Having finally recovered, Henry announced that he was taking his wife on progress to the north and east of the country. These plans were not new, for he had intended to take Jane Seymour on such a tour, possibly culminating in her coronation as Queen at York Minster, but the northern rebellion and Jane's death put an abrupt end to the project. Before the royal party even set out, the King issued orders for the execution of the Countess of Salisbury, heiress of the Plantagenets and mother of Cardinal Pole. On 28 May the sickly victim was helped to the block to suffer an horrific death at the hands of an incompetent headsman. She was 68 years old.

From London an obvious Yorkist sympathiser wrote afterwards, 'I do not hear that any of the royal race are left, except a nephew of the Cardinal [Pole] and the son of the Marquis of Exeter. They are both children, and in prison and condemned.'

Henry intended to demonstrate beyond all doubt that he was King of his entire kingdom. The north still hankered after the old ways, and more than 50 years after Bosworth loyalties to the Yorkist cause had not died. Harsh taxation, the dissolution of the monasteries in rural areas, enclosures and seizures of land caused as great a stirring of unrest as Catholic opposition to reform. The Tudors were seen as usurpers and tyrants who had overturned ancient kings and customs, riding roughshod over the people. It would take more than a glittering progress to placate their deep loathing.

In June Henry and his courtiers finally set out on his great progress, like a small army moving north. An immense train of 300 wagons, horses and artillery had already set out in advance to York-shire in case of trouble – Henry was taking no chances – but the main body of the procession was devoted to making the arduous journey as comfortable as possible. He took with him his furnish-ings, plate and even tapestries to line the walls of draughty north-ern castles. The intention was to create spectacle, to dazzle his rebellious subjects north of Watford into an acceptance that the Tudors were very much here to stay.

The King and Queen travelled slowly. Henry wanted to show himself off to the people with his beautiful young bride at his side. At every town on their route there were delegations and speeches at the county and parish boundaries followed by formal recep-tions. No doubt this soon proved repetitive, even tedious. They were fortunate to make ten miles a day.

Their slow journey was also hampered by rain. Unlike the very hot summer of 1540, when cattle died because of a water shortage, the summer weather was atrocious, with roads turned into muddy quagmires. Marillac wrote that 'the roads leading to the North ... have been flooded and the carts and baggage could not proceed without great difficulty'.

By the time they reached the manor of Grafton Regis there were doubts as to whether the progress could or even should con-tinue as Katherine announced that she was feeling 'unwell'. Such an admission could only add fuel to speculation about her condi-tion. No doubt that was Katherine's intention.

Marillac was convinced that the King was hoping for a second son, a future Duke of York, but others were less confident, afraid that history was repeating itself once again. It was still remembered that Catherine of Aragon had announced her first pregnancy at the beginning of her marriage to the King. After fruitless months of waiting for a sign that she had conceived, she panicked and lied, making a false declaration. She was then forced to carry on her pretence for months, hoping that she would eventually become pregnant, but the charade ended in public humiliation. The Queen's women were blamed, but Henry always remembered how she had lied to him and the nation.

There were already people ready to whisper that the new Queen was barren. After 11 months of marriage, Katherine too was becoming worried that she would not – could not – conceive.

The royal progress stayed with the King's great friend Charles Brandon, Duke of Suffolk, and his young wife Catherine Willoughby. The two couples were well matched as the King had followed Brandon's example by taking a very young wife. The Suffolks had produced two strong boys to prove that such marriages of 'crabbed age and youth' could work.

As long as Henry lived in hope of a pregnancy then Katherine's position was safe. But in order to convince the King that there could now be a second son, she had to endure nights in his bed, reassuring him that he was capable. Given her romance with Thomas Culpeper this must have proved increasingly distasteful to a young girl of scarcely 16.

For years Katherine had been told that the cardinal sin was to bear a child out of wedlock. She had learnt from the more experienced women at Horsham and Lambeth exactly how to 'meddle with a man' without conceiving, an irony that now returned to haunt her.

Whereas before she may have taken rue or savin to prevent a pregnancy, now she may have turned to a concoction of mugwort, sheep's urine, rabbit's blood and mare's milk to help her conceive. It was not only possible but increasingly a necessity if she was to remain Queen.

Henry would not wait for ever. His patience was already wearing thin, as the court had noted. Katherine knew what had happened to her cousin Anne Boleyn, who at least had succeeded in producing one healthy daughter, even if her other pregnancies had all ended in tragedy. How long would it be before Henry realised that all his dreams were an illusion and she must take the same path as her cousin?

Even Jane Seymour had been afraid that the King was not capable. It had taken eight months before she became pregnant with Edward, the much-awaited son. Surely the ambitious Seymour

family must have been growing frantic that their carefully contrived plot had failed?

Was Henry still capable of fathering a child? He had rid himself
of Anne of Cleves as he could not bring himself to consummate
the marriage. He claimed that she was no virgin but later contradicted himself by stating that he had left her a virgin. Was he still
capable of performing sexually with any woman?

Katherine endeavoured to do her duty but his age, his various
disabilities and illnesses were against her. The sooner she could
announce that she was with child, the sooner she would feel herself secure.

The King was often sick and probably impotent, as no one was
in a better position to know than his young wife and his favourite
Culpeper. Henry's chances of ever impregnating his child bride, let
alone getting a strong and healthy son by her, were minimal and
they both surely knew it.

Perhaps what had started out as a foolish mutual attraction suddenly metamorphosed into a conspiracy to defraud King and
nation as Katherine was under increasing pressure to provide a son
if she and the Howard family were to retain their power and position.

Norfolk was well aware that if Prince Edward should die
young, as so many children did in infancy, then the King would be
left once again without a male heir. Even if the boy survived, a second child would confirm the Howards' strong position to influence King and country in future years. If Henry died within the
next few years, both princes would be in need of a Regent or Lord
Protector to govern in their place. And should any misfortune
befall young Edward before he came of age, then who but the
Duke of Norfolk to take charge of the kingdom?

It was in Norfolk's interest for Katherine to bear a child but if
the King was incapable, he was possibly ready to suggest an alter-
native, a 'Plan B'. It seems highly probable that Katherine was
urged to become pregnant as soon as possible, regardless of the
paternity. Culpeper's bastard could be passed off as the King's legitimate son.

Katherine's affair with Culpeper, which reached a peak during the progress north, was not merely a heady romance that blinded the lovers to the risks involved. Culpeper was hardly a naïve Romeo. He knew the King almost better than anyone and had seen him in his worst moments, from his raging tantrums to sobbing pain. It is absurd to think that such an ambitious and sharp character, a rapist and murderer who always looked out for himself, would have dared to 'tup the old ram's ewe' under the same roof, virtually under the King's very eyes as they moved around the country, unless there had been something more in it for him than just sex.

Culpeper was intimate with the King and had served him through his sickness. Did he perhaps hope he was not long for this world? Henry was 50, not a great age even by the times, but his poor constitution and many ailments had aged him considerably. If Culpeper reasoned that the King had just a few years left, might he not gamble all on assisting the Queen, his cousin, to produce the second heir she so desperately needed in order to secure her position?

Surely it must have occurred to both lovers that the enormous risks they were running would only be worth it if the Queen found herself pregnant. There would be rich rewards for the favourite 'uncle' of a young prince. A widowed queen, even a Queen Regent, might well decide to marry again, offering her new husband a handsome dukedom. A similar suspicion had been behind the arrest of Anne Boleyn's accused lovers, in particular Sir Henry Norris who had aspired to rule England 'in the King's shoes'. That was sheer nonsense of course, contrived by Thomas Cromwell to be rid of Queen Anne, but Norris and Anne had paid for it with their heads.

Five years made all the difference. The King was a sick man on borrowed time, desperate to convince himself that he was still able to father a child. Culpeper may have rationalised the risk by thinking only of the rewards as he and Katherine resumed their trysts in the most dangerous of circumstances.

Chapter Fourteen

The Lover

THE ROYAL PROGRESS entered Lincolnshire, the hotbed of rural revolution only a few years before. Henry made little secret of the fact that he had not forgiven this betrayal by the county and its people, whom he had so openly castigated in 1536: 'How presumptuous then are ye, the rude commons of one shire, and that one of the most brute and beastly of the whole realm ...'

However, he made an effort for the royal occasion, arriving in the city of Lincoln lavishly dressed in Lincoln green and surrounded by a bodyguard of archers, as if he was Robin Hood. It is not recorded what the people of Lincoln thought of their King.

After changing into cloth of gold, he then led Queen Katherine to the cathedral where he pardoned those who had dared to rebel against him. After the ceremony the royal couple went to their quarters at the castle to rest.

On the night of 6 August when the castle watchmen were doing their rounds they came upon a door left open. Thinking that someone had been careless, they locked it again and went on their way. The door and staircase led up to the Queen Katherine's chamber. A short time later Culpeper and his servant arrived, discovered that they were locked out and had to pick the lock, one keeping guard in case they were caught.

Culpeper's man waited below while his master went up to keep his secret rendezvous. He was met by Lady Rochford and admitted to the Queen's room, where he remained from II to 3 in the morning. Culpeper later claimed that he and the Queen had simply talked. Lady Rochford, who stood guard outside the door, was later to tell a very different story. She confessed that from the noises she heard from inside they were clearly making love.

This sounds like folly, but the consequences were to be very severe. They were indeed seen and later evidence was given against them of that 'fatal night'.

Another of her ladies, Margaret Morton, was called upon to act as a lookout at Lincoln when Katherine 'went two nights out of her chamber, when it was late, to Lady Rochford's chamber'. At 2 am her companion Katherine Tilney awoke and asked, 'Jesus! Is not the Queen abed yet?' Margaret told her, 'Yes, even now.' The Queen had only just returned from her nighttime assignation.

Although they bear all the hallmarks of Katherine's earlier adventures, these backstairs fumblings and furtive nocturnal expeditions were apparently arranged by Lady Rochford. Whether eavesdropping or apparently sleeping in a chair in the very same room, there is something prurient and distasteful about Jane Parker and her connection to their affair.

Still only in her early thirties, she had known an unhappy married life with George Boleyn. She had given birth to one child, a son also called George, whom she appears to have 'placed out' at the earliest opportunity so that she might return to court. Her betrayal of her own husband fixed her reputation as a vindictive and envious woman with little or no scruples.

What was her motivation in helping Katherine? She was fully twice her age and must have known the terrible risks she was running in assisting her affair. Did she perhaps get some kind of vicarious thrill out of acting as bawd, deriving voyeuristic pleasure from being present and even watching? Or did she understand there was a motive behind Katherine's recklessness and from her own

Catholic perspective view the prospect of a Howard heir as a victory for the 'old faith'?

Jane Parker and Katherine discussed Culpeper, as they both later admitted. At the time the Queen allegedly warned that if these conversations 'came not out she feared not for no thing' and she brazenly told Jane to deny them 'utterly'.

Culpeper later testified that during their encounters Katherine was always 'as one in fear lest somebody should come in'.[3] On one occasion he was actually seen by one of her own chamberers, Lovekyn, and was forced to hide on the back stairs until the coast was clear and Lady Rochford came to lead him to the Queen's chamber.

Sometimes this was impossible, as Culpeper recalled of their first encounter in 'a secret and vile place' while on the progress, when Lady Rochford 'appointed him to come into a place under her chamber being, as he thinketh, the Queen's stool house'. He meant the privy.

The King all this time remained sublimely unaware that there was anything wrong.

The royal progress turned north from Lincoln towards the heart of the recent rebellion, Robert Aske's city of York, but on the way Henry took every opportunity to inspect sites for his new plans of fortification.

The harbour at Hull was protected by a heavy chain stretched across the river at its mouth into the Humber but the medieval fortifications were no longer capable of withstanding modern artillery. Henry decided that Hull was to have a new and 'notable fortress' in the same design as other vulnerable sites selected around the south coast at Walmer, Deal, Portland, Camber, Sandgate, Pendennis and St Mawes. He appointed Michael Stanhope as his lieutenant, housing him in King's Manor, the old home of the de la Pole family, although Stanhope found the place so large that he did not have enough furniture for one room.

Henry's coastal defence system was an innovative but expensive project to protect England from future foreign invasion. New castles and forts had been designed to incorporate modern artillery and new tactics developed to rain a coordinated barrage of fire on enemy shipping. Low squat turrets were being constructed at Falmouth and St Mawes to guard the sea defences against the Spanish or French fleets. These new fortifications were to be supplied with new breech-loading cannon or 'culverin'.

Afterwards, Henry also took some leisure to hunt. Ambassador Marillac, his guest, reported that the King killed over 200 deer and swans 'as near as if they had been domestic cattle'. He also enjoyed fowling expeditions on the lakes and marshes, catching 'a great quantity of young swans, two boats full of river birds and as much of great pikes and other fish'.

There was no opportunity for Katherine to meet her lover while they were housed in the countryside in great tent-like pavilions. But the affair resumed when they were on the move again, reaching Pontefract at the end of August. This was known as one of the finest castles in England and it was to provide another narrow escape for the lovers.

Upon arrival it was said that Katherine went straightaway 'in every house seeking for the back doors and back stairs herself'. If this is true, there is more than a hint of desperation here that cannot be explained away as sexual excess. Throughout the progress she was attempting to alternate her time between the King and her lover, risking all in order to satisfy them both, and yet time was passing and there was still no indication that she might be pregnant.

One evening at Pontefract the King sent Sir Anthony Denny with a message to inform the Queen that he was on his way to visit her but Denny found her door bolted. He kept this to himself at the time.

On 27 August while at Pontefract Katherine received another shock. A face from the past arrived to remind her that it was impossible to hide all her secrets. Katherine must surely have thought that she had seen off Francis Dereham by bringing him to court and making him gifts of money, but he had fresh demands. Perhaps he had caught some wind of her affair, perhaps he was even jealous, for now the only way she could buy his silence was by appointing him to become her Private Secretary and Usher of her Chamber.

This was little short of madness, for it placed Dereham at the very heart of her private household and he was not noted for his discretion. In fact his insolence and braggadocio were certain to cause trouble.

Katherine had to warn him to 'take heed what words you speak'. This proved to no avail for soon he was boasting about having the Queen's special favours and even that they might marry once the King was dead.

Dereham was more than foolish. What he had said was tantamount to high treason, for no one was permitted to mention the King's death. Others had gone to the block for trying to guess – by black magic or astrology – this very thing. By allowing Francis Dereham back into her circle, Katherine thought it would be safer to control him, but she was playing with fire. He may have intended to blackmail her, but his loose tongue was even more of a hazard. Besides which, he still clearly thought that they had an understanding, a precontract of marriage between them, consummated by their broken love affair, which made them true husband and wife.

It was astonishing, in these circumstances, that Katherine ever imagined that she had succeeded in concealing her affair with Culpeper.

At the castle of Sheriff Hutton in Yorkshire Culpeper and the Queen exchanged gifts. He gave her a ring and she presented him with two bracelets. She also cautioned him that when he made confession before a priest he should be careful, for 'the King was supreme head of the church and therefore the Queen bade him beware that whensoever he went to confession he should never shrive him of any such things as should pass betwixt her and him, for if he did, surely the King, being supreme head of the church, should have knowledge of it'.

Culpeper laughed and many writers have also taken the view that it was Katherine's naiveté and indeed stupidity that made her assume the King was somehow omnipresent like God and knew everything that happened in church. But Katherine had seen for herself the means by which her husband worked, employing informers and agents who reported back to him on the activities of his enemies. Her words indicate her fear that any confession recklessly made by Culpeper regarding the Queen would get straight back to the King's ears even though this would be break-ing the silence of the confessional.

The tour moved on and by 16 September the royal party was in York. There had been high expectations that by now there would have been great news, perhaps even the birth of a new Duke of York. Another major building project had been under way day and night, employing a thousand workmen to finish Henry's palace in the north. This was on the ruins of St Mary's Abbey, now known as King's Manor, for which the King had brought from London fine furnishings including his 'richest tapestry, plate and dress, both for himself and his archers, pages and gentlemen, with marvellous provision of victuals from all parts'.

Officially this was for a meeting between the King and James V of Scotland, who was expected to rendezvous for a peace confer-ence. But although Henry waited until the end of September, the Scots delegation failed to show. Being without an heir, James may well have distrusted Henry, fearing that he would be taken pris-oner or held hostage by the old enemy.

Were the preparations, Marillac wondered, for the meeting with James V of Scotland? Or were they for Katherine's coronation in the Minster, which would follow the birth of a Duke of York? But it was not to be; the long-expected coronation of the Queen did not take place. Instead Henry held another assembly offering par-don to those who had rebelled against him during the northern revolt.

Surrounded by clergy, those begging to be forgiven knelt in the street reciting their faults before the King: 'we wretches, for lack of grace and of sincere and pure knowledge of the verity of God's words have most grievously, heinously and wantonly offended your Majesty in the unnatural and most odious and detestable offences of outrageous disobedience and traitorous rebellion'.

To sway Henry's favour the City of York now offered up large sums of gold, which carried the day.

While her husband was preoccupied with affairs of state, Katherine was continuing with hers. King's Manor afforded the chance for more meetings with Culpeper and seems to have been so pleasant that she stayed on. But the summer was soon over and the royal progress drew to a close, with the court returning to London. There it would be even more dangerous to continue the affair, especially as there was no sign of a child and the King's moods were so unpredictable.

Whether Culpeper's affair with the Queen of England was her choice and responsibility alone, it has been the failure to grasp the reality of Katherine's age that deceives, creating a false assessment of her motives, participation and desires. She was neither the maligned innocent of Victorian biography nor the sexually liberated feminist of modern fiction.

In all this Henry has been the object of excessive pity for Katherine's betrayal of him, but a different explanation is required where a woman with her history is concerned. A child of 12 is a victim, not a promiscuous man-eater, nor is a 15-year-old bride married to a man 35 years her senior solely responsible for the failure of their marriage. But, to the 16th-century mind, the woman was always to blame. In Shakespeare's *Othello*, Iago's wife Emilia radically defies convention when she speaks up boldly on behalf of her sex:

'I do think it is their husband's faults if wives do fall ...
        Then let them use us well; else let them know,
The ills we do, their ills instruct us so.' (*Othello*, III iv.86–87,105–106)

Having inspected plans for his northern fortifications, the King and his great retinue moved south again, arriving back at Windsor Castle on 26 October. There he received the disturbing news that his son Edward, Prince of Wales, had been taken seriously ill, 'sick of a quartan fever, an unusual malady for a child of three or four years', as Ambassador Marillac records. 'All the physicians of the country' were summoned but the 'Prince was so fat and unhealthy as to be unlikely to live long'.

This was a severe blow to Henry, especially coming so quickly after his successful progress. From being in a calm and contented mood, he was now thrown into an immediate panic that he might lose his precious son and heir. It took considerable reassurances from the physicians and the Queen to keep him calm until he heard that the boy was past the crisis and would live.

Besides this, the news of the death of the King's sister Margaret, Queen Mother of Scotland, paled into insignificance. It did perhaps explain why her son James V had not turned up at the summit meeting in York, preferring to stay at his mother's bedside.

Henry's mood was jittery as the royal party moved on to Hampton Court. The King presented his wife with a new piece of jewellery to celebrate their return. This brooch extravagantly depicted 'the story of Noah' and was set with 35 diamonds and 18 rubies. The King's mood had swung from black despair and fear to high good humour.

For All Saints' Day, 1 November, Henry had commanded that all churches offer special prayers of thanksgiving for the Queen, his 'jewel of womanhood' and 'the good life he led and trusted to lead' with her at his side. The King's pride in her was reported to his Council.

Henry and Katherine now appeared to be enjoying a renewal of their honeymoon idyll. But this illusion was soon to be shattered. For when the King arrived to hear mass in the Chapel Royal at Hampton Court the following day, he discovered a letter left for him in the royal pew.

While the court had been touring the north of England, in London the Archbishop of Canterbury had been contacted with urgent news by John Lascelles, one of the sewers who served the King's food, tasting for poison every dish set before the monarch.

Who was John Lascelles? A courtier and member of the reform movement in London, born in 1510, he was the son of well-respected lesser gentry from Gateford in Nottinghamshire. John was very well educated and spoke Latin, Greek, court French and some German. He graduated from Oxford in 1530 and studied for the law at Furnivall's, one of the ten Inns of Chancery, gaining a place at Middle Temple in 1535. He was soon deeply involved in London's reform circles and sent his mother a copy of Tyndale's New Testament in English: 'I write not this to bring you into any heresies, but to teach you the clear light of God's doctrine ... for the Gospel of Christ was never so truly preached as it is now. Wherefore I pray to God that he will give you grace to have knowledge of his Scriptures.'

Lascelles was soon employed as one of Cromwell's messengers, listed as one of those 'Gentlemen most meet to be daily waiters upon my said Lord'. He was one of the few with cause to regret and mourn Cromwell's fall: 'so noble a man which did love and favour [God's holy word]'.

Lascelles had a sister, Mary, who had been 'placed out' in the household of the Dowager Duchess of Norfolk at Horsham and in Lambeth. There she had become very well acquainted with the young Katherine Howard.

It was Mary Lascelles who had been shocked by the nocturnal antics in the women's dormitories. It was Mary who, out of concern for Katherine's tender age and reputation, had even confronted Henry Manox, the music master who had seduced the girl, vowing to 'have her maidenhead'.

Mary Lascelles had stood up for Katherine at Horsham, but her opinion changed when the Dowager's household moved to London. There she witnessed at first hand Katherine's affair with Francis Dereham taking place in the long room with much 'puffing and blowing' over 'more than a hundred nights'. In consequence, she thought Katherine 'light in both living and conditions'. But she kept her silence, at least until she heard that Katherine was to marry the King.

Unlike Joan Bulmer, who saw Katherine's meteoric rise as an opportunity for personal advancement, her colleague Mary Lascelles was horrified that the girl she had grown to know so well was about to become Queen of England.

Although she had married and was now Mary Hall, her brother

John had suggested that she approach her friend and ask for a place in her household as Joan Bulmer had done. But Mary had refused, saying, 'I cannot think of the queen but with sadness.' When John asked why, she told him that Katherine was 'so frivolous in character and in life'. She was then obliged to explain what she knew of Katherine's past and, although there were extenuating circumstances because of her age during the Manox entanglement, it was harder to find excuses for her long affair with Francis Dereham.

Lascelles was undoubtedly shocked by his sister's revelations. He later claimed that they said nothing publicly at the time because of the speed with which the King had divorced Anne of Cleves and announced his secret marriage to Katherine. For a year they had been burdened with this unwelcome knowledge about the Queen, afraid to come forward and yet anxious about the consequences of keeping silent.

The King's savage reputation was well known and he was quite likely to turn on anyone who brought such news about his young wife, even if it was the truth. But then again Henry might react with equal violence if he discovered that this had been deliberately kept from him.

However, another version of the story suggests it was only in the summer of 1541 that John heard about the Queen when he visited his sister in Sussex after her marriage.

Brother and sister had nothing to gain from revealing secrets of the Queen's past. Mary felt no malice towards Katherine. She had, after all, tried to protect the girl from Manox. But Katherine had not followed her advice, plunging ahead into a fresh liaison with another adventurer and apparently enjoying every moment of it.

No one could have been more astonished than Mary when she learnt that Katherine was about to become the King's fifth wife. It was less of a surprise to discover that the Duke of Norfolk and Bishop Gardiner were involved in a plot to dangle her before the King. Her brother John owed his position at court to Thomas Cromwell, whom Norfolk and Gardiner had destroyed. The close servants of the King would hold Bible study meetings and on 15

September the group had still been lamenting Cromwell's fall. They blamed Norfolk and Bishop Gardiner, whom they saw as agents of the papal Antichrist, but Lascelles said, 'If we wait quietly and do not oppose Norfolk and Winchester, but rather suffer a while in silence, they will overthrow themselves. For they stand so obviously against God and their Prince that they cannot long survive.'

The victory of the Catholic party at court could only be a threat to the reform faith that the Lascelles family followed. Eventually John decided to approach the only person he could trust with these revelations, Archbishop Thomas Cranmer.

Spilling out his story to Cranmer may have eased Lascelles' conscience but it presented the Archbishop with a poisoned chalice. Cranmer was aware of Lascelles' reformist beliefs and had every reason to believe him. He also knew that he held dramatic information that could bring down the Queen, a Howard and the Catholic pawn of the enemies of the reform religion, Norfolk and Gardiner.

The Archbishop had seen the King's infatuation for his young bride and even after a year, with no sign of a pregnancy, there was no indication that Henry was tiring of her. It would be a brave man who dared to tell the King the truth about his unblemished rose.

Cranmer now faced a great dilemma. Should he boldly approach Henry with Lascelles' evidence or keep silent and pray that no whisper of the Queen's past would come to light? That seemed unlikely, for, as Lascelles had told him, there were many other witnesses to Katherine's exploits at both Horsham and Lambeth, not least the Dowager Duchess Agnes herself. Although she was unlikely to give her granddaughter away, any one of her chamberers, perhaps even the Queen's lovers, might come forward with their stories at some later date.

Shrewdly, Cranmer, 'being much perplexed', concluded that the 'weight and importance of the matter' obliged him to share the information with Lord Audley and Edward Seymour, Earl of Hertford, who was certainly no friend of the Howards. 'Having weighed the matter and deeply pondered the gravity thereof', they decided the King must be told.

'Unwilling to speak on so delicate a subject', Cranmer 'had not the heart to tell him by mouth' but penned the letter with the details of Lascelles' testimony: that Manox knew a privy mark on the Queen's body and Francis Dereham had lain with her. It was a hard task which 'no man durst take in hand to open him that wound', as Cranmer's secretary Ralph Morice records. All of this so far referred only to Katherine's affairs before she was married to the King. The Archbishop stated that he was concerned to warn the King before he heard it from someone else.

On 29 October Cranmer was waiting at Hampton Court when the royal party returned from its progress. It was only four days later that the opportunity arose for him to leave his letter in the King's private pew at mass. The King entered the Chapel Royal unaware of the storm about to break but as he broke the seal and began to read, the colour drained from his face.

It seemed as if history was repeating itself, but these accusations against the Queen were very different to those of 1536. Then it was the King himself who had instigated a scheme to be rid of his wife. He had demanded that Cromwell find a way out of a marriage that had split the Church, humiliated him in the eyes of the world and singularly failed to produce a male heir. Knowing that his career, if not his life was on the line, Cromwell set to work 'to fabricate and plot' the coup designed to bring down Anne Boleyn.

This time Henry was genuinely shocked to be told that his wife was not the pure, unsullied virgin bride that he had thought. His first reaction was one of disbelief. He could not accept that the girl who had restored his manhood and given him back his youth had been no better than a whore. Two lovers, perhaps more, before the age of 14? It seemed incredible.

Outwardly calm, yet inwardly seething, the King summoned Cranmer to a private conference and heard for himself the full story. Henry had been so confident of Katherine's innocence that at first he would not believe a word of the Archbishop's testimony.

Cranmer was now in great danger. Unless he could prove that John Lascelles was not lying, his own life was at risk.

The King then summoned the new Lord Privy Seal, William Fitzwilliam, and Russell, his High Admiral, together with Sir Anthony Brown and Wriothesley, the King's Secretary. Henry briefed them quickly, insisting he did not believe a word of Lascelles' story, yet his own innate jealousy and suspicion were already at work and he told them to put John Lascelles to the test.

The brother and sister were perhaps liars, hoping for money or a place at court. They were to be examined, new details gleaned and verified. In the words of Shakespeare's *Othello*, the rumours about his wife must also be proved:

> If I do prove her haggard,
> Though that her jesses were my dear heart-strings,
> I'd whistle her off, and let her down the wind
> To prey at fortune. (*Othello*, III.iii. 258–263)

These hawking and falconry terms express the relationship between the master and his bird, his possession in whom he takes the pride of ownership.

Fitzwilliam subsequently interrogated John Lascelles but could not shake his testimony. Lascelles, nervous but resolute, would neither change nor retract one word of his evidence. This was Fitzwilliam's report to the King at Hampton Court, much to Cranmer's relief.

Now the King had no option but to order a full and thorough investigation into his wife's past activities. Already Henry was raging about his 'ill-luck in meeting with such ill-conditioned wives'.

When Desdemona is exposed as sullied, no longer a 'jewel' (I. iii.60, 193) or, like Katherine, a rose, Othello laments,

> When I have pluck'd the rose,
> I cannot give it vital growth again,
> It must needs wither.

The thought that Katherine was no virgin when she came to the King was a bitter blow to Henry's fantasy of pure innocence. Although she was only a child when she witnessed the activities in the women's dormitory at Horsham, he found it impossible to excuse her. She had suddenly become tainted, dirty, transformed into a woman with a sexual appetite, and this at a time when women were viewed as more sexually voracious and susceptible to sin than men.

Shakespeare may well have had Henry in mind when he made Othello demand proof of Desdemona's guilt: Iago must 'prove (her) a whore' (III.iii.359), as Henry seeks evidence against Katherine. Othello cries,

> O curse of marriage!
> That we can call these delicate creatures ours,
> And not their appetites! I had rather be a toad
> And live upon the vapour of a dungeon
> Than keep a corner in the thing I love
> For others' uses. (III.iii.268–273)

There is no possibility of taking back the disgraced wife who has humiliated her husband by making him a cuckold and sullying their marriage bed. Henry's pride, his vanity and inherently vengeful character would never permit him to forgive the woman he had raised up to be his Queen.

Chapter Fifteen

Past Secrets

ON FRIDAY 4 NOVEMBER, Katherine was in her chambers at Hampton Court Palace, unaware of the horrors about to descend upon her. When the sound of boots rang in the corridor and armed guards suddenly burst into the room they found her practising dance steps. Abruptly she was told 'it is no more the time to dance' and that she was under arrest and must keep to her chambers.

Katherine was unable to understand what had happened. She demanded to see the King, but her request was ignored. She must have thought that Henry would sort out this obvious mistake if only she could see him. When the guards refused to let her leave her apartments, she became hysterical.

Katherine was rightly terrified. No one told her what had happened and her imagination must have run riot. Scarcely three days before the King had praised her as his jewel, his rose, appearing ecstatically happy with his young wife. What could possibly have happened in such a short space of time to bring about this swift turnaround in his mood and his opinion of her?

Left alone with her tumbling thoughts, she was aware that it could only signify one thing: someone had betrayed her to the King.

In her secret guilt, Katherine at first must have assumed that someone she trusted had informed upon her affair with Thomas Culpeper. What else could have happened to turn Henry from her? She was to spend the next anxious days and sleepless nights waiting for someone to talk to her. She had no idea that so far Henry only knew about her links with Manox and Dereham, before she was married.

Earlier on 4 November Fitzwilliam had set out from Hampton Court for a 'hunting trip' to Sussex in order to examine the crucial witness for the prosecution, Mary Hall. At the same time Henry Manox and Francis Dereham were secretly apprehended by the King's officers and taken for examination by Wriothesley and Archbishop Cranmer.

Everything was done with the utmost discretion in order to keep the growing royal scandal under cover until sufficient evidence had been found to prove conclusively that the Queen had deceived the King about her past.

Mary Hall confirmed every detail of her brother's story. She told her stern examiner that she had found the sexual games at Horsham and Lambeth shocking. She then related how she had sought out and confronted Manox herself to challenge him about his association with Katherine. Unfortunately, Manox was not at all intimidated and had openly boasted of his seduction of the young girl, claiming with callous brutality: 'I know her well enough, for I have had her by the cunt and I know it among a hundred.'

Manox was subsequently arrested and held for questioning at Lambeth. Thomas Wriothesley had worked for Cromwell and was regarded an expert in interrogation techniques, including the use of torture. There was no one better suited to prising out the full sordid details of hidden secrets.

Manox was surely aware of the great danger in which he stood, but although he readily admitted to his attempts to seduce Katherine, he insisted on his innocence. Yes, of course he had attempted to take her, he reasoned, and she teased him by granting him some favours, but they had never had full sexual relations. Manox admitted to Wriothesley that he was the instigator of the affair with the 11-year-old girl. He confessed that he had solicited her, urging her to 'Let me feel your secret … and then I shall think that indeed you love me.'

His persuasion had clearly worked and among those intimate favours Katherine granted him, Manox 'had commonly used to feel the secrets and other parts of the Queen's body'. He told Wriothesley that 'he felt more than was convenient', coming to discover a 'privy mark' there, and yet he still vowed 'upon his damnation and most extreme punishment of his body, he never knew her carnally.'

Manox must have been under no illusion that his fate was sealed.

Mary Lascelles-Hall was not the only one to know of his business with Katherine. The Dowager Duchess herself had caught them red-handed. But perhaps some residue of affection for the girl he once knew remained to keep him silent about the identities of the other occupants of the girls' dormitory who knew what else the Queen had done. Possibly he imagined that she might still be saved.

Francis Dereham, however, proved less than gallant. In his terror at being seized and arrested, he at once started confessing the truth about his relationship with Katherine. Without much persuasion he blurted out that he 'had known her carnally many times, both in his doublet and hose between the sheets and naked in bed'.

Wriothesley was encouraged but even this was not enough. The mere fact that the Queen had taken Dereham into her personal service in a position that gave him access to her private quarters provided sufficient grounds to suspect that their affair had continued after her marriage to the King. But he needed proof and Dereham hotly denied that their affair had been resumed.

The King found it difficult to sleep. When Wriothesley arrived to deliver his report on the interrogations so far, he called in his councillors for a secret midnight conference. Henry listened in silence as Wriothesley read out the confessions. He was forced to accept that John Lascelles and his sister had been telling the truth, but his instinct told him that there was yet more than either man had confessed.

On 5 November, about midnight, Henry summoned Thomas Howard, Duke of Norfolk, to Hampton Court. The King had been fooled and deceived. It was unlikely that the girl's uncle had known nothing about her activities.

The next morning he rose early and went to the Chapel Royal for mass before joining Norfolk and Audley on the pretext of hunting at a lodge nearby. As Henry knelt in his pew and listened to the sweet singing of the choir his mind may have been in turmoil but did he hear anything of a struggle outside in the corridor?

There is a legend at Hampton Court Palace that Katherine Howard made one last, desperate attempt to see her husband. The story goes that, knowing Henry was at service in the Chapel Royal, she broke free of her rooms and ran down the long gallery to try and talk to him and convince him of her innocence.

This gallery linking the chapel and royal apartments was built by Cardinal Wolsey. Today it is known as the Haunted Gallery, for it is said that Katherine's ghost is seen here, running and screaming in her panic as she calls Henry's name.

Katherine may have tried to reach Henry, but it is certain she did not succeed. She was presumably caught long before she came anywhere near the King and dragged away by her guards. Henry may have heard her but he certainly did not see her.

Once cast out of the King's intimate circle, it was as if the sun has gone out. Henry was far too much of a coward to come face to face with a prisoner once he was resolved to be rid of him. He had cut Anne Boleyn from his mind the moment Cromwell put his plan into action and it was the same with Katherine. Once he knew she had betrayed him, he blanked her out of his life, just as though she no longer existed.

After mass that Sunday, having perhaps heard his wife's screams in the gallery outside the chapel, Henry met with his councillors and dined 'at a little place in the fields'. Here, under the King's attentive gaze, Norfolk was confronted with the shocking news of his niece's reputation. We can imagine his reaction: the show of outrage and astonishment concealing his panic as he tried to convince Henry that he knew nothing about it.

Whether he really knew about Katherine and her early affairs or not, Norfolk surely realised that his performance now would either make or break the Howards. In the case of his other niece, Anne Boleyn, it had been much easier for him to reject and denounce her. Not only had the Boleyns broken away from the Howards on the issue of religion and patronage, but Anne had lost her power over the King and become a liability, so Norfolk became the initiator of her downfall.

With Katherine, the situation was quite different. Norfolk had selected the girl to be bait for the King on the recommendation of his stepmother Agnes. Looking her over in the house at Lambeth he had thought her perfect for the plan hatched with Gardiner. It is hardly likely that Norfolk was entirely unaware of what had gone on in his stepmother's house while Katherine was living there, but now he had to brazen it out while the real blame lay with the Dowager Duchess.

That evening Henry slipped away from Hampton Court in secret to return to London with the tide. He had turned his back on his wife, although at this point he knew only of her affairs prior to their marriage. They were neither adulterous nor treasonable. All that had been hurt was his pride, but that was enough for him to reject her completely and demand a way out of the marriage. Katherine would never see him again.

The Privy Council met in an emergency all-night session at Bishop Gardiner's palace in Southwark. Ironically enough, this was where Gardiner and Norfolk had first introduced the King to Katherine, but now it was the site of a meeting designed to bring about her removal. Henry was still at great pains to conceal the scandal but Ambassador Marillac soon realised something serious had happened for he noted curiously, 'They show themselves very troubled, especially Norfolk.'

The King vented his fury at being deceived. He was in one of his worst black rages, allegedly calling for a sword to kill the Queen. Then he broke down and began to cry copious tears of self-pity. Those present thought he had gone mad.

He is said to have denounced Katherine as 'That wicked woman!' insisting that 'She never had such delight in her lovers as she shall have torture in her death!'

If true, this shows that Henry was already contemplating her elimination, although no grounds yet existed for an annulment or divorce, let alone her execution. We must remember that so far he was still ignorant of her adultery with Thomas Culpeper.

Henry's character and past record offered little hope for clemency. He could not tolerate the humiliation of his wife's deception and was determined to extract vengeance. His parting words were ominous indeed: 'I blame my council for this mischief!'

Then he departed, taking barge for Westminster. His councillors, still shell-shocked, had been commanded to force a full confession from the Queen. It was decided that in the morning Cranmer and a delegation from the Council must return to Hampton Court to confront Katherine herself.

Norfolk was one of those who accompanied the archbishop. He was surely walking on eggshells. He knew that Wriothesley was carrying out a thorough investigation of Katherine's life at the Howard houses of Lambeth and Horsham. If he knew the truth about her past then he must have genuinely feared that the whole sordid business would come tumbling out to her shame and the disgrace of the entire family.

His many enemies would be quick to use the scandal to implicate the Howards and, by association, the entire Catholic party at court. The reform faction would take full advantage of this opportunity to blame them for making a fool of the King.

Norfolk knew of old that nothing would appease the King. The Howards were tottering on the edge of the abyss. He realised that unless he pushed Katherine over the precipice first, she would drag down the entire dynasty with her.

On Monday 7 November, Cranmer and Norfolk arrived to interrogate the Queen in her chambers. She was still in a terrified state, kept without information and tormented by fear, obliged to guess what had happened. She had no idea that the King, her once loving husband, had left the palace and abandoned her to her fate.

Katherine was crying when she met them, and apparently grew hysterical when she saw her uncle and his coldness towards her. Both Norfolk and Cranmer attempted to get her to confess, but in her panic they got nowhere and were forced to retire and think again.

An order was subsequently issued by the Council for the arrest of Agnes, the Dowager Duchess of Norfolk, Lord William Howard and his wife, together with various women who had been at Horsham and Lambeth and might know of Katherine's past. These included Katherine Tylney, Joan Bulmer and Margaret Morton, but the Dowager's former chamberer Mary Lascelles was not among them. The Council reported that she was 'an encouragement to others to reveal like cases, not to be troubled'.

Before her arrest the Dowager Duchess had the opportunity to burn certain incriminating papers, including letters she had retrieved by breaking into Dereham's coffers. She also attempted to hide her money. These actions suggest that she had received warning of an impending visit by the King's agents, surely from Norfolk, her stepson.

The story that came tumbling out only served to exacerbate the situation, involving more and more witnesses to the sexual goings-on under the Dowager's roof. Edward Waldegrave confessed that he had been a visitor, bearing his gifts of 'wine, strawberries, apples and other things to make good cheer' in the women's long room. There was no privacy and everyone there knew exactly what was going on.

Alice Restwold, who 'wist what matrimony meant', told of that 'puffing and blowing' in Katherine's bed. When questioned, Margaret Benet declared that she had seen 'Dereham pluck up clothes above her navel so that he might well discern her body'. She had heard 'Dereham say that although he used the company of a woman …yet he would get no child except he listed'.

Yet still no one had mentioned Thomas Culpeper.

On 8 November Cranmer returned to Hampton Court to see Katherine alone. She met him with trepidation, still uncertain exactly what was known or not known. The archbishop regarded her with sympathy, later recording, 'I found her in such lamentation and heaviness as I never saw no creature, so that it would have pitied any man's heart in the world, to have looked upon her.'

First he warned her of the 'grievousness of her demerits' and the penalty 'she ought to suffer' then he suggested that there was still the hope of forgiveness if she would only confess to him. 'This sudden mercy' put Katherine into a panic. Cranmer thought that his 'words of comfort coming last might peradventure have come too late' and feared that she would fall into 'some dangerous ecstasy'. At last he induced her to sit down, suggesting that if she would only confess her faults she would receive pardon. He urged her to write her confession in a letter for the King.

Katherine was neither sufficiently literate nor in any mood to compose such a traumatic declaration herself. The words were surely influenced by Cranmer, copied out by the frightened girl. Katherine was, of course, very young, still incredibly only 16 years of age. The extraordinary experiences of her short life make us forget just how immature she really was. She wrote in her childish hand:

I, Your Grace's most sorrowful subject and most vile wretch in the world, not worthy to make any recommendation unto your most excellent Majesty, do only make my most humble submission and confession of my faults. Whereas no cause of mercy is deserved on my part, yet of your most accustomed mercy extended unto all other men undeserved, most humbly on my hands and knees I do desire one particle thereof to be extended unto me, although of all other creatures I am most unworthy to be called either your wife or your subject.

Cranmer must have thought of the many letters that Thomas Cromwell, a self-educated but outstandingly intelligent prisoner, had written to the King in his desperation, albeit in vain. He no doubt recalled another Queen pleading for her life, whom the King had so cold-bloodedly abandoned to her fate, Katherine's own cousin, Anne Boleyn. Did Katherine think of her, too, as she laboriously copied out Cranmer's letter?

> My sorrow I can by no writing express, nevertheless I trust your most benign nature will have some respect unto my youth, my ignorance, my frailness, my humble confession of my faults, and plain declaration of the same referring me wholly unto Your Grace's pity and mercy.

Katherine allowed Cranmer to instruct her, confessing to her relationship with Manox and Dereham:

> First, at the flattering and fair persuasions of Manox, being but a young girl, I suffered him at sundry times to handle and touch the secret parts of my body which neither became me with honesty to permit nor him to require. Also, Francis Derehem by many persuasions procured me to his vicious purpose and obtained first to lie upon my bed with his doublet and hose and after within the bed and finally he lay with me naked, and used me in such sort as a man doth his wife many and sundry times, but how often I know not. Our company ended almost a year before the King's Majesty was married to my Lady Anne of Cleves and continued not past one quarter of a year or little above.

This was her 'abominable, base, carnal, voluptuous and vicious life' *before* she became Queen. But she surely marvelled that no mention had been made of Thomas Culpeper.

> Now the whole truth being declared unto Your Majesty, I most humbly beseech you to consider the subtle persuasions of young men and the ignorance and frailness of young women. I was so desirous to be taken unto Your Grace's favour, and so blinded by with the desire of worldly glory that I could not, nor had grace to consider how great a fault it was to conceal my former faults from

Your Majesty, considering that I intended ever during my life to be faithful and true unto Your Majesty ever after. Nevertheless, the sorrow of my offences was ever before my eyes, considering the infinite goodness of Your Majesty toward me from time to time ever increasing and not diminishing. Now I refer the judgement of mine offences with my life and death wholly unto your most benign and merciful grace, to be considered by no justice of Your Majesty's laws but only by your infinite goodness, pity, compassion and mercy without the which I acknowledge myself worthy of the most extreme punishment.

Katherine had heard that Culpeper was still at liberty, hunting with the King. She could not send to warn him, but according to the later testimony of Jane Parker, Lady Rochford: 'The Queen three or four times every day since she was in this trouble would ask what she heard of Culpeper?'

Katherine herself had a different version of events. When she begged Jane not to betray her affair, Lady Rochford had promised, 'I will never confess it, to be torn with wild horses.' Still no one had mentioned Culpeper, and Katherine could only pray that it would remain that way.

On 8 and 9 November so many new prisoners were arrested and taken to the Tower that there was scarcely room for all of them. The conscientious and ambitious Thomas Wriothesley instructed his team of interrogators to 'travail and labour to find out the bottom of the pot if it may be gotten out'. He asked for detailed reports of the examination of the witnesses who had known Katherine at Horsham and Lambeth. He told the Council it was necessary 'that we may peruse them and pick all such things out of them as may serve to the purpose of our business'.

During interrogation, Duchess Agnes was asked, 'in what sort she did educate and bring up Mistress Katherine and what change of apparel she was wont yearly and ordinarily to give her?' The questioners demanded to know when she had 'first knowledge that the King's Highness favoured Mistress Katherine?' This suggests they thought there was a conspiracy underpinning

Katherine's involvement with the King. The Dowager was examined 'both to make her confess [and] also to cough out the rest not yet discovered if any such dregs remain amongst them'. She was soon 'so meshed and tangled' that she 'fell on her knees' and confessed that she had hidden £800 from the King's agents. When Wriothesley learnt this, he became convinced that she must have even more to hide.

Lord William Howard, Katherine's uncle, was imprisoned for his failure to divulge the truth about his niece's character. He made his position worse by claiming that most of his silver and plate had been lost at sea en route home from France. The King's Council was darkly suspicious of this explanation, and while Lord William remained in the Tower, they gave orders to investigate whether this was true or some 'crafty means to conceal and embezzle the same'.

Francis Dereham was suddenly confronted with the testimony of his friend Robert Davenport, who had confessed that Dereham had called Katherine 'his own wife' before witnesses, which was tantamount to a precontract of marriage under canon law. He had claimed to be so sure of Katherine that he had rashly said if the King 'were dead I am sure I might marry her'.

Dereham's own words were enough to condemn him, for according to the 1534 treason act this was evidence that he had maliciously desired the death of the King.

This new law on the nature of treason permitted a charge based primarily on 'intent'. It was treason to 'maliciously wish, will or desire by words or writing, or by craft imagine' the King's death or harm.

Cranmer's focus now shifted to the possibility that the King's marriage might be annulled on the grounds of a precontract with Francis Dereham. If, as suggested by numerous witnesses, the couple had made promises to one another and called each other husband and wife, then the marriage to the King could be proved invalid, thus saving Katherine from a trial and probable execution.

Cranmer was all too experienced in such a business. He had been sent to Queen Anne when she was a prisoner in the Tower, trying to convince her to admit to a precontract of marriage with

Henry Percy of Northumberland. Although Percy had denied that their betrothal had been consummated by any sexual affair – the prerequisite for a valid precontract – Cranmer was able to convince the Queen to consent and therefore declare a divorce between her and the King. She had been persuaded to agree to what was certainly a lie only because Cranmer had offered her the chance of freedom. Cromwell had suggested that she would be sent abroad to live in exile with her daughter Elizabeth, but it proved not to be true. Although Cranmer had divorced Anne from the King, Henry still went ahead and executed her for the crime of adultery.

Such was the devious and treacherous master whom Cranmer served. The archbishop could have had few illusions about Henry, but he was determined to try and find an escape for Katherine if he could. Although she had sinned, she had also been just a child of 11 when Manox ruined her reputation. Surrounded by the experienced and wanton women in the Dowager's employ, what else did the girl know? The fault was surely that of her absent father, Duchess Agnes and her uncle Norfolk, who were responsible for her welfare.

Cranmer presented this way out to Katherine, seeking to get her admission that she and Dereham had made each other a pledge of marriage. But Katherine was not willing to cooperate. She only saw that to acknowledge a previous marriage or betrothal to Dereham would make her wedding to the King invalid, meaning that she had never been the rightful Queen.

Now all her Howard pride in the family heritage and name came out. She refused to sign, proudly exclaiming that a man such as Francis Dereham was too lowly to wed a Howard and that she had told him so. However much Cranmer tried to make her grasp this one last lifeline, she remained adamant that she was Queen.

Meanwhile in London the industrious Thomas Wriothesley had persuaded Francis Dereham under torture to talk freely. Such was his pain on the rack that he tried to divert his tormentor's attention by talking of his rival, one of the King's own gentlemen, Thomas Culpeper. Wriothesley's interest was immediately caught as he recognised 'an appearance of greater abomination', just as he had suspected.

Culpeper's room at court was secretly searched. At this point, Wriothesley did not want his new target alerted to his investigation, nor the King further troubled until evidence of the involvement of his favourite servant could be proved. Among Culpeper's private papers Wriothesley's agents discovered the letter from Katherine that she had written in April when he was sick.

He had foolishly kept this proof of their relationship, though whether from affection or as some kind of insurance policy for the future is unknown. Here was the kind of 'evidence' which Wriothesley's team were eagerly seeking. The Queen's letter to Culpeper left no one in any doubt that she had been involved in an adulterous affair.

Adultery was a far more serious crime than mere fornication. A wife was her husband's personal property and to interfere with that property in any way was an assault on his honour and that of his family. Even in Victorian times a husband could sue his wife's lover for personal damages. But in the 16th century the lovers were often required to pay the ultimate penalty. Isabella de' Medici was murdered by her husband Paolo Giordano Orsini for suspected adultery and in *Arden of Faversham*, the 'disloyal and wanton' wife is shown as destructive to all of society through her wicked ways.

Adultery was subversive because it compromised the true bloodline of a family with the possibility of an illegitimate child being passed off as the rightful heir. Nothing could be more dangerous to a society where inheritance and genealogical ties carried so much weight. In the case of the King, and a King with an uncertain line of succession, this was nothing short of treason.

That a mere servant, Thomas Culpeper, should have dared to touch the property of the King was an outrage. That the Queen had actively encouraged him was a national scandal. Her heartfelt words to Culpeper were incriminating enough to condemn her:

... send me word how that you do, for I never longed so much for a thing as I do to see you and to speak with you ... when I think again that you shall depart from me again it makes my heart die to think what fortune I have that I cannot be always in your company. It my trust is always in you that you will be as you have promised me ... Yours as long as life endures.

In an age when women were presented as dishonest and dangerous creatures who lusted after men and sought to entrap them in sin, Katherine's words seem naively romantic. To quote Helkiah Crooke, writing in 1615: 'Females are more wanton and petulant than Males, we think happeneth because of the impotency of their minds; for the imaginations of lustfull women are like the imaginations of brute beasts which have no repugnancy or contradiction of reason to restrain them.'

Perhaps Wriothesley and his investigators reasoned it was so with the Queen, who had been initiated into the wanton ways of women in the Dowager's household at such an impressionable age.

On 11 November the Privy Council ordered that the Queen's household was to be broken up. Most of her ladies were removed for questioning, leaving just a few to attend her. The Queen suddenly found herself confined to two rooms. All her jewels were seized, together with the dazzling gowns, diamond and pearl-encrusted headdresses and purses.

The Council also started to issue information to their ambassadors abroad, including Sir William Paget in Paris: 'The King ... being solicited by his Council to marry again took to wife Katherine ...thinking now in his old age to have obtained a jewel for womanhood, but this joy is turned to extreme sorrow ... having heard that she was not a woman of such purity as was esteemed.'

They concluded brutally, 'Now you may see what was done before marriage. God knoweth what hath been done since.'

Chapter Sixteen

The Cuckold's Vengeance

WRIOTHESLEY HIMSELF went to interrogate Katherine 'to get of her more information … (upon) the matter now come forth concerning Culpeper'. Her ladies were also being questioned further, this time in relation to their mistress's recent activities.

Anne Fox testified that she had known for 'a year past that the Queen was of ill disposition'. Katherine Tylney had already talked about the nocturnal parties held at Lambeth. Now she recalled how at Lincoln, on the royal progress, the Queen was away for hours visiting Lady Rochford's chamber on the staircase above her own. She had asked Margaret Morton, 'Jesus, is not the queen abed yet?' But when they pressed as to who the Queen might have been meeting there, her interrogators were disappointed. She had not seen anyone who could have been with the Queen in the middle of the night or who had left secretly before dawn.

It was Margaret Morton who named Culpeper. Deeply afraid, she confessed to her interrogators that she had never suspected the Queen of any misdemeanour until the time of the royal progress: 'I never mistrusted the Queen until at Hatfield I saw her look out of her chamber window on Master Culpeper after such sort that I thought there was love between them.'

She was also persuaded to recall that on a later occasion the Queen had been alone with Culpeper for more than five hours. From the noises coming from the Queen's chamber she thought they had 'passed out'. This was a common euphemism at the time for reaching orgasm.

While this was all music to Wriothesley's ears, it was still disappointing that none of the witnesses had actually been present when such an act took place. But the helpful Margaret Morton had named Jane Parker, Lady Rochford as 'the principal occasion of the Queen's folly' and she was now brought to explain her role in the Queen's affair.

Katherine's closest confidante was arrested and taken to the Beauchamp Tower in the Tower of London. It was no lowly dungeon but a series of rooms that housed those high-ranking prisoners who had earned the King's suspicion. However, it was still prison and there Lady Rochford suffered what appears to have been a complete nervous collapse – her contemporaries concluded that she had gone mad. Rightly terrified, Jane denied everything at first, trying to disassociate herself from Katherine and Culpeper. This singularly failed to convince anyone of her innocence and she was forced to accept that incriminating evidence existed against the Queen.

Jane Parker now denounced her mistress exactly as she had betrayed her own sister-in-law, Anne Boleyn, just four years before. The difference was that then she had acted as an *agent provocateur* for Anne's enemies and her previous 'evidence' had been false. Now she claimed that she had acted at all times upon the Queen's explicit instructions. She blurted out the times when Culpeper had visited Katherine, meeting in her room while she stood guard. She admitted that one night the King had sent Sir Anthony Denny to tell the Queen that her husband was on his way to share her bed, but discovered her door was bolted. Culpeper had to make a hasty escape down the backstairs.

In her testimony, Jane portrayed herself as a devoted servant, helpless to stop the lovers. She had just been following orders. She had never witnessed the act itself, although on one occasion she was actually asleep in a chair in the same room. But when asked whether she believed that adultery had taken place, she admitted 'that Culpeper hath known the Queen carnally, considering all things that she hath heard and seen between them'.

There can be no doubt that Jane Parker, Lady Rochford, was a strange and cold-blooded woman. She had been willing to send her husband George Boleyn and the Queen his sister to their deaths on a ludicrous charge of incest. Eventually reappointed to royal service, she seems to have won Katherine's trust, perhaps because she seemed more like an older sister or even a mother figure. That was the impression that Katherine herself conveyed when Wriothesley went to tell her he knew about Culpeper.

It was the fulfilment of her worst fears. Yet Katherine still attempted to avoid the truth, painting for Wriothesley the picture of courtly love, an unrequited romance that could have come straight from any number of poems or songs. Culpeper was simply a gallant knight sighing for his lady, fully aware that she is beyond him and physically unattainable.

Katherine admitted that she had been flattered, that she had called him her 'little sweet fool' and even given him tokens of her affection. She insisted that Lady Rochford had taken Culpeper's part, pleading his suit to her, urging her to speak to him. After her persistent nagging, the Queen had complained, 'Alas, madam, will this never end? I pray you, bid him desire no more to trouble me or send to me.' She finally agreed to see him on condition that he 'meant nothing but honesty'. Lady Rochford had sworn 'upon a book' that this was simply a game of courtly love.

Fitting the same mood of romantic love is the curious account written later by an anonymous Spanish chronicler. In *The Chronicle of Henry VIII* (also known as the *Spanish Chronicle*), a pretty but wildly inaccurate version of events, which is responsible for much of the legend surrounding Katherine Howard, he relates how Culpeper became obsessed with the young Queen and while dancing slipped her a note confessing his love for her. When Katherine passed him a reply in return, 'Culpeper was overjoyed beyond measure.'

In reality, Katherine claimed she had angrily warned Jane not to trouble her 'with such light matters' but the older woman had declared, 'Alas madame, this will be spied one day and then we be all undone.'

She hotly denied that she ever loved Culpeper, and insisted that although they had met secretly by night nothing at all had happened between them. She said it was Lady Rochford who 'would at every lodging search the back doors' for a way to let him in.

According to the anonymous Spanish chronicler, Katherine swooned when she was interrogated by Cromwell – as well she might, for he had then been dead for almost 18 months! In this version, Culpeper himself was interrogated by the Duke of Somerset, but Edward Seymour was then Earl of Hertford and would not become a duke for another five years.

Wriothesley returned to London to make his report, aware it was unsatisfactory without a full confession, which he felt certain that he could force from the Queen and her lover. For the present, the Council could only conclude that 'she hath not, as appeareth by her confession, so fully declared the circumstances of such communications as were betwixt her and Culpeper'.

That night, 12 November, Secretary Sadler wrote on behalf of the King, requiring Katherine to surrender her jewels, while in London a more significant event was taking place.

Thomas Culpeper was surprised on his return from accompanying the King hunting, arrested and taken to the Tower. There he was almost certainly put to the torture, as Dereham and Manox had been before him. According to Marillac, the French Ambassador, it was under torture that 'Dereham, to show his innocence since the marriage, said that Culpeper had succeeded him in the Queen's affections.'

The use of torture was controversial but highly regulated. Those officers who carried it out had royal immunity and were trained interrogators, keeping detailed reports of the questions and answers in each session. There was no official torture-chamber at the Tower, where prisoners were often questioned in their rooms or cells, or escorted to the basement of the White Tower.

It was usual to show a prisoner the rack first to persuade him that it was more sensible to talk. Only if he refused was the implement put into effect. The rack, also known as the Duke of Exeter's Daughter or 'the brake', was the invention of John Holland, Duke of Exeter, constable of the Tower in the 15th century under Henry VI. A search of the stores at the Tower in modern times discovered the remains of a rack, constructed of iron and with three wooden rollers, but minus its ropes. It was operated by turning levers in opposing directions to stretch the unfortunate victim, dislocating the limbs until they were finally torn from their sockets.

Variations existed in Spain, the *escalera* (ladder), in Germany, the *folter* (frame), and in France, the *chevalet* (little horse). The notorious 'Scavenger's Daughter', which compressed the body in a crouched position, was only found at the Tower, being named for Sir Leonard Skeffinton, a lieutenant there. Manacles suspended the prisoner off the ground, pilliwinks crushed the hands and pincers burnt flesh.

It is not known which methods were used on Katherine's lovers, but Wriothesley was pleased with the results. Robert Damport or Davenport confessed under torture that his friend Dereham had once bragged, 'An the King were dead I am sure I might marry her.' Wriothesley boasted to Secretary Sadler, 'And no torture could make him confess this before.' This was enough to secure a charge of high treason against Francis Dereham for desiring the King's death.

The heroic Culpeper portrayed in the *Spanish Chronicle* defied all torture, declaring valiantly that he had loved Katherine since childhood: 'Gentlemen, do not seek to know more than that the King deprived me of the thing I loved best in the world, and, though you may hang me for it, I can assure you that she loves me as well as I loved her, although up to this hour no wrong has ever passed between us. Before the King married her I thought to make her my wife, and when I saw her irremediably lost to me I was like to die.'

Although the idyllic yet platonic romance that is described never happened, in his agony on the rack Culpeper never admitted to having sex with the Queen. He later ungallantly claimed that she had been the instigator all along, trying to throw the blame on Katherine, stating that they met only at her insistence because she was 'languishing and dying of love for him'.

'He was then moved to set by others' but 'found so little favour at her hands' that he claimed to have been sleeping with someone else. Culpeper did admit, however, that 'he intended and meant to do ill with the Queen and that in like wise the Queen so minded to do with him'.

Now at last details of the scandal began to leak out. The Imperial Ambassador Chapuys reported to his master: 'This year on 13 November Sir Thomas Wriothesley, secretary to the king, came to Hampton Court to the queen, and called all the ladies and gentlewomen and her servants into the great chamber, and there openly before them declared certain offences she had committed in misusing her body with certain persons before the king's time, because of which he there discharged all her household.'

It was said, 'No pain so fervent, hot or cold as is a man to be called cuckold.'

A 'wittol' was a complacent husband who accepts being a cuckold and is perceived as a figure of fun, but there was nothing humorous about the King's reaction.

Henry saw himself as the wronged husband, who had trusted and raised up this simple girl to the heights as his wife in the assumption of her innocence and virtue. He had expected her to bear his sons, to establish the House of Tudor beyond all doubt before he died. The fact that she was not the pure and untouched virgin he had so hotly desired had shattered these illusions.

The Imperial Ambassador Chapuys declared cynically that the King's condition was like 'that of the woman who cried more bitterly at the loss of her tenth husband than she had on the death of the other nine put together ... the reason being that she had never buried one of them without being sure of the next, but that after the tenth husband she had no other in view, hence her sorrow and her lamentations'.

Henry's vanity had been touched and his pride had been rocked by the revelations against his wife, compounded by the shock of betrayal by his favourite Culpeper. Not only was she sullied by other, more lowly men and tutored in their basest desires but, he now suspected, she had chosen his own, devoted Culpeper to foist a bastard son upon the nation, passing it off as of royal blood.

That these two people whom he had raised from obscurity should have conspired together to make him appear ridiculous was a humiliation he could not – would not – forgive. Their fate was settled. He now instructed his Council to charge all those concerned with treason.

On 14 November Katherine was removed from Hampton Court and taken to Syon Abbey, where Lady Margaret Douglas was hastily freed to rejoin her friend Mary Howard at Kenninghall.

At Syon Katherine was held in a suite of rooms 'furnished moderately as her life and conditions hath deserved'. The new hangings were but 'mean stuff, without any cloth of estate'. Even her clothes were regulated, limited to six gowns, six pairs of sleeves and six French hoods unadorned with precious stones. Sir Thomas Seymour had confiscated all her collection of royal jewels and returned them to the King. There could be no greater indication that her term was over. It was not yet 16 months since her marriage.

All Katherine's attendants had now been dismissed with the exception of her half-sister Isabel, Lady Baynton, and two others. Isabel Legh had married Sir Edward Baynton, one of the largest landowners in Wiltshire, in 1532. He was the Queen's Vice-Chamberlain and had been in service since the time of Anne Boleyn, when the King had required him to spy on his mistress and to obtain evidence about her supposed lovers.

Whether he was once again commissioned to demonstrate his loyalty is uncertain but it appears that he and his wife now harangued Katherine, trying to make her understand the great danger in which she found herself. They persuaded her that she needed to offer up some defence, forcing her to sit down and write directly to Archbishop Cranmer, claiming that she was the victim of rape. Shortly afterwards Ambassador Chapuys heard that the King 'would show more patience and mercy than many might think – more even than her own relations wished, meaning Norfolk, who said, God knows why, that he wished the Queen was burned'.

He also reported on 19 November: 'I hear also that the Lady Anne of Cleves has greatly rejoiced ... and that in order to be nearer the King she is coming to, if she is not already at, Richmond.'

It seems that Anne's ostentatious demonstration of friendship towards her successor was something of a sham. Hearing of Katherine's trouble, Anne remarked, 'She was too much a child to deny herself any sweet thing she wanted.'

Could it be that after the humiliation of her experience with Henry she still hoped to be taken back? It appears so, for the official Cleves delegation at court pressed the King for the failed marriage to be resumed. Henry, however, was having none of it. On 15 December his Council issued the following rebuff: 'The separation had been made for such just cause that (the King) prayed the Duke (Anne's brother) never to make such a request.'

Henry himself was more concerned at removing another wife. On 22 November, Katherine had been publicly shamed by an official announcement: 'Proclamation was made at Hampton Court that she had forfeited her honour, and should be proceeded against by law, and was henceforth to be named no longer Queen, but only Katherine Howard.'

Norfolk cynically discussed his niece's predicament with the French Ambassador. He clearly felt no pity for her, claiming absurdly, in his desire to distance himself, that she had 'prostituted herself to seven or eight persons'. Her condition at Syon was one of despair in which she 'refuses to drink or eat and weeps and cries like a madwoman, so that they must take away things by which she might hasten her death'.

A formal indictment was published two days later that denounced her for 'an abominable, base, carnal, voluptuous and vicious life'. It stated that she had lived 'like a common harlot with

divers persons … maintaining however the outward appearance of
chastity and honesty'.

Such language was extraordinary before any trial had taken
place. Marillac reported that every 'foul detail' of her past had been
aired: 'Many people thought the publication of these foul details
strange, but the intention is to prevent it being said afterwards that
they were unjustly condemned.'

He wrote to his master that Culpeper had been brought up in
the English King's chamber from childhood and 'ordinarily shared
his bed' and 'apparently wished to share the Queen's bed too'.

The King of France expressed his concern to Paget, the English
Ambassador in Paris, remarking of Katherine that 'she hath done
wondrous naughty'. In an official letter of regret, he reflected to
'good brother' Henry that 'the lightness of women cannot bind the
honour of men'.

In the indictment, Katherine was described as deceitful and
conniving to trick the King into marriage, leading him 'by word
and gesture to love her'. She had 'arrogantly coupled herself with
him in marriage', concealing her precontract with Francis Dereham. She had placed her marriage to the King in jeopardy, 'to the
peril of the King and of his children to be begotten by her'.

Although Katherine repeatedly denied that she had promised to
marry Dereham, there were too many witnesses who had heard
them call one another husband and wife, and Dereham's own testimony under torture put the validity of her marriage to the King
in doubt. This did nothing to help Katherine, as Cranmer had discovered. As the indictment stated, the succession could have been
endangered had Katherine become pregnant, the paternity of her
child uncertain.

Was she pregnant? After 16 months of marriage, there were still
no outward signs of pregnancy, surely much to her regret and the
relief of the King and his ministers. By taking lovers behind
Henry's back, the Queen had put the whole line of succession at
risk 'to the most fearful peril and danger of the destruction of your
most royal person and to the utter loss, disherison and desolation
of this your Realm of England'.

Those members of her family who were not implicated quickly disowned her. The Duke of Norfolk made a point of attacking his 'ungrateful niece', even declaring that her only just punishment was to be burnt alive at the stake. Other Howard men appeared in the streets of London dressed in finery, out to enjoy themselves. Marillac commented, 'It is the custom and must be done to show that they did not share the crimes of their relatives.'

The contemporary chronicler Harpsfield concluded that Katherine was 'found an harlot' before her marriage and 'an adulteress after he married her'.

On 1 December Culpeper and Dereham were arraigned at the Guildhall on charges of high treason and adultery with the Queen. The unfortunate Robert Damport (or Davenport) was tortured and tried, purely because of his friendship with Dereham, being 'not only condemned by the order of the law but with such declarations of his offences as we think all the standers by did wonderfully both detest the man and the matter'.

There was a presumption of guilt, with the jury picked from the King's own ministers, including the Duke of Norfolk, Katherine's uncle, who presided over the trial.

The verdict was a foregone conclusion, and Thomas Culpeper's estate had already been seized and distributed. Yet the accused denied that they had committed any of the crimes with which they were charged and condemned.

Although there was no proof of adultery, the Queen and Culpeper were found guilty of the *intent* to have sex. This was enough to condemn them. Culpeper had always denied having a sexual relationship with the Queen but had admitted under torture that he 'intended and meant to do ill with the queen and that in like wise the queen so minded to do with him'. [31] It may have occurred to him that by denying physical adultery with the Queen he could escape the ultimate punishment. In this he was clearly deluded. All his experience of serving the King, of observing Henry in all his moods by day and by night, had not taught him to beware his vindictive and vicious nature. As Ambassador Marillac reported, Culpeper would die for intending to have carnal knowledge of the Queen 'although he had not passed beyond words; for he confessed his intention to do so, and his confessed conversations, being held by a subject to a Queen, deserved death'.

But what were the grounds for Dereham's conviction? He had only known Katherine when she was a young girl in her grandmother's house. How could he have guessed that one day she would become Queen of England? In any case, he and Katherine had not resumed their sexual relationship after his return from Ireland. But when she became Queen she had listened to pleas to help him and finally had rashly appointed him to the position of secretary in her own household. This, of course, looked bad to outsiders, but from Katherine's point of view must have seemed a shrewd move at the time, in order to keep Dereham close, where she might control him.

Her object was to stop him from spreading abroad his claim that they were precontracted or promised to one another. When arrested and put to the torture, Dereham had stated that when he and Katherine indulged in their nightly antics under the Dowager's roof they were in fact man and wife in the sight of God and according to common and canon law. His crime, therefore, could only be that he had failed to warn the King of this at the time of the royal marriage, thus allowing Katherine to commit bigamy.

Dereham was accused of this, that he had kept silent about his precontract 'to the intent of preferring the Queen to her royal marriage by which they deceived the King'. But he was also accused on charges that he had 'traitorously imagined and procured that he, Dereham, should be retained in the service of the Queen, to the intent that they might continue their wicked courses'.

It was claimed that 'his coming again to the Queen's service was to an ill intent', enabling their earlier relationship to continue. Dereham's appointment as secretary was explained by Katherine's chamberer and 'friend' Katherine Tylney as 'proof of her will to return to her abominable life'.

The court tried to have it both ways: accusing Dereham of

hiding his 'marriage' with Katherine but then planning to commit 'adultery' with her, although he was her 'husband' and not the King. Was it any wonder that public opinion considered that Dereham had been treated unjustly?

Dereham pleaded for Henry to spare him the full penalty of a death usually reserved for traitors, but the King chose to vent the full blast of his anger on the man he believed had first taken Katherine's virginity, Henry, the Council reported, 'thinketh he hath deserved no such mercy at his hands and therefore hath determined that he shall suffer the whole execution'.

Henry believed that it was Dereham who had destroyed her innocence, and for this he must suffer the ultimate punishment of hanging, drawing and quartering.

In this the King deceived himself. It was not Francis Dereham who had first initiated Katherine into the adult world, but Henry Manox, her music master, at the tender age of ten or eleven. Whether he 'had her maidenhead' or not, he did still admit to Wriothesley that he had known her so intimately that he could recognise 'a privy mark' in the 'secret parts' of her body 'for I have had her by the cunt and I know it among a hundred'. Yet 'upon his damnation and most extreme punishment of his body, he never knew her carnally'

Nevertheless, it was Francis Dereham who bore the brunt of the King's full retribution for his humiliation. Both he and Culpeper were sentenced to die at Tyburn, first being hanged, then cut down while still alive, castrated, split open, their entrails burnt, and finally beheaded. Thomas Culpeper, who at least knew that he was getting involved with the Queen, would have his sentence reduced to decapitation. Norfolk was said to have laughed out loud during the trial, 'as if he had cause to rejoice'.

On 10 December Dereham and Culpeper were drawn on hurdles to Tyburn and executed. Culpeper was a gentleman and for this reason, or because the King still felt some sympathy for him even after all the evidence, he was informed at the last moment that he would not face disembowelment. Francis Dereham was not so fortunate: 'Culpeper and Dereham were drawn from the Tower of London to Tyburn, and there Culpeper, after an exhortation made to the people to pray for him, he standing on the ground by the gallows, kneeled down and had his head stricken off; and then Dereham was hanged, membered, bowelled, headed, and quartered, their heads set on London Bridge.'

Their heads remained there as late as 1546, four years, but Culpeper's body was buried at St Sepulchre's church near Newgate.

Norfolk immediately left London for his family estate at Kenninghall. The King's moods were unpredictable and he must have thought it safer to be out of sight until his niece's fate was decided. He complained of gout, though few believed him. He had rebuilt the house more than ten years before, as the Howards rose to their greatest influence with Anne Boleyn.

But Kenninghall was no longer the family seat of a great dynasty, for the wheel of fortune had turned and the Howards were now at a very low ebb. The Duke's daughter Mary was no longer the wife of the King's bastard son, the Duke of Richmond, but a widow who had turned her back on the Catholic faith and showed little interest in finding herself a new husband. She spent her time with her friend Margaret Douglas, who through her reckless romantic affairs had destroyed two of the Howard family: first Thomas, who had died in the Tower, then Charles, brother of the Queen, who had been forced into exile abroad. Even Surrey, Norfolk's heir, was in disgrace, having made dangerous enemies of the Seymour brothers and the King.

More Howards were sent to join the large numbers already being held in the Tower. There were so many of them in fact that the Royal Apartments had to be opened up to make room for them. They included the Dowager Duchess, together with her eldest son Lord William Howard, who had both been parties to the cover-up of Katherine's affair with Henry Manox. The fact that the Dowager had destroyed certain letters and papers and had also broken into Dereham's coffers was considered to be 'marvellous presumption', indicating that her 'intent' had been to remove 'letters of treason'.

Remembering the dismal end suffered earlier that year by the Countess of Salisbury, the Dowager must have feared that her age would not save her. Duchess Agnes 'most abundantly besought God to save His Majesty and to preserve him in long and prosperous life'. She then helped her case by surrendering to the King the £800 she had been concealing.

The Howards were in a desperate dilemma, with the French Ambassador asserting of Norfolk himself that 'of his future many presume ill and none good'. As soon as he arrived at Kenninghall, Norfolk decided to plead for mercy. In a letter of 12 December he sought to distance himself from his 'ungracious' stepmother, his 'unhappy' brother and his 'lewd' sister. He had already denounced his 'whore' of a niece but knowing Henry's violent moods, he feared the King might 'conceive a displeasure' against him.

This fawning letter tells us all we need to know about Norfolk's character. His obsequious crawling for favour also shows the nature of the monarch he served:

The most abominable deeds done by two of my nieces hath brought me into the greatest perplexity that ever poor wretch was in ... prostrate at your royal feet, most humbly I beseech Your Majesty that by such, as it shall please you to command, I may be advertised plainly, how your Highness doth weigh your favour towards me; assuring your Highness that unless I may know your Majesty to continue my good and gracious Lord, as ye were before their offences committed, I shall never desire to live in this world any longer, but shortly to finish this transitory life as God knoweth, who send your Majesty the accomplishments of your most noble heart's desires.

This level of abasement was clearly effective with Henry, showing what was required to survive being close to the King's person.

On 22 December the Duke was exempted from the trial of those Howards and others held at the Tower. They were all found guilty:

Jurors further find that the said Katherine Tylney, Alice Restwold, wife of Anthony Restwold, of the same place, Gentleman; Joan Bulmer wife of William Bulmer, of the same place, Gentleman; Anna Howard, wife of Henry Howard late of Lambeth, Esq.; Robert Damporte late of the same place, Gentleman; Malena Tylney late of the same place, widow; and Margaret Benet, wife of John Benet, late of the same place, Gentleman; knowing the wicked life of the Queen and Dereham, did conceal the same from the King and all his Councillors. And that this said Agnes, Duchess of Norfolk, with whom the Queen had been educated from her youth upward; William Howard, late of Lambeth, uncle of the Queen and one of the King's Councillors; Margaret Howard, wife of William Howard; Katherine, Countess of Bridgewater, late of Lambeth, otherwise Katherine the wife of Henry, Earl of Bridgewater; Edward Walde-grave late of Lambeth, Gentleman; and William Asheley, late of Lambeth, in the county of Surrey, knowing that certain letters and papers had been taken from a chest and concealing the information from the King ... Katherine Tylney, Alice Restwold, Joan Bulmer, Anna Howard, Malena Tylney, Margaret Benet, Margaret Howard, Edward Waldegrave, and William Asheley are brought to the Bar by the Constable of the Tower, and being severally arraigned as well upon the Surrey Indictment, as the Indictments for Kent, and Middlesex, they pleaded guilty.

JUDGEMENT: they shall be severally taken back by the Constable of the Tower, and in the same Tower, or elsewhere, as the King shall direct, be kept in perpetual imprisonment and that all their goods and chattels shall be forfeited to the King, and their lands and tenements seized into the King's hands.

Ambassador Marillac reported that the King 'will not hear of business' and insisted on escaping. 'He is gone twenty-five miles from here, with no company but musicians and ministers of pastime.' He indulged in 'marvellous excess ... and was so fat that three of the biggest men that could be found could get inside his doublet'. His time was spent socialising 'with the ladies, as gay as I ever saw him'.

Chapter Seventeen

The Final Journey

THE KING HAD NO INTENTION of repeating the fiasco of the trial of Anne Boleyn, when the Queen and her brother George had spoken up so courageously that they swayed public opinion. This time his wife would not get the chance to defend herself in court. Katherine would be tried in absentia by Parliament and to spare himself having to hear all the 'wicked facts of the case' Henry would issue letters patent under the great seal of England for *The Bill of Attainder of Mistress Catherine Howard, late Queen of England, and divers other persons her complices.*

Parliament duly assembled on 16 January 1542. The Lord Chancellor, Thomas Audley, made a speech praising the King that rivalled Norfolk's letter for flattery. How happy England was to have as its sovereign such a wise and just monarch as Henry Tudor! The Lords and Commons stood 'as if to acknowledge the truth of his words', giving 'thanks to Almighty God who had preserved for so long a time such an exceptional prince over this kingdom'. Then the Attainder from both Houses of Parliament against Katherine was read out:

In their most humble wise beseech your most royal Majesty the lords spiritual and temporal and all other your most loving and obedient subjects the commons of this your most high court of parliament assembled; that where, besides any man's expectation, such chance hath happened, by Mistress Katherine Howard which Your Highness took to your wife, both to Your Majesty chiefly and so consequently to us all that the like we think hath scarce been seen, the likelihoods and appearances being so far contrary to that which by evident and due proof is now found true ... for which treasons being manifestly and plainly proved, as well by the confession of the said queen and other the said parties as by divers other witnesses and proofs, the said Francis Dereham and Thomas Culpepper having been lawfully and truly and according to the laws of the realm convicted and attainted, and the said queen and Jane, lady Rochford, be lawfully indicted, insomuch that Thomas Culpepper and Francis Dereham have justly suffered therefore pains of death according to their merits ....

The Bill did not bear the King's signature but only the Royal Seal. When the document was re-examined in the reign of Queen Mary, it was therefore declared to be void and of no effect.

Even at the time, it was apparent that there was rebellion among the ranks. The Lords expressed concern that the Bill of Attainder against Katherine might condemn the accused to death without any hearing or chance of defence – which, of course, had been the King's intention.

Even the Lord Chancellor warned that Katherine had been the Queen of England and not some common criminal. Lord Audley declared that she 'was in no sense a mean and private person but an illustrious and public one ... therefore her case had to be judged with ... integrity'.

It was 'but just that a princess should be tried by equal laws' before the peers of the realm. She must be seen to have justice. Conscious of her 'womanish fear', he suggested that an official delegation should visit Katherine at Syon to hear her defence.

Their problem was to appease the King yet find adequate grounds to kill Katherine. What exactly was her crime? That she had lost her virginity before she married the King? Or that she had slept with Dereham and called him husband long before she ever dreamt of meeting the King?

No one had admitted to adultery, nor could there be adultery if, as the indictment stated, she was already precontracted to Francis Dereham. Few husbands at that time would have forgiven their wives and continued to live with them after an adulterous affair. Such 'fallen women' could be rehabilitated through a life of penance and charitable works, but they could not be expected to be taken back into the family they had betrayed. Henry's hypocrisy is shown by the fact that he forced Sir Thomas Wyatt to take back his adulterous wife.

Was Katherine's 'violent presumption' enough to condemn her?

It seems it was. The Bill of Attainder went through second and third readings and on 11 February Katherine's death warrant effectively became law.

To Henry, Katherine was already as good as dead. On the same day, the King held a banquet to show his lack of concern. In his own mind at least, he was still young and virile, and needed to be seen as such, therefore inviting 50 ladies of the court to dine with him with 'great and hearty cheer'. It was noted that Henry paid particular attention to the wife of Sir Thomas Wyatt, Elizabeth Brooke, the reformed adulteress whom the King had forced her unhappy husband to take back. Chapuys reported cynically, 'She is a pretty young creature with wit enough to do as badly as the others if she were to try.' The King also noticed young Anne Basset, who reacted with understandable nervousness.

It was difficult for any woman to put aside the image of Katherine Howard imprisoned at Syon Abbey. Only Jane Seymour previously had shown herself insensitive and callous enough to allow herself to be fondled by the King while his wife was in the Tower awaiting execution. As with Anne Boleyn, the King's mind was already fixed upon destruction. In *Othello*, the Moor rationalises his decision to kill his wife Desdemona as the need to stop her trapping other innocent victims: 'Yet she must die, else she'll betray more men.'

It was now made a crime for any woman to conceal her sexual

history before marrying the King. Should the monarch take to wife someone who appeared to be 'a pure and clean maid when indeed the proof may or shall after appear contrary', she would be guilty of treason. Should such a lady 'couple herself with her Sovereign Lord' without declaring 'her unchaste life' then 'every such offence shall be deemed and adjudged High Treason'. 'Few, if any, ladies at court would henceforth aspire to such an honour', concluded the Imperial Ambassador cynically.

If word got through to Katherine at Syon of her husband's behaviour, she appeared unaffected. Chapuys reported that late in January she was 'making good cheer, fatter and handsomer than ever she was, taking great care of her person, well dressed and much adorned; more imperious and commanding, and more difficult to please than ever she was when living with the King her husband'.

If the report is true, what accounts for her sudden resilence? Was she valiantly concealing her own natural terror or merely deluding herself as to her fate? It is possible that Katherine may have remained ignorant of the evidence against her. Isolated in her rooms among the nuns, was she even informed of events in London? Did she hear of the interrogation and torture of her lovers and not realise the implications for herself? It is quite possible that, almost to the end, she had little idea of the danger she faced or what had befallen Dereham and Culpeper.

The delegation of lords had called, but Katherine seemed in a daze. It was stated that she had 'openly confessed and acknowledged to them the great crime of which she had been guilty against the most High God and a kind prince'. She hoped the King 'would not impute her crime to her whole kindred and family' and that he would also give her fine clothes to her attendants, 'since she had nothing now to recompense them as they deserved'.

Then on Friday 10 February, even before the Act of Attainder was passed, a new delegation headed by the Duke of Suffolk arrived to tell her she must leave behind the comforts of Syon for the stark realities of the Tower of London.

Katherine could not fail to understand that this was the end.

Once again, the ghost of her cousin Anne overwhelmed her and she broke down in despair and terror. It was said that she had to be forced into the waiting barge, with 'some difficulty and resistance'.

The Act of Attainder would not receive the King's approval for another day, but her death was already determined. The men who came to fetch her to her last resting place knew that within three days she would be dead.

Much of the traditional account of Katherine's last days is fiction. Her story has always inspired pity, but little understanding. This was a girl, possibly not yet 17. She had already gone through more in one lifetime than most women of three score and ten. From the age of seven when she was sent away by her father, unwanted, an encumbrance; she was on her own, without friends or any dependable family member in whom she could confide.

The women in her grandmother's house became her surrogate family, but her status as niece of the great Duke of Norfolk was a magnet for fortune hunters and ambitious young men. Pushed by her family into the King's bed, she was under intense pressure to provide a child before his interest dwindled away and she would be destroyed. Everyone betrayed her and, in the end, she betrayed herself, taking the reprobate Culpeper to be her ally.

Stories of last-minute confessions and appeals to save her family ring false. Her fate was already determined the moment that Henry read Cranmer's letter. Already his patience had been wearing thin as months passed and there was no sign of a second son. The revelation of her past misdemeanours shattered his fantasy of his precious little bride, a virgin with the power to revive his manhood and restore his youth. How could he ever forgive her?

As the solemn procession approached its destination by river, they passed under London Bridge, now adorned with two new heads. Francis Dereham and Thomas Culpeper stared down on Katherine as she approached the Tower on her final journey. They were there as a dread warning to others, as Hilles wrote to his friend in Zurich, the theologian Bullinger, 'But, to say the truth, people did not inquire much, as it is no new thing to see men hanged, quartered, or beheaded, for one thing or another, sometimes for trifling expressions construed as against the King.' They were not justly condemned, people said.

Sir Thomas More had recognised the danger of being close to a King such as Henry and had paid with his life: 'And so they said that these matters be Kings' games, as it were stage plays, and for the more part played upon scaffolds.'

Katherine entered through the Water Gate, now known as Traitors' Gate. Waiting for her at the top of the steps were her jailors, ready to escort her inside. Sir Edmund Walsingham, the Lieutenant of the Tower, showed her the newly refurbished apartment that had been prepared for her.

Lady Rochford was said to be in a state near madness as she realised that her betrayal of Katherine would not save her. The two women were kept separate and, according to Chapuys, Jane 'had shown symptoms of madness until the very moment when they announced to her that she must die'. On the Sunday evening both women received the news that they were to die next morning. Katherine was advised to 'dispose her soul and prepare for death'.

Chapuys now relates the pretty story that she rehearsed her own execution. He claims that she called for the block to be brought to her in order to 'make trial of it' so 'that she might know how to place her head on it'. Two kinds of block were in use, one much lower than the other, requiring the victim to lie down in an almost prone position. This made it much more difficult for the headsman to achieve a clean blow with just one stroke of his axe, and there were many inept executions. In 1541, Margaret Countess of Salisbury was butchered by an inexperienced executioner who 'hacked her head and shoulders to pieces' and it took three blows to sever the head of Mary, Queen of Scots at Fotheringhay Castle in 1587.

According to Chapuys, the block was brought to Katherine and 'she herself tried and placed her head on it by way of experiment'.

If true, this was a remarkable recovery from her earlier horror and rejection. She had scarcely 24 hours to come to terms with the harsh reality of her situation. There would be no trial, no chance to appeal. She was abandoned, ultimately all alone again, with no way out.

Yet she grew calm. She had been surrounded by death in an age when its prospect was ever present, from the death of her mother right up to the moment when she looked up and saw Culpeper's head on London Bridge. She accepted her fate and her thoughts must have turned inward, perhaps for the first time in her young life considering her own mortality.

February 13 1542 dawned cold and clear. At seven o'clock the Tower began to fill up with members of the King's Council and a number of foreign ambassadors arriving to witness the executions. Suffolk had excused himself, claiming to be ill and the Duke of Norfolk still skulked away on his estate at Kenninghall. But the 25-year-old Henry Howard, Earl of Surrey, was there to see his young cousin beheaded, just as he had witnessed the death of Anne Boleyn.

Just before nine, Katherine appeared and faced the short walk to the wooden scaffold that had been built for her final journey. It was a cold morning and the few trees standing sentinel near the scaffold were still bare. It was the same dread place where, less than six years earlier, her cousin Anne Boleyn had suffered the same penalty.

Katherine climbed the steps up to the scaffold, built four feet above the ground. Ambassador Marillac, who was not there, later wrote that she was 'so weak that she could hardly speak'. The anonymous Spanish chronicler goes even further, attributing to Katherine a dramatic last speech in which she seeks to justify her romance with Culpeper:

Brothers, by the journey upon which I am bound, I have not wronged the King. But it is true that long before the King took me, I loved Culpeper, and I wish to God I had done as he wished me, for at the time the King wanted to take me he urged me to say that I was pledged to him. If I had done as he advised me I should not die this death, nor would he. I would rather have had him for a husband than be mistress of the world, but sin blinded me and greed of grandeur; and since mine is the fault, mine also is the suffering, and my great sorrow is that Culpeper should have had to die through me.

Then she told the executioner, 'Pray hasten with thy office.' According to this uncorroborated and unlikely version, before she submitted to the axe her last words to those watching were: 'I die a Queen, but I would rather die the wife of Culpeper. God have mercy on my soul. Good people, I beg you pray for me.'

The least prejudiced witness on that day was Otwell Johnson, who worked for the Comptroller of the Royal Household, Sir John Gage. Johnson was there, and just two days later wrote to his brother John in Calais his own account of the execution: 'I see the Queen and the Lady Rochford suffer within the Tower ... whose souls be with God, for they made the most godly and Christian end.'

He describes how Katherine made a very different speech, speaking of her 'lively faith in the blood of Christ only' and confessing that she had sinned against 'God heinously from youth upward in breaking all his commandments'.

Far from remembering her doomed affair with Culpeper, Katherine and her fellow victim that morning, Jane, Lady Rochford, concentrated upon religion and their own salvation: 'with goodly words and steadfast countenances, they desired all Christian people to take regard unto their worthy and just punishment with death ... (sinning) also against the King's royal majesty very dangerously ... justly condemned by the laws of the realm and parliament to die'.

Katherine then begged 'the people to take example of them', to amend 'their ungodly lives, and gladly to obey the King in all things, for whose preservation they did heartily pray'.

Then Katherine removed her cloak, to reveal her long hair caught up under a coif and cap. She turned to face the axeman in his black suit, just the slight figure of a frightened young girl meeting her killer.

In a low voice, according to tradition she forgave him for the task that he was about to carry out and paid him well for his work. Unlike her cousin Anne, who was beheaded by a sword, Katherine had to kneel down before a wooden block set up on the straw that had been spread on the scaffold to absorb her blood.

One of her attendants took out a large kerchief and blindfolded her, then guided her forward to the block.

As the crowd watched, Katherine knelt in the straw, feeling for the edges of the wooden block. Then she laid her head down on the rough wooden surface and stretched out her arms. There was silence, as if the whole world had ceased to turn and held its breath.

Then suddenly the headsman swung his axe and abruptly it was all over. The ravens croaked as those people gathered around let out a cry of horror.

The body was quickly moved aside and covered with a cloth. Then Jane Parker, Lady Rochford, who had been watching all this time standing to one side, stepped up onto the scaffold in her turn.

Although she had been hysterical since her arrest, according to eyewitness reports she recovered her senses and was able to make 'a long discourse' on the 'several faults which she had committed in her life': 'Good Christians, God has permitted me to suffer this shameful doom as punishment for having contributed to my husband's death. I falsely accused him of loving in an incestuous manner, his sister, Queen Anne Boleyn. For this I deserve to die. But I am guilty of no other crime.'

Then Jane Parker knelt down in the sodden straw at the block still wet with Katherine's blood and paid the ultimate price for all her betrayals.

It was over. For the second time in under a decade, a Queen of England had been brutally dispatched by her husband, cementing his reputation as a tyrant for posterity.

Katherine Howard's body was later borne away to the Tower's own Chapel of St Peter ad Vincula. There she was buried beside the grave of another Queen, her cousin Anne Boleyn, as close in death as their stories had echoed one another in life.

Aftermath

WHEN KATHERINE WAS EXECUTED, Henry was hunting at Waltham. The following day he returned to Whitehall to celebrate Shrovetide with a carnival of three days of feasting before the start of Lent. Ambassador Chapuys records, 'The King did nothing else ... than go from one chamber to another to inspect the lodgings prepared for the ladies.'

The 'King's sister', Anne of Cleves, never really gave up hopes of restoring their marriage. She and the King had exchanged New Year presents and on Katherine's death she offered him sympathy, but was eventually disappointed when Henry announced the following year that he would marry the widow Catherine Parr.

The fate of others involved in Katherine's brief life includes the release of Joan Bulmer, who later remarried and had five children, dying in 1590. The father of Jane, Lady Rochford, was the Catholic intellectual Sir Henry Parker, Lord Morley. Shortly after his daughter's execution he dedicated a translation of Boccaccio's '*Of the ryghte renoumyde ladyes*' to the King. This attack on female promiscuity may reflect his view of the disgrace he had suffered as a result of his daughter's betrayal.

John Lascelles, brother of Mary, who informed Cranmer of

Katherine's past, became an influential leader of London Protestants, associated with Queen Catherine Parr. Five years later, he was imprisoned with the Protestant martyr Anne Askew, who was tortured on the rack by Thomas Wriothesley. They were both burnt at the stake, their bodies being covered in gunpowder, on 16 July 1546 at Smithfield, just outside London Wall.

Perhaps the person most affected by the death of Katherine Howard was a small girl approximately the same age that Katherine had been when placed out in the country, left to make her own way in life. The parallels of her lonely existence struck home.

Elizabeth Tudor, the eight-year-old daughter of Anne Boleyn, had already suffered much at the hands of her father, being robbed of her mother and publicly declared illegitimate. From the sidelines she had watched a procession of other wives come and go, but none troubled her quite so much as the young Katherine, who had paid her some kind attention. Then in little more than a year she was gone, her head struck off, just like her own mother.

Long after, Robert Dudley, Earl of Leicester, told the Spanish Ambassador that as a child Elizabeth had vowed she would never marry but die a virgin. Lord Burghley later declared that 'marriage with the blood royal was too full of risk to be lightly entered into'. It was a lesson that his mistress Queen Elizabeth had learnt at a tender age: *The closer you are to Caesar, the greater the fear.*

And what of the Howards and the third Duke of Norfolk, Thomas Howard, who had been so ready to manipulate Katherine for his own security and the future of his dynasty?

Katherine's uncle saved himself with his grovelling letter to the King and kept his post as Treasurer. The Dowager Duchess Agnes did not suffer the same fate as the wretched Countess of Salisbury. By handing over her fortune, she escaped further punishment and left the Tower in May along with her son Lord William Howard and the rest of their relatives. Duchess Agnes died in 1545, aged 68.

Chesworth was among the manors passed over to Norfolk until 1547 when it was granted by the King to Thomas Wriothesley, then Earl of Southampton. [7] Katherine's brothers, Henry and Charles

Howard, were both shortly restored to the King's favour, receiving pensions and a knighthood.

Nor could Henry manage for long without Norfolk. On 24 August 1542 the Privy Council recorded Henry's plan to invade Scotland 'for the distruccion of their country'. The King sent Norfolk and his rival Edward Seymour, Earl of Hertford, into Scotland, where they burnt villages in Teviotdale. But a Scottish army 18,000 strong moved west into the Debateable Land between the two countries. On 24 November they clashed with the greatly inferior English forces under Lord Wharton at Solway Moss, where the Scots were caught in boggy ground and forced to surrender. Legend has it that King James V, who was too ill to lead the battle, died of shame. His heir, Mary, Queen of Scots, was born one week later.

Norfolk's heir, the hotheaded Earl of Surrey, was with the English army in France. In an attack on Montreuil he was seriously wounded and left for dead, but saved by his squire, Thomas Clere, who was wounded during the rescue and later died of his wounds. He returned as Commander-in-Chief but a reverse at St Etienne on 7 January 1545 led to his recall and replacement by his old enemy Hertford.

There was much personal competition between the Howards and the Seymours, the old aristocracy against the new, the Catholic party versus the reforming Protestants.

Hertford's success forced the old fox Norfolk to seek a reconciliation between the families, proposing a number of influential marriages to restore good relations, including that of Surrey's son and heir, Thomas, with Hertford's eldest daughter, although Surrey reportedly said he would 'sooner see his children dead in their coffins than married to Seymour's brats'.

Speculation increased as to who would become regent or 'Protector' for Prince Edward if the King died before he came of age. Hertford, as Edward's uncle, was the leading contender, but Surrey made his opposition known, deriding Hertford for 'having ever God on his lips'. Norfolk and the Howards had pre-eminence over the court and Surrey, 'the most relish prowde boye that ys in England', rashly boasted what they would do when the King died.

Surrey's claim to the throne was better than that of the Tudors, as he was descended from the bloodline of King Edward III through John of Gaunt and his mother's Stafford heritage, and it was now suggested that the Howards were plotting to overthrow Prince Edward, once the King was dead.

On 2 October 1546 Surrey was summoned to appear before the Privy Council in Wriothesley's house in Holborn, where he was accused of conspiring against the crown. His accusers included Sir Richard Southwell, who had been brought up at Kenninghall, Sir Edmund Knyvet, his cousin and son of Lady Muriel Howard, Norfolk's own sister, and George Blage, once his friend.

Surrey was accused of harbouring Italian spies, corresponding with the traitor Cardinal Pole and discussing the date of the King's death. This was treason. Norfolk himself had been seen at a secret nighttime rendezvous at the house of Charles de Marillac, the French Ambassador. One of his letters to Bishop Gardiner proved that they were in contact with Cardinal Granville, in a plot to restore Roman Catholic control in England.

The King read Wriothesley's handwritten report of the interrogation. Although his health was poor and his eyesight weak, Henry furiously underlined the charges against the Howards:

> If a man coming of the <u>collateral line to the heir of the crown</u>, who ought not to bear the arms of England but on the second quarter... do presume ... to bear them in the first quarter ... <u>how this man's intent is to be judged</u> ...If a man compassing <u>with himself to govern the realm do actually go about to rule the king</u>, and should for that purpose advise his daughter or sister to become the king's harlot, thinking thereby to bring it to pass ... what this importeth.
>
> If a man say these words, 'If the king die, who should have the rule of the prince but my father or I?' what it importeth.

Henry's doubts about the Howards' loyalty were clearly expressed. Men of ambition were manoeuvring to take control of the future boy King and make themselves Protector during his minority. Surrey's ambition and pride were to cause his downfall.

In Wriothesley's report, Surrey was accused of bearing the heraldic arms of Edward the Confessor which belonged 'only to the King of this realm'. He had spoken irreverently of His Majesty, and had speculated upon what might happen after his death. What had Surrey written to his father at the time of the King's sickness? Surrey had boasted, 'They will let me alone as long as my father lives and after, I shall be well enough.' Wriothesley's notes referred to 'my lord of Surrey's pride and his gown of gold'. It was suggested 'that Mr P. should be chancellor of England'.

Had Surrey plotted with the Emperor Charles V at Landrecy? Why was Norfolk holding secret meetings with the French? Had he contacted the Vatican to seek the restoration of church powers? Was he using secret code in his letters? Sir Henry Knyvet's death in France was linked to 'my lord of S. dissembling'. The Howards had discussed 'Dr Butts and the matter of Denny'. Sir Anthony Denny was the King's closest servant and his name came up again in a list of 'things in common: Paget, Hertford, Admiral, Denny'.

What the men had in common was their evangelical reform beliefs. They were Protestants and determined to keep England out of the Vatican's and the Emperor's control. They were therefore the natural enemies of the Howards and would have to be removed before any Howard coup.

On Saturday 12 December Norfolk appeared before Lord Chancellor Wriothesley to be charged with his son. They were both dispatched to the Tower; because of his age Norfolk was allowed to travel by barge but Surrey was paraded through the crowded streets. That evening Sir Richard Southwell, Sir John Gates and Wymond Carew were sent to Kenninghall in Norfolk to seek evidence. Gates and Carew were part of the reformist party and both brothers-in-law of Sir Anthony Denny.

They travelled at speed, covering the hundred miles by dawn. Southwell's report to the King tells what happened next: '... we did declare our desire to speak with the Duchess of Richmond and Elizabeth Holland, both which we found at that time newly risen, and not ready. Nevertheless, having knowledge that we would speak with them, they came unto us without delay into the dining chamber, and so we imparted unto them the case and condition wherein the said Duke and his son, without your great mercy, did stand.'

Mary Howard was shocked by the news but told them 'although nature constrained her sore to love her father, whom she hath ever thought to be a true and faithful subject, and also to desire the well doing of his son, her natural brother, whom she noteth to be a rash man, yet for her part, she would nor will hide or conceal any thing from your Majesty's knowledge'.

Her apartment was searched but 'hitherto we have found no writings worthy sending ...'. Nothing compromising was discovered, although they made a list of jewels discovered in Norfolk's mistress's chamber.

On 15 December the Privy Council informed England's ambassadors abroad that Surrey and Norfolk had conspired to overthrow the regime and that Surrey had confessed. The next day Wriothesley told the Imperial Ambassador that Norfolk and Surrey's intention was to 'usurp authority by means of the murder of all the members of the Council, and the control of the prince by them alone'. There were no details about Norfolk's secret meetings and codes or plots with Rome, but Van der Delft, the Imperial Ambassador, wrote to the Emperor Charles V on 24 December: 'The majority of the people are of these perverse sects (reformers) and in favour of getting rid of bishops and they do not conceal their wish to see Winchester (Bishop Gardiner) and other adherents of the ancient faith in the Tower with the Duke.'

Mary, Duchess of Richmond, now arrived in London with Bess Holland. Under further questioning, she stated that her father had told her 'the King was sickly, and could not long endure; and the realm like to be in an ill case through diversity of opinions'. This corroborated the charge against Norfolk. She agreed that her brother Surrey had adopted the arms of their attainted and executed grandfather, the Duke of Buckingham, the royal lions and lilies with a white border inherited from Thomas of Woodstock, younger son of Edward III. This suggested that Surrey was boldly reinstating a claim to the throne and therefore challenging the Tudor dynasty.

Depositions were taken from at least 22 witnesses. These included Edward Warner, Surrey's cousin Edmund Knyvet, Edward Roger and Gawain Carew who, like Southwell, had served with Surrey in France. But Surrey saw himself as the victim of his family and former friends who betrayed him. His accuser Southwell had been a childhood friend, raised in the Howard household.

Surrey had dabbled briefly with the evangelical faith, perhaps at his sister's urging. He appears to have sought out known reformers at court, including George Blage, who had been accused of heresy, and Sir Anthony Denny. Surrey's 'simple' faith was tested and found wanting by these established reform figures.

> My Deny, then myne errour depe imprest,
> Began to worke dispaire of libertye,
> Had not David, the perfyt warriour, tought
> That of my fault thus pardon shold be sought. (Sonnet 35, 5–8)

However, that did not prevent the embittered Surrey writing from prison poetry that portrayed himself as an evangelical martyr: *Ecclesiastes* paraphrases, Psalms 54, 72, and 87 (Vulgate numbering).

> Myne old fere and dere frende, my guyde that trapped me;
> Where I was wont to fetche the cure of all my care,
> And in his bosome hyde my secreat zeale to God.
> (Psalm 54; 54.24–26)

How accurate is Surrey's view of himself? If he and his father were really embroiled in a plan to overthrow the King then they had set about it in a remarkably clumsy and amateur fashion. Surrey's vanity had alienated most of those who knew him, including his sister, whom he insulted and from whom he probably stole poetry later attributed to him, and his new evangelical friends, who saw through his superficial and self-obsessed interest in their affairs.

Unlike Surrey, men like Denny were serious and hard-working

administrators who had risen through their own merits and possessed a rigorous and enduring faith that could withstand the flames of Smithfield. They were not playing games, for they had already witnessed the King's casual cruelties when he destroyed their patroness, Queen Anne Boleyn.

If there was any plan to safeguard the succession after Henry's death, then it was in favour of the Protestant heritage for young Edward VI, and those closest to the King were not about to permit the likes of the Howards and their allies to turn back the clock.

On 12 January Norfolk made a confession to members of the Privy Council, perhaps hoping to save his son by making an admission on his behalf:

> I, Thomas, duke of Norfolk, do confess and acknowledge myself ... to have offended the king's most excellent majesty, in the disclosing ... of his privy and secret counsel ... to the great peril of his Highness ... That I have concealed high treason, in keeping secret the false and traitorous act ... committed by my son ... against the king's majesty ... in the putting and using the arms of Edward the Confessor ... in his scutcheon or arms ... Also, that to the peril, slander, and disinherison of the king's majesty and his noble son, Prince Edward, I have ... borne in the first quarter of my arms ... the arms of England ... Although I be not worthy to have ... the king's clemency and mercy to be extended to me ... yet with a most sorrowful and repentant heart do [beg] his Highness to have mercy, pity, and compassion on me.

The next day, 13 January, Surrey was tried before a jury at Guildhall on a single charge: of quartering the arms of King Edward the Confessor with his own. He was found guilty after the King sent a message to the court.

Surrey was beheaded on 19 January 1547 on Tower Hill. He was 29. The body was first buried in All Saints church in Barking, but later the remains were transferred to Framlingham. Afterwards, his widow Frances de Vere was 'relieved' of her children, who were brought up by their aunt Mary Howard, Duchess of Richmond, at

Reigate Castle. They were joined by Charles Howard, the son of Lord William Howard of Effingham, and taught by the reformer John Foxe.

Henry seemed determined to be done with his old enemy but Norfolk could not be condemned with so little formality as Surrey. As a peer of the realm, he could not be tried by a common jury but by his own peers. The consequent delay was to save his life.

A Bill of Attainder against him was hurried through the House of Lords in three readings on 18, 19 and 20 January. It was completed by the Commons on 24 January and signed with Henry's signature stamp on the last day of his life. The King was gravely ill but he had frequently used the convenience of this 'dry stamp', which was kept in the safekeeping of Sir Anthony Denny. Henry was on his sick bed at Whitehall but still *compos mentis*, as proved by his notes in the margins of the document in a shaky hand.

No one had dared to tell the King that he was dying, as it was treason even to discuss the possibility. But as his condition deteriorated, Sir Anthony Denny alone had the courage to tell him the truth and urge him to make his peace with God.

Henry said he would see only Cranmer, but by the time the Archbishop of Canterbury arrived the King could no longer speak but squeezed his hand, which Cranmer took as a sign of his repentance. He died at two o'clock in the morning, aged 56. It was Friday 28 January 1547.

Norfolk was condemned to die that very day, but was saved by the King's death.

His relief was short-lived. All the Howard lands and titles had been forfeit under the attainder and the new young King Edward VI was no friend to him. It has been suggested that the confiscation and redistribution of the Howard estates was the motivation for bringing Norfolk and Surrey down. Certainly many of those who accused them received benefits subsequently, including George Blage, Southwell, Knyvet, Warner, Devereux, Barker, Hussey, Bellingham and Fulmerston.

Norfolk spent the next six years in the Tower until the accession of Mary who restored him to his dukedom, aged 80. He died at Kenninghall on 25 August 1555.

He was a monolithic figure, a monster and ruthless in his cold-blooded use of those around him, including the members of his own family, who were just pawns for his ambition. For more than 30 years he was the leader of the conservative Catholic party at court and in the country, seeking to coax and wheedle a contrary King into a return to the traditions and powers of the old order and faith. His survival was just part of his astonishing luck, ironically cheating the scaffold of another Howard victim at the last hour and dying in his bed.

The Howard tombs can still be seen in the Church of Saint Michael the Archangel in Framlingham, having withstood the onslaught of time and the worst excesses of Reformation and Civil War zeal. The second Duke's body was removed from Thetford Priory and buried with his son. The famous Flodden Helmet, borne at his funeral in memory of his defeat of the Scots in 1513, hangs over their tomb, which is carved with images of the 12 Apostles, Aaron the priest and St Paul. Nearby is the tomb of his son-in-law, Henry's VIII's illegitimate son, the Duke of Richmond, who died in mysterious circumstances in 1536, also brought from Thetford after the dissolution of the monasteries; later Mary Howard was buried at his side, still a widow after 21 years. Their tomb is richly carved with scenes taken from the Old Testament, including Adam and Eve, Noah's Ark, Sodom and Gomorrah, and Moses receiving the Ten Commandments

And what remains of Katherine? A plaque in the Tower of London and the fleeting memory of her existence in the place where she suffered her traumatic and sudden fall.

A ghostly figure has been reported in what used to be the Rose Garden of King's Manor in York, where she dallied in the hope of more meetings with Culpeper. A woman in a green Tudor gown is seen carrying fresh roses as she passes through the walls.

Hampton Court Palace is reputedly one of the most haunted places in Britain, with sightings of more than 30 spectres. Visitors have reported they could feel a 'presence' in the so-called Haunted Gallery leading to the Chapel Royal. From 1897 there have been repeated sightings of Katherine's ghost, dressed in white and screaming as she runs down the 40-foot-long gallery to hammer on the door of the chapel, hysterically begging for mercy. Her fear and terror have been re-enacted many times since by her ghost.

In the 1930s a curator at the palace saw a hand with an elaborate ring knocking furiously on the chapel door. When he described the ring, it was found to match that worn by Queen Katherine in one of her portraits. It is a nice story but unlikely. Portraits of Katherine are rare enough and false attributions were common in the 1930s.

In April 2000, two visitors on separate guided tours felt as if something invisible had punched them, then fell down in a dead faint outside the door to the chapel.

On recovering, they both described feeling hot and were sweating profusely. In December 2003 closed-circuit security cameras revealed on video a figure violently pushing through the doors of an emergency exit. Security guards checked to see who kept leaving open one of the palace's fire doors.

James Faukes, one of the guards, reported, 'It was incredibly spooky because the face just didn't look human. It is actually quite unnerving.'

In the still photograph, the figure is shown bursting through the door, one arm reaching out for the handle. The clothing could be Tudor, with its parted skirt and large sleeves.

A team of ghost-busting psychologists, led by Dr Richard Wiseman, installed thermal-imaging cameras, air movement detectors, pressure gauges, electromagnetic sensors and humidity monitors in the gallery.

'It could be the best ghost sighting ever,' Wiseman told the media. 'I haven't seen anything that would match that at all.'

But as of today Katherine has failed to put in another appearance.

Notes on Sources

Abbreviations used in the notes:

BIHR   Bulletin of the Institute of Historical Research

BL   British Library

JHI   Journal of the History of Ideas

Lisle Letters   *The Lisle Letters*, ed. M.St Clare Byrne, 6 vols, Chicago, 1981.

LP   *Letters and Papers, Foreign and Domestic of the Reign of Henry VIII*, ed. J.S. Brewer, J. Gairdner, and R. H. Brodie (21 vols, London, 1862-1932).

MUP   Manchester University Press

OUP   Oxford University Press

PRO   Public Record Office

SP.   *State Papers of King Henry VIII* (II vols, London, 1830-52).

SP.Span.   *Calendar of Letters, Despatches, and State Papers, relating to the Negotiations between England and Spain, preserved in the Archives at Vienna, Simancas, BesanVon and Brussels*, ed. Pascual de Gayangos, G. A.Bergenroth, M. A. S. Hume, Royall Tyler, and Garrett Mattingly (13 vols, London, HMSO,1862-1954).

SP.Ven.   *Calendar of State Papers and Manuscripts Relating to English Affairs, Existing in the Archives and Collections of Venice and in Other Libraries of Northern Italy*, ed.R.Brown, G. Cavendish-Bentinck, H. F. Brown, and A. B. Hinds (38 vols, London, 1864-1947).

CHAPTER 1

Biller, Peter, 'Medieval Childbirth', *History Today* 36, August 1986, pp. 42–9; Rawcliffe, Carole, 'Women, Childbirth and Religion in Later Medieval England', in Webb, D., *Women and Religion in Medieval England*, Oxbow, 2003; Gibson, Gail McMurray, 'Scene and Obscene: Seeing and Performing Late Medieval Childbirth', *Journal of Medieval and Early Modern Studies*, 29, 1999; Eccles, Audrey, *Obstetrics and Gynaecology in Tudor and Stuart England* London, 1982; Lee, Becky R., 'A Company of Women and Men: Men's Recollections of Childbirth in Medieval England', *Journal of Family History,* 27, 2, 2002, pp. 92–100; Outhwaite, R. B., ed., *Marriage and Society: Studies in the Social History of Marriage*, London, 1981, pp. 35–57.

Guy, John, *Tudor England,* OUP, 1988, pp. 30–4; Clay, G. A., *Economic Expansion and Social Change: England, 1500–1700.* Cambridge, 1984, i. 13; Wrigley, E. A. and Schofield, R. S., *The Population History of England*, London, 1981, pp. 174–210, 531–2, 568, 645–85.

Marillac guessed Katherine's age from her 1541 confession of her affair with Francis Dereham, ending in 1539: *Original Letters*, I, p. 201; L.P., xvi, 426. The *Spanish Chronicle* states she was fifteen in 1540 when she first met Henry VIII: Hume, David, *The History of England from the Invasion of Julius Caesar to the Revolution in 1688*, Vol. 3., 1788, xxxi. Other writers noted that she was exceptionally young: Hilles to Bullinger in 1540: *Original Letters from Zurich*, Parker Society, i.205. The year 1525 is given by Weir, Alison, *Britain's Royal Family: A Complete Genealogy*, London, 1999, p. 154; www.thepeerage.com.

For Katherine's age see: 15 Bodfield, 24 Bennet, 3 Crymes, 18 Porch in the *Surrey Archaeological Collections*, LI, pp. 85–90; *Visitations of Cornwall* (ed. Vivian, J. L.), pp. 4–5; *Inquisitions Post Mortem, Henry VIII*, I. 820; *Archaeologia Cantiana*, IV, p. 264; *Visitations of Surrey*, H.S., XLIII, pp. 20–1; *Visitation of Kent*, H.S., LXXIV, pp. 41–2 and 81; Hasted's *Kent*, vol. v, pp. 63–4; Brenan and Statham, *House of Howard*, I, pp. 268–9; *Sussex Arch. Col.* XLVII, pp. 72, 80; XLVIII, p. 56; *Visitation of Kent*, H.S. XLII, p.11; *Visitations of Surrey*, H.S., XLVIII, pp. 20–1; *D.N.B.,* article: 'Katherine Howard'; LP., 2nd edn., I, ii, 3325; *Colepeper of Aylesford Pedigree; V.C.H., History of Hampshire,* IV, pp. 185, 295–6; *Remains, Historical and Literary of Lancaster and Chester,* Chetham Society, LI, p. 72; LXXXI, p. 3; Strickland, *Queens of England*, III, p. 101; Howard,

H., *Memorials of the Howard Family*, pp. 1–26; Smith, Lacey Baldwin, *A Tudor Tragedy*, Jonathan Cape, 1962, pp. 194–6; www.gen.culpepper.com.

Stone, Lawrence, *The Family, Sex and Marriage in England*, 1500–1800, New York, 1977; Webster, C., ed., *Health, Medicine and Mortality*, Cambridge, 1979; Coster, William, 'Purity, Profanity, and Puritanism: The Churching of Women, 1500–1700,' *In Women in the Church*, ed. Sheils, W. J., and Wood, Diana, Oxford, 1990,. pp. 377–87; Cressy, David, *Birth, Marriage, and Death: Ritual, Religion and the Life Cycle in Tudor and Stuart England*, Oxford, 1997; Gies, Frances and Joseph, *Marriage and the Family in the Middle Ages*, New York, 1987, p. 278.

Ozment, S., *When Fathers Ruled: Family Life in Reformation Europe*, Cambridge, Mass., 1983, pp. 25–37; Houlbrooke, Ralph. *The English Family, 1450–1700*, London and New York, 1984; Emerson, K. L., *Everyday Life in Renaissance England: 1485–1649*, Ohio, 1996; Hanawalt, Barbara, *The Ties that Bound: Peasant Families in Medieval England*, Oxford University Press, 1986, pp. 44,113,129,177; Orme, Nicholas, 'Child's Play in Medieval England', *History Today*, October 2001; Orme, Nicholas, *Medieval Children*, Yale University Press, 2001.

The Lisle Letters, ed. M. St. Clare, Byrne, 6 vols, Chicago, 1981; Furnivall, *Early English Meals and Manners*, London, Early English Text Society, 1868, pp. 48, 94, 120; Gairdner, J., *The Paston Letters*, 1422–1509 ed., 6 vols, 1904, 69714; Sather, K., 'Sixteenth and Seventeenth Century Child Rearing: a Matter of Discipline', *Journal of Social History*, 22, 1988/9.

CHAPTER 2

Robinson, John Martin, *The Dukes of Norfolk: A Quincentennial History*, New York: Oxford University Press, 1982.

Richard III's right to the crown was enshrined in the parliamentary bill, *Titulus Regius*, as a result of the revelation that Edward IV's marriage was bigamous and his children all illegitimate: 'King Edward's sons were bastards' see Pronay and Cox, *Crowland Chronicle*, pp. 161,192; Commynes, *Rotuli Parliamentorum*, 1783, vol. 6, pp. 240–2; *Memoires*, i.455, ii.64–5. Henry Tudor attempted to destroy every copy of *Titulus Regius* 'so that all thinges said and remembred in the said Bill and Acte thereof maie be for ever out of remembraunce, and also forgott': York Civic Records, 1, p. 122. But the truth was still recognised 50 years later as the Imperial Ambassador Chapuys records in 1533: LP. HVIII. vi. 618; vii.1368.

Collier, Payne, *Household*, pp. 383–4; Crawford, Anne, ed., *The Howard Household Books, 1462–71 and 1481–83*, 1992, entry for 1 July 1483; *Correspondencia de Gutuerre Gomez de Fuensalida*, ed. Duque de Berwick y de Alba, Madrid 1907, p. 449; Hall, Edward, *The Triumphant Reign of King HVIII*, 1904, vol.1.

BM – Navy Records Soc. x., 145; LP relating to the war with France in 1512–13, pp. xxxvi–ix, 132–9, 147–8; Allen et al., eds, *The Letters of Richard Fox*, 1928, p. 58; S.P. Hen.VIII. 3, f. 202;

Charles, Cruickshank, *Henry VIII and the Invasion of France*, St Martin's Press, 1990; 'The Ballad of Sir Andrew Barton', in *Percy's Reliques of Ancient English Poetry; Child's English and Scottish Popular Ballads.*

Bates, C. J., *Flodden Field*, Newcastle 1894, p. 9; Robson, James, *Border Battles and Battlefields*, Kelso, 1897; Barr, Niall, *Flodden*, Tempus, 2003; Reese, Peter, *Flodden: A Scottish Tragedy*, 2003; *Archaeologia*, XXV, p. 376; Leadam, I. S., ed., *Select Cases before the King's Council in the Star Chamber, commonly called the Court of Star Chamber, 1509–1544*, Selden Society, 1911; Stow, *Annales*; Hall's *Chronicle*; Holmes, Martin, 'Evil May Day 1517: the Story of a Riot', *History Today*, 15, 1965, pp. 642–50.

CHAPTER 3

Bergenroth, G. A., ed., *Supplement to Vols. I and II of the Calendar of State Papers, Spanish*, London, 1868, i.265; ii.38; ii.suppl.19; iii.ii.38.suppl.134; iv.1133; v.i.410; vi.i.68, 134,142, 211,410,559–60; Vatican Archives, Arm. 39,23, 689.

Hanawalt, Barbara, *Growing Up in Medieval London*, Oxford University Press, 1993, pp. 114,179–180; Fitzherbert, John, *A Book of Husbandry*, 1525; Sim, Alison, *The Tudor Housewife*, Sutton 2002; Ellis, ed., *Original Letters*, London, 1825,3, pp. 34–9; Hall, pp. 798–805; Cranmer, *Works*, ii.245–61; BL. Sloane MSS; Vives, Juan Luis, *Instructions of a Christian Woman*, 1529, p.165; Travitsky, Betty, *The Paradise of Women: Writings by Englishwomen of the Renaissance*, Westport: Greenwood Press, 1981, p. 5; Hull, Suzanne W., *Women According to Men: The World of Tudor–Stuart Women*, London: Altamira Press, 1996, pp. 135,153.

CHAPTER 4

The Paston Letters, n. 83, pp. 174–5; Swetnam, Joseph, *The Arraignment of Lewd, Idle, Froword, and Unconstant Women,* London, Thomas Archer, 1615; Eales, J. *Women in Early Modern England 1500–1700,* UCL Press, London, 1998; Mendelson, S., Crawford, P., *Women in Early Modern England,* Clarendon Press, Oxford, 1998.

Sessions, William, *History Today* 41, 6, June 1991, Sessions, W. A., *Henry Howard, Earl of Surrey,* G. K. Hall & Co., 1986; Knecht, R. J., *Francis I,* Cambridge University Press, 1982; Grace, F. R., 'Life and Career of Thomas Howard', M.A., Thesis, Univ. of Nottingham, 1961, p.137.

Dowling, Maria, 'Anne Boleyn and Reform', *Journal of Ecclesiastical History*, 35, I, January 1984, pp. 30–46; Wyatt, *Life of Anne Boleigne,* 18; Latimer: *A Brief Treatise or Chronicle of . . . Anne Boleyn,* Oxford, Bodleian MS C. Don. 42, fos. 20–33.

Devonshire MS., British Library Additional MS 17,492; Remley, Paul G., 'Mary Shelton and Her Tudor Literary Milieu', pp. 40–77 in Herman, Peter C., ed., *Rethinking the Henrician Era: Essays on Early Tudor Texts and Contexts,* Urbana: University of Illinois pp. 44,46; Ray Siemens' ongoing project, *Epistolary Politics and the Poetic Miscellany: An Exploration of the Devonshire Manuscript;* Heale, Elizabeth 'Women and the Courtly Love Lyric: The Devonshire MS, BL Additional 17,492,' *Modern Language Review* 90, 1995, pp. 296–313, edition in print and electronic form, of the *Devonshire MS;* Southall, Raymond, 'The Devonshire Manuscript Collection of Early Tudor Poetry, 1532–41', *Review of English Studies* [n.s.] 15 (1964): 142–50, p.146; Stevens, John, 'The Game of Love', pp. 154–202 in *Music & Poetry in the Early Tudor Court,* London: Methuen, 1961; Thomson, Patricia, 'Courtly Love'. pp. 10–45 in *Sir Thomas Wyatt and His Background,* London: Routledge and Kegan Paul, 1964.

CHAPTER 5

Wriothesley, Charles, *A Chronicle of England during the Reigns of the Tudors,* Hamilton, W., ed., Camden Soc.i.,1874, i.33,189–226; Ives, E. W., 'Faction at the Court of Henry VIII: The Fall of Anne Boleyn', *History,* LVII, 190, June 1972, pp. 169–88.

Savine, A., *English Monasteries on the Eve of the Dissolution,* Oxford, 1919;

Fuller, *Church History*, 1655, p. 317; Zahl, Paul F. M., *Five Women of the English Reformation*, Eerdmans, 2001, p. 5; De Carles, in Ascoli, *L'Opinion*, lines 861–4; James Froude, Anthony, *History of England from the Fall of Wolsey to the Death of Elizabeth*, 6 vols, *Atlantic Monthly*, Vol. 10, No. 57, July, 1862; Ales, 'Letter', pp. 530–1. Early street ballads will be found in Ritson's *Ancient Songs and Ballads*, revised by Hazlitt, W. C., 1877; Ballads from MSS ed. by Furnivall, F. J., Ballad Soc. 1868–77.

CHAPTER 6

Stone, Lawrence, *The Family, Sex and Marriage in England 1500–1800*, New York, 1977, p. 607; Ruether, Rosemary Radford, 'Sex and the Body in the Catholic Tradition', *Conscience: A News Journal of Prochoice Catholic Opinion*, Winter 1999/2000; Bullough, Vern L., and Brundage, James, *Sexual Practices and the Medieval Church*, Buffalo, NY: Prometheus Books, 1982, pp. 22–33; Sennert, *Practical Physick*, pp. 115–116; Sommerville, Margaret, *Sex and Subjection*, Arnold, 1995; Crawford, Patricia, and Mendelson, Sara, *Women in Early Modern England*, Oxford, 1998; Henderson, Katherine Usher, and McManus, Barbara F., *Half Humankind: Contexts and Texts of the Controversy about Women in England, 1540–1640*, University of Illinois Press, 1985.

Ingram, M., *Church Courts, Sex and Marriage in England*, Cambridge, 1987, pp. 227—30; Quaif, Q. R., *Wanton Wenches and Wayward Wives*, 1979, pp. 128f; Reay, B., *Popular Cultures in England, 1550–1750*, London, 1998, p.11, n. 31; Adair, Richard, *Courtship, Illegitimacy and Marriage in Early Modern England*, Manchester & New York, 1996, p.146; O'Hara, Diana, *Courtship and Constraint: Rethinking the Making of Marriage in Tudor England*, Manchester University Press, 2000; Amundsen D. and W. Diers, C. J., 'The age of menopause in medieval Europe', *Human Biology*, 45, 1973, pp. 605–12; Friedrich, W. N., 'Sexual victimization and sexual behaviour in children: A review of recent literature', *Child Abuse and Neglect*, 17, 1993, pp. 59–66.

Skelton, John, 'The Tunnyng of Elynour Rummyng,' *The Poetical Works of John Skelton*, vol I, Dyce, Rev. Alexander, ed., Boston: Little, Brown, and Company, 1866, pp. 109–131; Knox, John, *First Blast of the Trumpet against Monstrous Regiment of Women*, 1558; Harris, Barbara, 'Women and Politics in Early Tudor England', *Historical Journal* 33, 1990, pp. 259–81; Becon, Thomas, *The Christian State of Matrimony*, 1546.

CHAPTER 7

Margaret Douglas became Countess of Lennox and her son, Lord Darnley, married Mary, Queen of Scots. The Devonshire Manuscript is now in the British Library, BL Additional 17492, and work is being carried out in electronic form to determine the identity of its various authors. Head, 'Being Ledde and Seduced by the Devyll', pp. 8–10; *Schutte Appendix*; Muir, 'Unpublished Poems', pp. 247,255; Fox, Alistair, 'The Unquiet Mind of Sir Thomas Wyatt', pp. 257–85 in *Politics and Literature in the Reigns of Henry VII and Henry VIII*, Oxford: Basil Blackwell, 1989, pp. 268,271; Statutes of the Realm, 28 H VIII, c.24; Lehmberg, 'Parliamentary Attainder in the Reign of Henry VIII', pp. 691–2.

Maculloch, Diarmud, 'Vain, Proud, Foolish Boy: The Earl of Surrey and the Fall of the Howards', in Starkey, *Rivals in Power*, p. 93; Brigden, Susan, 'Henry Howard, Earl of Surrey and the Conjured League', *Historical Journal*, 37, 1994, p. 516; D'Aubigny, vol. 2, p. 243; Duffy, Eamon, *The Stripping of the Altars: Traditional Religion in England 1400–1580, Yale 1994, pp. 422, 479–80*; Dickens, A. G., *The English Reformation*, 1991 edn, p. 13; Dickens, A. G., 'The Early Expansion of Protestantism', in Todd, Margo, *Reformation to Revolution Politics and Religion in Early Modern England*, 1995, p. 13.

Hoyle, Richard W., *The Pilgrimage of Grace and Politics and Politics of the 1530s*, OUP, 2001; Bush, Michael, *The Pilgrimage of Grace, A Study of the Rebel Armies of October 1536*, MUP, 1996; Dodds, Madeleine Hope, and Dodds, Ruth, *The Pilgrimage of Grace 1536–1537 and the Exeter Conspiracy 1538*, 1915, repr. F. Cass 1971; Fletcher, A. and MacCulloch, D., *Tudor Rebellions*, 1997; Bush, Michael, *The Defeat of the Pilgrimage of Grace*, OUP, 1999.

Loach, *Edward VI*, pp. 4–7; de Molen, R. L., 'The Birth of Edward VI and the Death of Queen Jane: the Arguments For and Against Caesarian Section', *Renaissance Studies*, iv.1990, pp. 359–91; see also: Copeman, W. S. C., *Doctors and Disease in Tudor Times*, London: 1960; Webster, Charles, *Health, Medicine and Mortality in the Sixteenth Century*, Cambridge University Press, 1979.

CHAPTER 8

Erasmus, *Polite Manners for Boys*, 1530; Tusser, Thomas, *Five Hundred Goode Pointes of Husbandrie*, 1573; Emerson, K. L., *Everyday Life in Renaissance England: 1485–1649*, Writers Digest, Ohio, 1996, p.54.

Blanton, Suellen Clopton, *The Clopton Chronicles: A Project of the Clopton Family Genealogical Society.*

'Sermon on Marriage at Merseburg', 1545, Wing, John, 1620; Kelly, K. C., *Menacing Virgins: Representing Virginity in the Middle Ages and Renaissance*, University of Delaware, 1999. 25 – *Aldhelm: Prose Works*, trans. Lapidge, Michael, and Herren, Michael, Cambridge: D. S. Brewer; Tottowa, NJ: Rowman & Littlefield, 1979, p. 75; Castelli, Elizabeth, 'Virginity and Its Meaning for Women's Sexuality in Early Christianity', *Journal of Feminist Studies in Religion*, 2, 1986, pp. 61–86; Salisbury, Joyce, *Church Fathers, Independent Virgins*, London: Verso, 1991, ch.1, 'The Early Fathers on Sexuality: The Carnal World'; McLaren, Angus, *Reproductive Rituals, The Perception of Fertility in England from the Sixteenth to the Nineteenth Century*, Methuen, London, 1984, p. 142; Himes, Norman E., *Medical History of Contraception*, New York, 1963; Reay, B., *Popular Cultures in England, 1550–1750*, London, 1998, p.11, n.31; Ingram, M., *Church Courts, Sex and Marriage in England*, Cambridge, 1987, pp. 227–30; Adair, *Courtship*, pp. 146; Parisot, Jeannette, *Johnny Come Lately: A Short History of the Condom*, London: The Journeyman Press, 1985; Tannahill, R., *Sex in History*, pp. 74,128.

Bryan, Francis, *A Dispraise of the Life of a Courtier*, 1548; Castiglione, B., *The Book of the Courtier*, trans. Hoby, T., 1946, pp. 39, 89; Greenblatt, Stephen, 'Power, Sexuality, and Inwardness in Wyatt's Poetry', pp. 115–156 in Greenblatt, Stephen, *Renaissance Self-Fashioning: From More to Shakespeare*, University of Chicago P, 1980; Rebholz, *Wyatt*, poem CLI.68. Tottel's *Songes and Sonettes*, 1557; Spearing, A. C., 'Wyatt as Satirist', *Medieval to Renaissance in English Poetry*, Cambridge UP, 1985, pp. 235–6; Zagorin, Perez, 'Sir Thomas Wyatt and the Court of Henry VIII: The Courtier's Ambivalence', *Journal of Medieval and Renaissance Studies*, 23, 1993, pp.113–4; Starkey, D. R., 'The Court: Castiglione's ideal and Tudor reality', in *Journal of the Warburg & Courtauld Institutes*, 45, 1982, pp. 232–9.

CHAPTER 9

Statutes of the Realm, III 26 Henry VIII cap– 13. p– 508; Smith, 'English Treason Trials and Confessions in the Sixteenth Century', *J.H.I.*, xv. no. 4, October 1954, pp. 472–5; Cardinal Pole, *Epistolae Poli*, ii, 191; Durant, Horatia, *Sorrowful Captives, The Tudor Earls of Devon*, The Griffin Press, 1960, p. 46; Turner, William, *Huntyng and Fyndyng out of the Romishe Fox*, 1543; Foxe, *Actes and Monuments*, p. 529; Scarisbrick, J. J., *Henry VIII*, London, 1968, pp. 490–9; Riordan, Michael, and Ryrie, Alec, 'Stephen Gardiner and the making of a protestant villain', *Sixteenth Century Journal* 34/4, 2003, pp. 1039–65; Redworth, Glyn, *In Defence of the Church Catholic: the Life of Stephen Gardiner*, Oxford, 1990, pp. 234, 287, 321; Cranmer, *Doctrinal Treatises,* Parker Soc., pp. 74–6; Scarisbrick, J. J., *Henry VIII,* London, 1968, p. 296; BL.Cotton MS Cleopatra EVI ff. 234–5; Foxe, *Actes and Monuments*, 1583; Strype, *Ecclesiastical Memorials*, 1,ii.

CHAPTER 10

Parker, K.T., *Drawings of Hans Holbein in the Collection of His Majesty the King at Windsor Castle*, 1945, no. 62; Strong, Roy, *National Portrait Gallery: Tudor and Jacobean Portraits*, London, 1969, pp. 41–4; Roberts, Jane, *Holbein and the Court of Henry VIII: Drawings and Miniatures from the Royal Library, Windsor Castle*, National Galleries of Scotland, 1993, p. 90. Many thanks to Martin Clayton, Deputy Curator of the Print Room at Windsor Castle and Susan Owens of the Royal Collection.

'In the Lower Rhineland and Westphalia, the dynasty of Cleves and Juliers united some duchies and counties in which the 'Oesterse' dialect became the official Chancellory language. Despite Saxon and High-German influences it was very similar to the ancestors of the Dutch language, and has influenced it greatly. It was widely used in what is now the Eastern and Northern Netherlands also.'
www.home.versatel.nl/gerardvonhebel/burgundy.htm

Kelly, *Matrimonial Trials*, pp. 250–9, 268–9; Slavin, A. J., 'The Politics of Conspiracy', *Albion*, 9, 1977, pp. 316–36; Robson-Scott, *German Travellers in England*, pp. 22–3; Pseudo-Albertus Magnus, *De Secretis Mulierum (On the Secrets of Women*, trans., Lemay, Helen Rodnite, Albany, NY: State University of New York, 1992, p.129; *The Book of Women's Love and Jewish Medieval Medical Literature on Women,* ed. and trans. Caballero-Navas, Carmen, London: Kegan Paul, 2004, pp. 142–4; Karras, Ruth, *Common Women: Prostitution and Sexuality in Medieval England*, New York: Oxford University Press, 1996; Stow, John, *The Survey of London*, ed, Ernest, Rhys, London: J. M. Dent & Sons Ltd, 1929, p. 362; Mitton, G. E., ed., *Maps of Old London*, London: Black, 1908, I, II, IV, V, VI; D'Aubigny, *The Reformation in England*, vol. 2, p. 430; Gibbons, Geoffrey, *The Political Career of Thomas Wriothesley, First Earl of Southampton*

1505–1550, Henry VIII's Last Chancellor, Studies in British History, vol. 64, Edwin Mellen Press, 2001; Warnicke, Retha W., *The Marrying of Anne of Cleves: Royal Protocol in Tudor England*, Cambridge: Cambridge University Press, 2000.

CHAPTER 11
Thomson, Patricia, 'Courtly Love', *Sir Thomas Wyatt and His Background*, London: Routledge and Kegan Paul, 1964, p. 23; Blanton, Suellen Clopton, *The Clopton Chronicles:* A Project of the Clopton Family Genealogical Society; Clopton, Gene Carlton, *The Ancestors and Descendants of William Clopton of York*, County, Phoenix Printing, Inc., Atlanta, Georgia, 1984.

Clowes, William, *Selected Writings*, 1579, ed. Poynter, FNL, BA, FLA, Harvey & Blythe Ltd, London, 1948; MacNalty, A. S., *Henry VIII: a Difficult Patient*, pp. 180, 199; Brinch, 'The Medical Problems of Henry VIII', p. 367; Currie, Dr A. S., 'Notes on the Obstetric Histories of Catherine of Aragon and Anne Boleyn', *Edinburgh Medical Journal*, I, 1888, pp. 1–34; Dewhurst, Sir John, 'The Alleged Miscarriages of Catherine of Aragon and Anne Boleyn', *Medical History*, 28, 1984, pp. 49–56; Hall, ii. 209; Bell, Rudy, *How to Do It: Guides to Good Living for Renaissance Italians*, University of Chicago Press, 1999.

Elton, G. R., 'Thomas Cromwell's Decline and Fall', *Cambridge Historical Journal*, x.1951; D'Aubigny, *The Reformation in England*, vol. 2, pp. 416–22; Smith, Lacey Baldwin, *Treason in Tudor England: Politics and Paranoia*, Jonathan Cape, 1986; Hackett, Francis, *The Personal History of Henry the Eighth*, New York: Horace Liveright, Inc., 1929; reprinted London: Jonathan Cape, 1946. p. 395.

CHAPTER 12
Hall, Edward, *Henry VIII*, 2 vols, 1904; Hume, *Chronicle of Henry VIII*, p. 77; Kaulek, *Correspondence Politique de M. De Castillon et de M. Marillac*, Paris 1885, p. 218; Williams, James, 'Hunting, hawking and the Early Tudor Gentleman', *History Today*, 53, Aug. 2003, p. 8.

Strong, Roy, *The English Renaissance Miniature*, London, 1983, pp. 36–7; James, Susan E., 'Lady Margaret Douglas and Sir Thomas Seymour by Holbein', *Apollo Magazine*, May 1998, pp. 15–20; Smither, Larissa Taylor, 'Elizabeth I: A Psychological Profile', *Sixteenth Century Journal*, 15, 1984, pp. 47–72.

Starkey, David R., 'The King's Privy Chamber', Ph D. diss. Cambridge University, 1973, p. 8; LP.xvi.284ff; Maria Hayward, *The 1542 Inventory of the Palace of Westminster: The Palace and its Keeper*, Illuminata Publishers for the Society of Antiquaries of London, 2003; Foxe, John, *Actes and Monuments*, London, 1563, Sig. Pp.5, 562; *The Whole Works of Roger Ascham*, ed Rev. Dr Giles, 3 vol, London, 1865, I.i.65,73; Narasingha Sil, P, *Tudor Placemen and Statesmen: Select Case Histories*, Cranbury, N. J.:Fairleigh Dickinson University Press, 2001; Lerer, Seth, 'Errata: print, politics and poetry in early modern England', in Sharpe, Kevin and Zwicker, S. N., eds., *Reading, Society and Politics in Early Modern England*, Cambridge University Press, 2003.

CHAPTER 13

Genealogy Culpepers, p.197; *Culpepper Connections! The Culpepper Family History Site*: http://gen.culpepper.com.; Strickland, iii.p.115; *Chancery Town Depositions*, Henry VIII, Bundle 9, No. 7; Wentworth, *Advice to his Son*, pp. 14,18; Baldwin, *Morall Philosophie*, f.180; Starkey, D. R., 'The Court: Castiglione's ideal and Tudor reality', in *Journal of the Warburg & Courtauld Institutes*, 45,1982, pp. 232–9; Ridley, Jasper, *The Tudor Age*, pp. 80, 83, 87.

Margaret Plantagenet, Countess of Salisbury was interred in the Tower. She was made a saint by Pope Leo XIII on 29 December 1886.

CHAPTER 14

Wilson, Derek, *A Tudor Tapestry: Men, Women and Society in Reformation England,* Heinemann, 1972, pp. 91,94–6,106; D'Aubigny, *The Reformation in England*, vol. 2, pp. 440–6.

CHAPTER 15

Cranmer, *Works,* Parker Society, ii.pp.408–9; Smith, 'English Treason Trials and Confessions in the Sixteenth Century'. *J.H.I.,* xv. 4, October 1954, pp. 472–5.

Crooke, Helkiah (1576–1648), *Microcosmographia* 1615; Sennert, *Practical Physick,* pp. 115–116; Diethelm, Oscar, *Medical Dissertations of Psychiatric Interest before 1750*, Basel: Karger, 1971, pp. 62, 139; Bienville, M. D.T., *Nymphomania, or a Dissertation concerning the Furor Uterinus,* trans. Edward Sloane Wilmot, London: J. Bew 1775.

Chapter 16

LP. xvi. 1334–9,1366; Statutes of the Realm, III, 33 Henry VIII, Cap. 21. p. 857; 33 Hen VIII: PRO KB 8/13/1; Smith, 'English Treason Trials and Confessions in the Sixteenth Century', *J.H.I.,* xv. no. 4, October 1954, pp. 472–5.

Historical Manuscript Commission: Calendar of the Ms. of the Marquis of Bath preserved at Longleat, Wiltshire, 3 vols 1904–8, ii. pp.9 –10; Ashbee, Jeremy, Assistant Curator, Historic Royal Palaces, The Tower of London, *History Today,* 2003.

Chapter 17

1542. 33 Henry VIII. c. 21. 3 S. R. 857–9; Modern Short Title: Royal Assent by Commission Act 1542; *Journal of the House of Lords,* pp.165,171; Lehmberg, Later Parliaments, pp. 144–5; LJI, p. 176.

Aftermath

Some sources give Norfolk's death as 1554.

Clopton Family Genealogical Society, *The Ancestors and Descendants of Sir Thomas Clopton,* Phoenix Printing, Inc., Atlanta, Georgia, 1984; Simpson, James, 'The Sacrifice of Lady Rochford: Henry Parker, Lord Morley's Translation of De claris mulierbus', in *Triumphs of English,* British Library, 2000, pp.154, 164–5; Wright, H.G, ed., *Forty–Six Lives, translated from Boccaccio's De claris mulieribus by Henry Parker, Lord Morley,* London: Early English Texts Society, 1943.

Beilin, *The Examinations of Anne Askew,* xix; Foxe, pp. 667, 1425–27.

Sessions, W. A., *Henry Howard, The Poet Earl of Surrey: A Life ,*Oxford University Press, 1999, pp. 358–87; Moore, Peter R., 'The Heraldic Charge Against the Earl of Surrey, 1546–47', *English Historical Review,* 116, 2001, pp. 557–83; Padelford, Rev., ed., *Henry Howard, Earl of Surrey: Poems,* Seattle: University of Washington Press, 1928; Zim, Rivkah, *English Metrical Psalms: Poetry as Praise and Prayer 1535–1601,* Cambridge University Press, 1987, pp. 88–91; Brigden, pp.507–37.

CNN, 19 December 2003; Graber, Janna, 'The Hauntings at London's Hampton Court Palace', *Favorite Haunts Travel Guide Book,* Fall 2001.

Picture Credits

p. 1   *(top and bottom)* The Royal Collection © 2005, Her Majesty Queen Elizabeth II

p. 2   *(top and bottom)* National Portrait Gallery, London

p. 3   *(top)* National Portrait Gallery, London, *(bottom)* Kunsthistorisches Musuem, Vienna/ www.bridgeman.co.uk

p. 4   *(top)* National Portrait Gallery, London, *(bottom)* Louvre, Paris/www.bridgeman.co.uk

p. 5   *(top)* Mary Evans Picture Library, *(bottom)* akg-images / Erich Lessing

p. 6   *(top)* National Portrait Gallery, London, *(bottom)* Mary Evans Picture Library

p. 7   National Archives

p. 8   *(top)* National Portrait Gallery, London, *(bottom)* Royal Palaces

Primary Sources

Becon, Thomas, *The Catechism of Thomas Becon, S. T. P.* ed. John Ayre, Parker Society 3, Cambridge: Cambridge University Press, 1844.

Brewer J.S., Brodie, R.H. eds., *Letters and Papers, Foreign and Domestic, of the Reign of Henry VIII*, 21 vols. London: HMSO, 1862-1920.

Byrne, M. St. Clare, ed., *The Letters of Henry VIII*, 1968.

Castiglione, B., *The Book of the Courtier*, trans. T. Hoby, 1946.

Coates, Tim, ed., *The Letters of Henry VIII, 1526-1529*, HMSO, 2001.

Cranmer: *Works*, ed. J. E. Cox, 2 vols., Cambridge 1844-6.

De Carles, in Ascoli, *L'Opinion*.

Devonshire Mss., British Library Additional MS 17,492.

Ellis, Henry, *Original Letters*, London, 1825-46.

Extracts from State Trials, 1 Mary, 1553 – and others, for High Treason, from Cobbett's Complete Collection of State Trials, 1809, London.

Foxe, *The Acts and Monuments of John Foxe*, ed. G. Townsend, 8 vols, reprint, 1965.

Hall, Edward, *The triumphant reigne of King Henry the VIII*, ed. Charles Whibley, 2 vols, London: T. C. and E. C. Jack, 1904.

Holinshed, Raphael, *Chronicles of England, Scotland and Ireland*, 1807-8

Kaulek, Jean, *Correspondence politique de Castillon et de Marillac*, Paris 1885.

Latimer, *A Brief Treatise or Chronicle of . . . Anne Boleyn*, Oxford, Bodleian MS C. Don. 42, fos. 20-33.

Loades, D. M., *The Papers of George Wyatt*, 1968.

Merriman, R. B, *The Life and Letters of Thomas Cromwell*, 2 vols, Oxford, 1902.

Muller, J. A., *Letters of Stephen Gardiner*, Cambridge University Press, 1933.

Strype, John, *Annals of the Reformation*, Oxford, 1824.

Swetnam, Joseph, *The Araignment of Lewd, Idle, Froward, and Vnconstant Women*, London: Thomas Archer, 1616.

Vives, Juan Luis, *Instructions of a Christian Woman*, 1529.

Wriothesley, Charles, *A Chronicle of England during the reigns of the Tudors*, ed. W. Hamilton, Camden Society i., 1874, i.33.

Secondary Sources

Adair, Richard, *Courtship, Illegitimacy and Marriage in Early Modern England*, Manchester, 1996.

Archer, John, *Sovereignity and Intelligence: Spying and Court Culture in the English Renaissance*, Stanford, 1993.

Aughterson, Kate, ed., *Renaissance Woman: A Sourcebook: Constructions of Femininity in England*, Routledge, 1995.

Beckingsale, B. W., *Thomas Cromwell: Tudor Minister*, Macmillan, 1978.

Bell, Rudy, *How to Do It: Guides to Good Living for Renaissance Italians*, University of Chicago Press, 1999.

Bellamy, John G. *The Tudor Law of Treason. An Introduction*, Routledge and Kegan Paul, 1979.

Block, J. S., *Factional Politics and the English Reformation 1520–1540*, Woodbridge, 1993.

Bowker, M., 'Lincolnshire 1536: heresy, schism or religious discontent?', in *Studies in Church History*, 9, 1972.

Brenan, G. Statham, E. P. *The House of Howard*, 1907.

Brigden, S., *London and the Reformation*, Oxford, 1989.

Brigden, S., *New Worlds, Lost Worlds: The Rule of the Tudors*, Penguin 2000.

Brinch, Ove, 'The Medical Problems of Henry VIII', *Centaurus V*, 1958, 3, p. 367.

Brigden, Susan, 'Henry Howard, Earl of Surrey and the Conjured League', *Historical Journal*, 37, 1994.

Brundage, James, *Law, Sex, and Christian Society in Medieval Europe*, Chicago, 1987.

Bush, Michael, *The Pilgrimage of Grace, A Study of the Rebel Armies of October 1536*, Manchester University Press, 1996.

Bush, Michael, *The Defeat of the Pilgrimage of Grace*, OUP, 1999.

Carlson, Eric J., 'Courtship in Tudor England' *History Today*. August, 1993.

Casady, Edwin E., *Henry Howard, Earl of Surrey*, New York, 1938.

Crawford, Anne, ed., *The Howard Household Books, 1462–71 and 1481–83*, 1992.

Cressy, David *Birth, Marriage and Death in Tudor England*, Oxford 1997.

D'Aubigny, J.H.Merle, *The Reformation in England*, 2 vols. Banner of Trust, London, 1962–3.

Davis, J. F., *Heresy and Reformation in the South-East of England 1520–1559*,

London, 1983.

Dickens, A.G., *The English Reformation*, 2nd edn, London, 1991.

Dickens, A.G., 'The Early Expansion of Protestantism,' in Margo Todd, *Reformation to Revolution: Politics and Religion in Early Modern England*, 1995.

Dodds, M.H., Dodds, R., *The Pilgrimage of Grace 1536–1537 & the Exeter Conspiracy 1538*, 1915, repr. F. Cass 1971.

Donaldson, Peter, 'Bishop Gardiner, Machiavellian', *Historical Journal*, XXIII, 1 March 1980.

Drummond, Jack C. and Wilbraham, Anne, *The Englishman's Food. A History of Five Centuries of English Diet*, London, J. Cape, 1939.

Duffy, Eamon, *The Stripping of the Altars: Traditional Religion in England 1400–1580*, Yale 1994.

Durant, Horatia, *Sorrowful Captives, The Tudor Earls of Devon*, Griffin Press, 1960.

Dusinberre, Juliet, *Shakespeare and the Nature of Women*, Macmillan, 1996.

Eales, J., *Women in Early Modern England 1500–1700*, UCL Press, London, 1998.

Elton, G.R, *The Tudor Revolution in Government,* Cambridge, 1953.

Elton, G.R. 'Thomas Cromwell's Decline and Fall', *Cambridge Historical Journal*, X. 1951.

Emmisson, Frederick George, *Tudor Food and Pastimes*, London: Benn, 1965.

Fletcher, A. and MacCulloch, D., *Tudor Rebellions*, 1997.

Fox, Alistair. 'The Unquiet Mind of Sir Thomas Wyatt', 257–85 in *Politics and Literature in the Reigns of Henry VII and Henry VIII*, Oxford: Basil Blackwell, 1989, pp. 268, 271.

Fraser, Antonia, *The Wives of Henry VIII*, New York: Alfred A. Knopf, Inc., 1993.

Gibbons, Geoffrey, *The Political Career of Thomas Wriothesley, First Earl of Southampton 1505–1550, Henry VIII's Last Chancellor*, Studies in British History, V.64, Edwin Mellen Press, 2001.

Grace, F. R. 'Life & Career of Thomas Howard', M.A. Thesis, University of Nottingham, 1961.

Greenblatt, Stephen, 'Power, Sexuality, and Inwardness in Wyatt's Poetry', 115–156, in Greenblatt, Stephen, *Renaissance Self-Fashioning: From More to Shakespeare*, University of Chicago P, 1980.

Guy, J. A., 'The Privy Council: Revolution or Evolution?', in Coleman C., and Starkey, D., eds., *Revolution Reassessed: Revisions in the History of Tudor Government and Administration*, Oxford, 1986.

Guy, J. A., *Tudor England*, New York, NY.: Oxford University Press, 1991.

Hanawalt, Barbara A., *Growing Up in Medieval London*, New York: Oxford University, 1993.

Harris, Barbara, 'Women and Politics in Early Tudor England', *Historical Journal*, vol. 33, 1990, pp. 259–81.

Head, David M., *The Ebbs and Flows of Fortune: The Life of the Duke of Norfolk*, Georgia University Press, 1995.

Heale, Elizabeth, 'Women and the Courtly Love Lyric: The Devonshire MS, BL Additional 17, 492', *Modern Language Review* 90, 1995, pp. 296–313.

Hopkins, Lisa, *Women Who Would Be Kings: Female Rulers of the Sixteenth Century*, London: Vision Press, 1991.

Hoyle, Richard W., *The Pilgrimage of Grace and Politics of the 1530s*, OUP, 2001;

Hull, Suzanne W., *Women According to Men: The World of Tudor-Stuart Women*, London: Altamira Press, 1996.

Ingram, Martin., *Church Courts, Sex and Marriage in England, 1570–1640*, Cambridge, 1987.

Ives, E. W., *Faction in Tudor England*. London: Historical Association, 1979.

Ives, E. W., *Anne Boleyn*, Oxford, 1986.

Laurence, Anne, *Women in England 1500–1760: A Social History*, London: Phoenix, 1996.

MacCulloch, Diarmaid, ed., *The Reign of Henry VIII: Politics, Policy and Piety*, London, 1995.

MacCulloch, Diarmaid, 'Vain, Proud, Foolish Boy: The Earl of Surrey and the Fall of the Howards', in Starkey, *Rivals in Power*, p. 93.

MacCulloch, Diarmaid, *Cranmer*, Yale, 1996.

MacFarlane, Alan, *Witchcraft in Tudor and Stuart England*, 1970.

MacFarlane, Alan, *Marriage and Love in England. Modes of Reproduction 1300–1840*, Oxford, 1986.

MacNalty, A.S. *Henry VIII: a Difficult Patient*, London, 1952, pp.180,199.

Marks, Richard, 'The Howard Tombs at Thetford and Framlington: New Discoveries', *Archaeological Journal*, 141, 1984, pp. 254–5.

Mendelson, S., Crawford, P., *Women in Early Modern England*, Clarendon Press, Oxford, 1998.

Molen, R.L.de, 'The Birth of EVI and the Death of Queen Jane: the Arguments for and against Caesarian Section', *Renaissance Studies,* iv, 1990, 359–91.

Muller, J. A., *Stephen Gardiner and the Tudor Reaction,* 1926, repr. 1970.

Murphy, Beverley A., *Bastard Prince: Henry VIII's Lost Son,* Sutton, 2001.

Nott, G.F., ed., *The Works of Henry Howard,* New York, 1965.

O'Hara, Diana, *Courtship and Constraint: Rethinking the Making of Marriage in Tudor England,* Manchester University Press, 2000.

Outhwaite, R.B. (ed.), *Marriage and Society: Studies in the Social History of Marriage,* London, 1981, pp. 35–57.

Ozment, Stephen, *When Fathers Ruled: Family Life in Reformation Europe,* Cambridge, Mass.: Harvard UP, 1983.

Picard, Liza, *Elizabeth's London,* Weidenfeld & Nicolson, 2003.

Pinchbeck, Ivy and Margaret Hewitt, 'Children in English Society', Vol. 1, *From Tudor Times to the Eighteenth Century,* London: Routledge & Kegan Paul, 1969.

Plowden, Alison, *Tudor Women: Queens and Commoners,* 1998.

Pollard, Albert F., *Henry VIII,* London: Longmans, Green and Co., 1905,1951.

Quaife, G.R., *Wanton Wenches and Wayward Wives: Peasants and Illicit Sex in Early Seventeenth-Century England,* London, 1979.

Reay, B., *Popular Cultures in England, 1550–1750,* London and New York, 1998.

Rebholz, R.A., ed., *Sir Thomas Wyatt: The Complete Poems,* Cornell, 1995.

Remley, Paul G., 'Mary Shelton and Her Tudor Literary Milieu', 40–77 in Herman, Peter C., ed., *Rethinking the Henrician Era: Essays on Early Tudor Texts and Contexts,* Urbana: University of Illinois 1994.

Richardson, E.M., *The Lion and the Rose,* New York, 1922.

Robinson, John Martin, *The Dukes of Norfolk: A Quincentennial History,* Oxford University Press, 1982.

Savine, A., *English Monasteries on the Eve of the Dissolution,* Oxford, 1919.

Scarisbricke, J. J., *Henry VIII,* London, 1968.

Schutte, Kimberley, *Margaret Douglas,* Edwin Mellen, 2002.

Sessions, W. A., *Henry Howard, the Poet Earl of Surrey: A Life* Oxford, 1986.

Simpson, James, 'The Sacrifice of Lady Rochford: Henry Parker, Lord Morley's Translation of De claris mulierbus,' in *Triumphs of English,* British Library, 2000.

Smith, Lacey Baldwin. 'English Treason Trials and Confessions in the Sixteenth Century', *Journal of the Historical Ideas*, XV, No.4 (October 1954).

Smith, Lacey Baldwin, *Henry VIII: The Mask of Royalty*, Boston, Houghton Mifflin, 1971.

Smith, Lacey Baldwin, *A Tudor Tragedy – The Life and Times of Catherine Howard*, Jonathan Cape, 1962.

Smith, Lacey Baldwin, *Treason in Tudor England: Politics and Paranoia*, Jonathan Cape, 1986.

Somerset, Anne, *Elizabeth I*, 1991.

Southall, Raymond, 'The Devonshire Manuscript Collection of Early Tudor Poetry, 1532-41', *Review of English Studies* [n.s.] 15 1964: 142-50.

Spearing, A. C, 'Wyatt as Satirist', *Medieval to Renaissance in English Poetry*, Cambridge UP, 1985.

Spearing, A. C, 'Surrey' 311-26 in *Medieval to Renaissance in English Poetry*, Cambridge UP, 1985.

Starkey, David, *The Reign of Henry VIII: Personalities and Politics*, London, 1985.

Starkey, David, 'Privy Secrets: Henry VIII and the Lords of the Council', *History Today*, Vol.37,8, August 1987, pp. 23–31.

Starkey, David, *Six Wives: The Queens of Henry VIII*, London, Chatto & Windus, 2003.

Stevens, John, 'The Game of Love', 154-202, in *Music & Poetry in the Early Tudor Court*, London, Methuen, 1961.

Stone, Lawrence, *The Family, Sex and Marriage in England 1500–1800*, New York, 1977.

Strickland, Agnes, *Lives of the Queens of England*, 1866.

Strype, John, *Ecclesiastical Memorials*, London, 1820–40.

Tucker, M. J., *The Life of Thomas Howard, Duke of Norfolk*, The Hague, 1964.

Thomson, Patricia, 'Courtly Love', 10-45 in *Sir Thomas Wyatt and His Background*, London, Routledge and Kegan Paul, 1964.

Warnicke, Retha M., *The Marrying of Anne of Cleves: Royal Protocol in Tudor England*, Cambridge University Press, 2000.

Weir, Alison, *The Six Wives of Henry VIII*, New York, Ballantine Books, 1993.

Weir, Alison, *Henry VIII King and Court*, Jonathan Cape, 2001.

Weisner, Merry, *Women and Gender in Early Modern Europe*, Cambridge University Press, 1993.

Williams, Neville, *Thomas Howard, 4th Duke of Norfolk,* London, Barrie and Rockliff, 1964.

Williams, Neville, *Henry VIII and His Court*, London, Weidenfeld & Nicolson, 1971.

Wilson, Derek, *In the Lion's Court*, Hutchinson, 2001.

Wright, H. G., ed., *Forty-Six Lives, translated from Boccaccio's De claris mulieribus by Henry Parker, Lord Morley*, London: Early English Texts Society, 1943.

Zahl, Paul F. M., *Five Women of the English Reformation*, Eerdmans, 2001.

Index